# INTERIOR PLAYS

# Interior Plays

PEOPLE ARE LIVING THERE

STATEMENTS AFTER AN ARREST
UNDER THE IMMORALITY ACT

DIMETOS

THE GUEST

A LESSON FROM ALOES

Athol Fugard

*Edited with an Introduction by*
DENNIS WALDER

OXFORD
UNIVERSITY PRESS

# OXFORD
## UNIVERSITY PRESS

Great Clarendon Street, Oxford OX2 6DP

Oxford University Press is a department of the University of Oxford.
It furthers the University's objective of excellence in research, scholarship,
and education by publishing worldwide in

Oxford New York

Athens Auckland Bangkok Bogotá Buenos Aires Calcutta
Cape Town Chennai Dar es Salaam Delhi Florence Hong Kong Istanbul
Karachi Kuala Lumpur Madrid Melbourne Mexico City Mumbai
Nairobi Paris São Paulo Singapore Taipei Tokyo Toronto Warsaw

with associated companies in Berlin Ibadan

Oxford is a registered trade mark of Oxford University Press
in the UK and in certain other countries

Published in the United States
by Oxford University Press Inc., New York

British Library Cataloguing in Publication Data

Data available

ISBN 0-19-288035-7

1 3 5 7 9 10 8 6 4 2

Typeset in Baskerville
by RefineCatch Limited, Bungay, Suffolk
Printed in Great Britain by
Cox & Wyman Ltd Reading, Berkshire.

# PREFACE

I am a storyteller. Not one of my plays has been driven by an 'idea', political or otherwise. All of them have had their genesis in an image or incident, mostly from my own life but occasionally from second-hand sources. The experience which provided the setting and characters of *People Are Living There* dates back to the time in Johannesburg in 1958, when my wife Sheila and I were living in a ramshackle old boarding house in Johannesburg and I was writing *No-Good Friday* and *Nongogo*. The only truly fictional character in the play is that of the drop-out student Don—though even he is something of a portrait of the author as an obnoxious young student. I have a special fondness for the character of Mildred Constance Jenkins. I am very proud of the gallery of female portraits in my work and dear Milly was the first.

Also direct from my own personal experience is the setting and characters of *A Lesson From Aloes*. I was one of the 'comrades' at that sad birthday party which was rudely broken-up by a raid from the Security Branch of the police and the arrest of Steve. And even though Piet is an attempt at a loving portrait of a friend of those years, there is a lot of Fugard the Afrikaner in my writing of him. This play is dedicated to my mother because in Piet Bezuidenhout I tried to celebrate those qualities which as an Afrikaner, my mother had taught me to admire. And Gladys? In talking about the play I always say that the two men are victims of an unjust and evil system; whereas Gladys is God's victim. She is the dark heart at the centre of the play.

*Statements after an Arrest under the Immorality Act* came to me via a newspaper story, with photographs, of an actual case in a small country town in Port Elizabeth's hinterland. At the time I was deeply involved in my professional and hugely creative relationship with the actress Yvonne Bryceland. Using the techniques I had evolved with the making of *Sizwe Banzi* and *The Island*, I wrote *Statements* for the opening of the theatre in Cape Town, *The Space*, which Yvonne and her husband Brian Astbury had started.

This play stayed 'in process' longer than anything else I have written, and went through several different productions before ending up as the text that is now in print.

And then *Dimetos*. This is an intensely personal play. Provocations for the writing of it came from incidents and images in my own life and very decisively, a little paragraph in one of Camus' *Notebooks*. Its examination of alienation and the resulting sense of uselessness relies heavily on the hell I lived through during a sustained period of writer's block.

Athol Fugard
October 31, 1999

# CONTENTS

Notes to the texts of the plays can be found on
page 271 and are cued by asterisks.

# INTRODUCTION

I

The five works in this new collection by South Africa's foremost dramatist, Athol Fugard, suggest the need to rethink the relation between drama and politics in that country. Most worthwhile South African theatre has until recently been marked by an overriding concern with politics, and Fugard's plays are no exception. Public matters such as the pass laws, detentions, or conditions in the 'townships' have been at the forefront of attention. But the plays I have collected here are more remarkable for their exploration of the troubled interior lives of their characters. The people of these plays are shown living through an awareness of suffering—their own, or that of others. Pain, guilt, betrayal, and survival are the main themes. The dominant tone is serious, even anguished; but there are also moments of absurdity, high comedy, and a moving tenderness. These 'plays of the interior' reveal a new, or at least forgotten, emphasis in Fugard's work, confirmed by such recent works as the autobiographical memoir *Cousins* (1994) and *The Captain's Tiger* (1997)—the most personal of his plays.

But if Fugard seems to have found the space, in the 'post-apartheid' 1990s, to ruminate upon his personal past in a quite detailed, nostalgic way, this volume relates to an earlier time when there were different reasons to explore the inner life—although that is not all they do. The production of these plays over the decade from 1968 to 1978 coincided with the collapse of liberal politics in the country, and the rise of the Black Consciousness Movement. The South African Liberal Party dissolved itself in 1968, when non-racial political parties were prohibited; in the same year Steve Biko founded the exclusively black South African Students Association (SASO). By 1978 SASO had been banned, Biko murdered by the police, and thousands of young black South Africans had fled abroad, many to train for the forthcoming conflict. White opposition from within had become futile and irrelevant; international opposition was, as Leonard Thompson remarks, 'though strong in rhetoric, weak in substance'.[1]

These plays, then, emerge from an embattled society; and indeed, from an embattled segment within that society: a segment which might be characterized as that of 'the colonizer who refuses'; those whose dissent, though principled, appears to have little influence beyond arousing the hatred of fellow citizens, while leaving the colonized indifferent.[2] It is difficult, if not impossible, to gauge the precise nature and extent of Fugard's influence within South Africa, or beyond; but he was certainly perceived by the authorities as a danger (put under surveillance, his passport cancelled); and by the active minority of theatreworkers, critics, and audiences as a significant voice. How far dissenting, liberal, or left-wing artists and intellectuals unconsciously share the assumptions of the dominant power-structure which they consciously reject remains a difficult question, particularly when trying to understand the behaviour of people in colonized or formerly colonized communities. It is a question raised by these plays, with varying degrees of self-awareness. In any case, by means of their common focus upon the inner dimension of experience—the dimension of fantasy, dream, or nightmare—the plays offer a compelling opportunity to experience and reflect upon the way in which we are all intimately touched by situations of tyranny, especially by what we might nowadays call ethnic tyranny.

'The notion that there could be a South African story that doesn't have a political resonance is laughable,' the playwright asserted during a talk in New York on 16 October 1990, as events in his home country were reaching the final crisis which precipitated the release of Nelson Mandela, and the transformation of the country into a multiracial democracy four years later. He was, he explained, taking the word 'political' in its 'broadest and most meaningful sense'. Living in South Africa, 'there is no area of my life, even my most private moments, which does not have a

---

[1] *A History of South Africa*, rev. edn. (New Haven: Yale University Press, 1995), 215.

[2] Albert Memmi, *The Colonizer and the Colonized*, introd. J.-P. Sartre, trans. Howard Greenfield (1957; London: Souvenir Press, 1974), 19 ff.

political resonance. Politics is there in everything we do in South Africa. So the notion of telling a story in South Africa and not being political is naïve. I know, particularly as I have an interest in the dispossessed of my country, with whom I identify very strongly, it is inevitable that there is going to be a political byproduct to what I make. But that is not my focus as I start out.'[3]

Fugard's focus as he starts out has always been a story, embodied first in an image, or complex of images, which has caught his imagination, prompting long, slow germination, sometimes over decades, before emergence as a script, or a staged performance— not always the same thing, since some of his works (such as *Statements after an Arrest*) were first performed when their written version was still little more than a set of notes for a production. While not political in any narrow, programmatic, or very specific sense, these plays of the interior all carry a resonance in terms of the politics of their time and place—which means initially, the time and place of their first production. Further, that politics may be understood as the broader politics which engages both personal and public, both inner and outer spheres of life—insofar as these are finally separable. Fugard's overriding interest lies, he says, in 'the dispossessed of my country'—not in any particular group defined by race, gender, or class.

Of course, those dispossessed by the apartheid system which dominated the country during most of his adult life—a system which, to an alarming degree, survives the dismantling of its legal superstructure—belong mainly to the black majority. But there are others, such as the 'poor whites', historically disabled by the development of South Africa's capital-intensive, mining-based economy, for example, whose deprivations made them uniquely unwilling to acknowledge the rights of others, while struggling—as Shorty, the postman-boxer of *People Are Living There* struggles—to maintain some sense of self. For Fugard, the disempowered are not definable only in terms of race. Apart from the Man in *Statements*, the central characters of all these plays are white South

---

[3] 'Some Problems of a Playwright from South Africa', *Twentieth Century Literature: Athol Fugard Issue*, ed. Jack Barbera, 39 (Winter 1993), 385.

Africans; of these, several are women, ranging from the middle-aged Milly (of *People*), who rages wonderfully against the dying of the light, through the sad librarian of *Statements* and the frustrated housekeeper of *Dimetos*, to the psychologically wounded Gladys (in *A Lesson from Aloes*), who teeters despairingly on the edge of insanity. The diversity and depth of character displayed in these neglected works is remarkable, as is the variety of dramatic resource: most striking, perhaps, in the symbolic or mythical element in *Dimetos*, arguably the pivotal play of this group.

II

Like all Fugard's work, the plays in this collection are rooted in the specifics of their time and place—a rootedness which is not uniformly apparent in setting or character, but which the language and history of the plays connect with their local origins. The South African experience over the last four decades—the decades of the rise and fall of apartheid—has provided the world with a remarkable and creative form of cultural expression, a distinctive form of political or, more precisely, oppositional theatre involving a varied mix of African and Western traditions, all serving to undermine or at least question the status quo. Fugard's striking contribution—most notably but not exclusively in collaborative productions such as *Sizwe Bansi Is Dead* (1972) and *The Island* (1973)—has been to demonstrate the potential of such theatre to bear witness to the lives of those daily ground down by the oppressive, racist structures of the state. This is not to deny the remarkable efforts of compatriots such as Fatima Dike, Ronnie Govender, Zakes Mda, Gcina Mhlophe, Mbongeni Ngema, Paul Slabolepsky, and Pieter-Dirk Uys—to name some of those who have operated in English. But what is undeniable is the original, sustained, and lasting impact of the Fugardian intervention, represented today by more than twenty plays, a novel, and three screenplays.

Looking back over this large corpus from the present perspective, at least two important considerations emerge: one is that, although plays such as *Sizwe Bansi Is Dead* and *The Island* (available in a companion volume, *The Township Plays*) helped define the nature of oppression in the country, crossing racial boundaries and breaking censorship restrictions by the very nature of their production at a time of fierce attempts to crush opposition in thought, word, or deed, they were accompanied by, indeed closely linked with, much more inward, even contemplative work—such as *Statements after an Arrest under the Immorality Act* (1972) which, despite its title, was predominantly concerned with the psychological, if not spiritual, impact of the notorious laws against interracial sex. Secondly, although it is arguable that a play like *Statements* carried an explicitly anti-apartheid message (which can now be read in terms of the politics of race more widely understood), there are other Fugard plays which appear to take us some distance from the immediate, socio-historical domain. The most shocking example at the time of its first appearance was the semi-mythological, seemingly obscure drama *Dimetos*, which, in 1975, provoked an outcry against its 'unexpected non-political nature'.[4]

Yet, while *Dimetos* unquestionably departed from explicitness about the daily experiences of the black victims of apartheid to explore instead the inner doubts and self-questioning of a white man among whites in a remote and timeless setting, the play made a claim which helps us to understand something that has been lacking from past (and present) assumptions about South African theatre: the claim of the inner life, of interiority—an interiority which implicitly repudiates firm boundaries between the political and the non-political, the public and the private. The landscape of *Dimetos* is the shifting, uncertain, complicit landscape of guilt and responsibility. Far from denying the public sphere, the play draws us into acknowledging its importance, as inseparable from the private life, in a society seeking irrevocably to demarcate the two. If, as Michael Rustin has argued, the difficult but necessary task today is to connect the representation of the interior, perhaps unconscious experiences of individuals with their wider social determinations and representations,[5] then *Dimetos* is a work which helps to point the way.

---

[4] Ned Chaillet, 'One Play Down', *Plays and Players*, 23 Aug. 1976, 26.
[5] See Michael Rustin, *The Good Society and the Inner World: Psychoanalysis, Politics and Culture* (London: Verso, 1991), 197.

So, too, does its companion-piece, *The Guest at Steenkampskraal* (later retitled simply *The Guest*), Fugard's screenplay about an incident in the life of the tormented Afrikaner poet-naturalist Eugène Marais. Created in collaboration with South African filmmaker Ross Devenish, it was first shown on BBC TV in 1977, and, like *Dimetos*, has languished ever since. Both works deal with the tormented self-examination of isolated artist-figures (Dimetos is an engineer); but while *Dimetos* retains a somewhat abstract, mythical air, *The Guest* is specific and detailed about both character and setting to a degree quite exceptional in Fugard. It goes back furthest in time, and furthest into the interior of the country: it is set on a farm in the remote Heidelberg district of the Transvaal in 1926. Marais (played by Fugard himself, in one of the most compelling performances of his career as an actor) is a writer and thinker who tries to understand himself in relation to his people— the Afrikaners—and his environment, animal and natural; but with disastrous, self-destructive consequences.

*Dimetos* and *The Guest* were undeniably further from the social and political realities of their time than their predecessors. But they were also revealing and symptomatic, in a way confirmed by the last work in this volume, *A Lesson from Aloes* (1978), a sombre psychological drama set in 1960s suburban Port Elizabeth which questions the passivity of the white Afrikaner at its centre, Piet Bezuidenhout—an aloe-enthusiast who finds in the plant's survival through drought a parable for himself, which apparently does not apply to his friend, the 'Coloured' activist Steve, who is about to leave the country on a one-way 'exit permit'. It is no coincidence that, when these plays appeared, other white South African writers were producing works that veered away from directly addressing the crises then facing their country, towards more symbolic, unspecific modes of storytelling—a trend most obvious in the novels of J. M. Coetzee, like Fugard a half-Afrikaner who writes in English. Yet the results, in works such as Coetzee's *In the Heart of the Country* (1977), suggest that the impotence of white dissidents to effect change in the face of the rising generation of politically conscious blacks was leading to a retreat into self-scrutiny, fantasy, and an obsession with the psychopathology of the isolated consciousness, described in terms of relatively unspecific, symbolic modes.

III

*People Are Living There*

But, long before this happened, Fugard had already begun to conceive of a play which, as he remarked in 1974, struck him as in many respects 'an aberrant work', lacking the Port Elizabeth setting of its predecessor *The Blood Knot* (1961) and 'seemingly, a socio-political context of any significance'.[6] That play, the first in this collection, was called *People Are Living There* (1968). The title implies a challenge: to acknowledge the living reality of a group of despised and forgotten people—the lower middle class and 'poor whites'. The novelist André Brink has recalled attending one of the first local productions of this play in Cape Town in 1969, and 'when one character on stage accused another of hiding behind his white skin, the entire audience jumped to their feet and shouted "Yes!"'[7] This was after the government had prohibited racially mixed audiences in all public theatres (private clubs or venues still managed to get round the segregation laws). In March 1995, when I attended a revival of the play at the Baxter Theatre in Cape Town as part of a predominantly 'Coloured' audience, I witnessed a very different response. Clucks of disapproval, cries of 'Shame!' as the landlady Milly exclaimed to Shorty that Don 'once called you a perfect specimen of a retarded poor white', and Don piled on the humiliation by adding 'You're saved by your white skin . . . I'm amazed at your survival. According to Darwin you should be dead' (pp. 58–9).

Underlying this cruel taunt is an awareness of the inbred ancestry of many Afrikaans-speaking 'poor whites', who frequently intermarried with near relatives to keep land within the family—in

[6] Introduction, *Boesman and Lena and Other Plays* (Cape Town: Oxford University Press, 1980), xi.
[7] 'On Culture and Apartheid' (1970), in *Mapmakers: Writing in a State of Siege* (London: Faber & Faber, 1983), 88.

vain, as it turned out, when they were forced to join the drift to the towns after the Boer War, becoming part of a competing proletariat with rural blacks, a situation which fostered the call for job-protection through racial segregation (the so-called Colour Bar) during the inter-war years. Changing attitudes towards this group as evinced in the responses of two audiences thirty years apart suggest precisely a changing and continuing, rather than an indifferent response to the play, which effectively survives the radical transformations of the environment in which it was set. That environment was a boarding-house in the run-down, inner-city area of Braamfontein, Johannesburg, where the Fugards lived briefly in 1958, in fairly poor conditions. The only job the aspirant playwright could get at the time was as clerk in the Fordsburg 'Native Commissioner's Court', which handled pass law cases. He lasted six months: 'It was like a factory. We sent an African to jail every two minutes. It was the ugliest thing I've ever been part of. I think my basic pessimism was born there, watching that procession of faces and being unable to relate to them.'[8]

The difficulty, if not impossibility, of relating to the Other is the central dilemma of Fugard's plays. Yet out of that court experience grew a sense of the need to represent the everyday lives of black people, which led to playmaking with a brilliant generation of intellectuals, artists, and actors met in the multiracial township Sophiatown—then facing extinction under the Group Areas Act. Fugard's earliest successful plays emerged out of that interaction (*No-Good Friday*, 1958, and *Nongogo*, 1959, reprinted in *The Township Plays*, Oxford University Press, 1993). But so, too, did the recollections upon which *People Are Living There* is based. According to his *Notebooks*, Fugard had already begun notes towards the play during a stay in London (1959/60): recalling the earlier 'old complex of ideas' two years later, one image in particular helped focus renewed attempts to write the play: 'Milly's "cri de cœur" when she finds she's been in her dressing-gown all day.' That cry echoes through the play, reaching its climax as the ageing boarding-house keeper asks Don, 'You are telling me this is all I get?' and he

---

[8] 'Afrikaner Humanist', *Observer*, 18 July 1971, 9.

exclaims 'Yes!': 'Then somebody's a bloody liar . . .' she exclaims, launching into an aria of self-assertion, by turns comic, pathetic, and defiant (p. 61). 'Came across these notes made in London', Fugard confided to his notebook in May 1962:

*Milly*—divorced three times. Living with Ahlers for about ten years. 'He was nothing when I met him.' She took him in and built up his business, working as his secretary in the factory. It is flourishing and now he is (apparently) no longer interested. He left her once—and came back. Is there another woman?

It is Milly's birthday and he is taking someone else out.

Milly is proud of her past—her ties with a big family.

She lives a lot in her dressing-gown.

*Don*—intellectual—books, music—knows a lot—knows what is wrong with the world outside. Knows that he is doing nothing.

*Shorty*—a small man—amateur boxer. Earns his living precariously as a postman. Married Cissy—a child bride. No sex (except maybe for the first night). Keeps silk worms and loves Mario Lanza's singing.[9]

The central importance of the character of Milly is already clear, as is the process of Fugard's imagination, fixing on the dramatic essentials so that, for example, we never learn precisely what was involved in Milly's earlier relationship with the invisible German lodger Ahlers (who in the final version is said to make plastic flowers for funerals), although we share her fury as she yells down the corridor at the invisible figure returning from the evening out which has prompted her 'party'—

That's right, shut your door. But you'll still hear me! [*She is back in the kitchen now and shouting up at the ceiling.*] If it's the last thing I do, I'll make you hear me! [*To the others.*] Sing! Come on! [*Singing.*] 'Why was she born so . . .' COME ON! (p. 70)

In the end, her 'protest' is 'about making a noise so that "they don't forget we're here"' as Fugard noted (Jan. 1963, p. 69), rather than simply a pitiful, vengeful outburst. Revising and reworking the play during 1964, while starting work on *Hello and Goodbye*

---

[9] *Athol Fugard: Notebooks 1960/1977*, ed. Mary Benson (London: Faber & Faber, 1983), 51–2 (May 1962). This text will be referred to from here on. The first title of the play was *The Silk Worms*.

(1965) and simultaneously rehearsing Brecht's *The Caucasian Chalk Circle* with the Serpent Players from New Brighton township in Port Elizabeth, Fugard noted that Milly's 'predicament' had a 'tremendous and moving relevance to all I think, feel and do. She deserves her chance' (*Notebooks*, Sept. 1964, p. 119).

In retrospect it is astonishing that Milly's chance took so long to arrive. To begin with, Fugard was unable to obtain a satisfactory local producer for the completed work, which premièred in Glasgow on 13 March 1968, directed by Robin Midgley (who had directed *The Blood Knot* for BBC TV the year before) with Carmen Silvera as the mercurial Milly, playing the part 'with a rich South African accent', according to Allen Wright in the *Scotsman*. Wright went on to say that the play revealed 'another form of apartheid—between the loved and the unloved', and could have been located in Glasgow itself.[10] But the South African accent of the play is the key to its success, however strong the resonances elsewhere. Yet the Alexander Theatre in Johannesburg turned it down as unsuitable for local audiences. On the other hand, when the PACT offered to produce it in March 1967, Fugard refused, on the grounds that PACT was a government-sponsored organization and 'I'd rather work here, decently, with impoverished Serpent Players' (*Notebooks*, Mar. 1967, p. 149). It was the playwright's friend and early collaborator Barney Simon (1932–95) who persuaded him to do it in Cape Town for the CAPAB, with a performer who was to make the role of Milly the beginning of a crucial collaboration: Yvonne Bryceland (1926–92).

Fugard had already interviewed several performers in vain; Bryceland, whom he dimly recalled having met in Cape Town in the late 1950s, immediately gave him the sense that here was a performer who would give Milly what was needed; and even before the première of *People*, he began conceiving the major role of Lena in *Boesman and Lena* (1969) for her. By all accounts, Bryceland's performance as Milly at Cape Town's Hofmeyr Theatre was electrifying. An editorial in *The Cape Times* exclaimed:

[10] 'Boarding House with the Lid Off', *Scotsman*, 14 Mar. 1968, 10.

Something happened at the Hofmeyr a week ago after which South African theatre can never be the same again—the opening before a wildly enthusiastic audience of an indigenous play dealing powerfully and tellingly in the modern idiom with the confusions and disorientations of modern urban man . . . perhaps the Government could share in our gratitude to the modest extent of giving Mr. Fugard his passport back.

Just over a month later, the playwright himself told the local branch of the English Association that theatre in the country 'faced a sterile future unless the Government changed its censorship policies . . . I can only presume my passport was taken away because of what I express as a writer', namely a 'sense of values . . . in direct conflict to [*sic*] what prevails in South Africa at the moment'. All that had come his way was 'at the expense of millions of less-privileged people', but if he were to depict this 'rotten society', he did not think he would get the opportunity to 'put it on the South African stage'.[11]

*Statements after an Arrest*

Ironically, given the subsidized, semi-government status of CAPAB, it was this body which then—bolstered by the success of *People*—commissioned Fugard to exploit their Theatre Laboratory, producing the one-act Grotowskian *Orestes* (1971), with Yvonne Bryceland, Wilson Dunster, and Val Donald, in which the three CAPAB performers enacted the story of John Harris, executed for exploding a bomb on Johannesburg station as a protest against apartheid seven years before, an image superimposed upon the myth of Clytemnestra and her two children, Orestes and Electra. 'Harris stood in relation to his society as Orestes did to Clytemnestra. An intolerable burden of guilt for the crimes committed—the act of violence an attempt to escape the burden of guilt' (*Notebooks*, Sept. 1970, p. 188). Led by his reading of Grotowski and R. D. Laing, as much as by collaborative playmaking with the black Serpent Players, to rethink the linear, 'mechanical' linkage of his previous work, Fugard embarked on a

---

[11] [Anon.], 'Happening at the Hofmeyr', *Cape Times*, 21 June 1969, 6; 'Sterile Future for SA Theatre Forecast', *Cape Times*, 31 July 1969, 11.

'dialogue' with Bryceland. He wished to find a new way of 'communicating my sense of self and the world as experienced by that self'. Bryceland shared the struggle to 'discover or feel, if there were not in fact regions of our experience of ourselves that had not been articulated . . . We both felt that there were things to say, and ways of saying them, that we had not yet encountered' (*Notebooks*, Sept. 1970, pp. 189–90).

The material for exploring these new regions had already been noted, in the early to mid-1960s—for a play about Dimetos from Camus's *Carnets*, a play about Robben Island, a play about an informer in Algoa Park, Port Elizabeth, and another about a white librarian caught and photographed by the police *in flagrante* with a 'Coloured' Anglican missionary in the small Karroo town of De Aar. The first set of images eventually became *Dimetos* (1975), the second, the collaborative work *The Island* (1973), the third, *A Lesson from Aloes* (1978), and the fourth, *Statements after an Arrest under the Immorality Act* (1972). *Statements* was to prove the most radically inward of these. Less a play than a choreographed set of variations upon the opening image (shocking for its first South African audiences) of a naked white woman and 'Coloured' man lying in a state of post-coital tenderness on a blanket on the floor, *Statements* transgressed a fundamental assumption of racist ideology: that desire across racial lines is unnatural and should be resisted, if not forcibly stamped out.

The law forbidding 'unlawful carnal intercourse', or indeed 'any immoral or indecent act' alluded to by the title has long been consigned to the dustbin of history; but it existed for nearly three decades (1957–85) as the cornerstone of apartheid interference in private life. The Immorality Act of 1957 was the product of numerous earlier attempts (supported by all three Dutch Reformed Churches) to regulate individual behaviour so as to 'preserve' racial distinctiveness; and it brought humiliation, misery, and despair to many thousands of ordinary people before it was abolished for having 'made enemies for South Africa'.[12] As

---

[12] P. W. Botha, qtd. Roger Omond, *The Apartheid Handbook: A Guide to South Africa's Everyday Racial Policies* (Harmondsworth: Penguin, 1985), 26.

Jeanne Colleran has pointed out, while many plays by Fugard, and by other South African dramatists, have presented the effects of apartheid, few have addressed directly this 'very core of the heart of South African racism: the prohibition against skin contact'—a prohibition reflecting a fear so strong it required the vast bureacratic machine of the state to prevent, and to punish. Colleran makes a persuasive claim for the continuing validity of Fugard's 1970s depiction of an interracial affair which, while it exposes the limits of liberal tolerance (in the white librarian's reactions to her lover), reveals also a deep sense of the couple's 'insurmountable dread. The depth of their fear swamps any occasion for intimacy and overwhelms easy platitudes about reconciliation and forgiveness. However dark, this statement about what had been legally erected but is less easily eradicated, is an extraordinarily vital one, well worth the re-listening.'[13]

*Statements* was Fugard's most Grotowskian, ritualistic, and physically explicit play, taking actors and audiences further from social reality than before, but doing so to suggest the profoundly instinctual dimensions of a relationship which breaks fundamental taboos. In his notes, the playwright revealed his sense that he was creating a new and uniquely theatrical reality to explore transgressive desire: 'The De Aar Immorality Case: outsiders. Violation of a social taboo: incest, homosexuality, adultery. Impossible (absurd), because doomed, love. The essence of love=absurdity. Possession and loss' (*Notebooks*, June 1970, p. 187). Initial reactions were confused and disappointing: Owen Williams of the Cape *Argus* admired Yvonne Bryceland's 'haunting pathos', Fugard's own 'grimy realism', and the bored, conscientious policemen (there were two for the first Cape Town Space Theatre production); he applauded the honesty of a situation 'which has never before been dramatised in so immediate a fashion'; but concluded that 'such things are better at least partly concealed'.[14]

The revised production in London nearly two years later attracted full houses, although critical responses were muted, partly

---

[13] 'Re-situating Fugard; Re-thinking Revolutionary Theatre', *South African Theatre Journal*, 9 (Sept. 1995), 47–8.
[14] 'Honesty, Integrity, but dullness in Play', *Argus*, 29 Mar. 1972, 17.

because the play was the last in a South African Season at the Royal Court, preceded by stunning performances from John Kani and Winston Ntshona in *Sizwe Bansi* and *The Island*, which overshadowed the sensitive and nuanced acting of Yvonne Bryceland and Ben Kingsley as Frieda Joubert and Errol Philander (a name which could have been better chosen). But critics were also affected by the play's static, repetitive structure, its indecisive hovering between realist and non-realist dimensions—most suggestively in the 'sub-textual' moments when the guilty couple are caught by the flashes of police cameras, their panic-stricken gestures and excuses becoming confessions of guilt despite themselves. As John Elsom observed, part of their minds

supports the authoritarian logic which condemns them . . . Frieda doesn't want her body to be seen even in the safe light of a flickering match, while Errol suffers from the divided instincts of an adulterer whose betrayal of his wife is also a racial desertion. They both regard the temporal justice which snaps them up as some mark of divine retribution. But their bodies do not accept the habits of their minds, which is why, despite the surface bickering, one instinctive movement of the hand or loin destroys the destructive alienation. Physical love, their very nakedness, overcomes the years of conditioning. Throughout the play, Fugard emphasizes those forces, such as evolution and the need for water, which the will of man can't control, only violate. Love is one of those forces, and to separate the lovers is an act of mutilation.[15]

Fugard has always held a strong belief in this play, as he has in *Dimetos*—his next attempt to explore guilty desires, but in the more personal context of the artist's role in society.

## *Dimetos*

Here, too, John Elsom was almost alone among English critics in responding with sympathy and understanding. His response towards the first, stumbling 1975 Edinburgh Festival production, revised for the Nottingham Playhouse and then London's West End the following year, with Paul Scofield replacing the Afrikaner Carel Trichardt in the lead, identified *Dimetos* as

[15] 'The Coloured', *Listener*, 31 Jan. 1974, 159.

not Fugard's least, but perhaps his most, 'South African' play. He has journeyed, not away from his home, but deeper into the heart of it. The mythological framework is not an escape from 'reality' but a sort of shield to protect himself and others from the painful glare of self-examination . . . [it] is a stern, demanding play, an authentic tragedy seen from the angle of an Afrikaner, which makes no concessions to Western liberalism. Apartheid is not mentioned, although it would be the obvious illustration for the attempt to crush nature.[16]

When he was revising the play after its disastrous Edinburgh première, Fugard changed the 'remote province' of Act One to Nieu Bethesda, the Karroo village (near his birthplace Middelburg) where he used to escape from Port Elizabeth; Act Two's setting 'beside the ocean' became Gaukamma Beach, a desolate spot on the eastern Cape coast. But success does not depend upon specifying these locations, as was effectively demonstrated by the German director Dieter Reible, whose ingenious 1981 production at The People's Space (Cape Town) with leading Afrikaans actor Marius Weyers in the title role highlighted the central conflict between guilty withdrawal and taking responsibility. The 'strongly atmospheric production' helped focus Weyers's 'strongly controlled playing, building from the relatively placid, withdrawn, ostensibly avuncular figure, to the ultimately raging, demented guilt-ridden soul whose scientific knowledge cannot rescue him from his moral dilemma', as the *Argus* reviewer observed.[17]

Responsibility requires a confrontation with the inner self; and the development of a sense of the Other. The self-exiled engineer Dimetos fails to manage this, with tragic results; a predicament Fugard found in an enigmatic paragraph from his favourite French philosopher, Albert Camus (1913–60). Fugard came across this entry in his *Carnets*, dated August 1939:

Dimetos had a guilty love for his niece, who hanged herself. One day, the little waves carried on to the fine sand of the beach the body of a marvelously beautiful young woman. Seeing her, Dimetos fell on his knees,

[16] 'The True and False Pilgrim', *Listener*, 4 Sept. 1975, 311–12.
[17] Derek Wilson, 'Powerful Fugard Play Gets Deserved Airing', *Argus* Supplement, 28 Dec. 1981, 3.

stricken with love. But he was forced to watch the decay of this magnificent body, and went mad. This was his niece's vengeance, and the symbol of a condition we must try to define.[18]

Desire, betrayal, guilt, and vengeance are the key elements in this mythical kernel (derived from a little-known first-century BC Greek poet, Parthenius).[19] As he 're-read and thought about it many times', this situation 'commanded his imagination' until finally, despite being 'very far away, both in time and distance, from my own social realities', the moment came to keep the 'appointment I had made with myself' to represent it.[20]

Fugard's stage Dimetos echoes the playwright's own words when he tells the young man who claims him for the troubled city that he is 'tired of other men's needs, other men's disasters' (p. 136). Dimetos goes on to use the unwitting emissary to arrange a sexual assault on his orphaned niece, which he watches from an adjoining lemon grove. The tell-tale lemon smell on his hands reveals his complicity, which leads the girl to hang herself, using knots her uncle taught her. This concludes the first act. The second act, some years later, finds Dimetos and his housekeeper Sophia beside the sea, where the smell from a rotting off-shore creature drives him mad. After Sophia reveals her complicity in the niece's suicide, she delivers a nightmare vision which was Yvonne Bryceland's gift to the playwright—a monologue prompted by Fugard's request to her to go and look at Blake's *Hecate* in the Tate Gallery in London, an image of the triformed moon goddess and guardian of the underworld derived from *Macbeth's* Queen of the Witches.[21] Blake's prophetic writings, which appeal for a reconciliation of self and Other, provide an interesting intertext for this play, with its resounding Blakean epigraph, 'May God us keep | From Single vision & Newton's Sleep'.

The ending of the play is evidently intended as prophetic: the

[18] *Notebooks: 1935–1942*, trans. Philip Thody (New York: Marlowe & Company, 1996), 136; first pub in English as *Carnets 1935–1942* (London: Hamish Hamilton, 1963).
[19] See Richard Whitaker, 'Dimoetes to Dimetos: The Evolution of a Myth', *English Studies in Africa*, 24 1 (1981), 45–59.
[20] Programme Note, *Dimetos* (Edinburgh International Festival, 1975).
[21] Personal interview with Yvonne Bryceland, London, 21 Sept. 1983.

dead niece's spectral, off-stage voice offers Dimetos the chance to redeem himself by turning everything into a story, and he begins again at the beginning with 'Once upon a time . . .', his hands imitating a juggler who could 'give and take with the same action'. The key to what might redeem the broken engineer appears to lie in forgiveness for the sinful exercise of power; although we may feel that the hands he holds out to us at the end (like Prospero at the end of *The Tempest*, particularly as played by Paul Scofield shortly before he was cast as Dimetos)—these hands remain tainted. A 'gesture of humanist complicity' one critic called it,[22] but the Afrikaner identity of the character suggests an undertow of brooding Calvinism, of suffering without grace, which becomes more explicit in *The Guest*.

## The Guest

Suffering is the key to consciousness, according to the troubled meditations of Eugène Marais (1871–1936), naturalist-poet and author of such founding texts of Afrikaans literature as 'Die Lied van Suid-Afrika' ('The Song of South Africa'), in which South Africa speaks with a woman's voice, demanding everything, giving nothing. The woman's voice in *The Guest* is expressed by the Afrikaner mother-figure Tant Corrie (Wilma Stockenström, who replaced Fugard's first choice, Yvonne Bryceland). She tells of her suffering in the British concentration camps. More interestingly, her small daughter Little Corrie enables the afflicted Marais at least momentarily to connect with his creativity, as her fantasy of fairies enables him to create 'Die Spinerak-rokkie' ('The little cobweb dress'). This Romantic, almost visionary alternative to the environment of endless, incomprehensible suffering which dominates the film, as it dominated Marais's suicidal career, remains unrealized, however.

The idea for the film came from Ross Devenish, at the time of his collaboration with Fugard on the film version of *Boesman and Lena* with Yvonne Bryceland in 1973. Long based in London, Devenish (born 1939) came from an English farming

---

[22] Michael Billington, 'Dimetos', *Guardian*, 29 Aug. 1975, 10.

background—near Pietersburg in the Transvaal. He was an experienced documentary filmmaker, trained at the London Film School. Seeing *Boesman and Lena* in London in 1971 made him want to work with the South African playwright: first on the film version of that play, then on *The Guest*, finally on a film about squatters outside Port Elizabeth, *Marigolds in August* (1980). In his view, *The Guest* was the best of these collaborations, because 'the most filmic', and because 'Athol's theatrical scriptwriting was not allowed to dominate'.[23] Marais appealed to him as a cultured, freethinking Afrikaner educated in English, who began his lifelong study of the nature of consciousness while in London studying law in 1896, before writing the poetry and natural history which brought him a kind of fame; he attracted Fugard as another South African 'man alone' whose story would enable exploration of the consequences of withdrawing from public life.

In 1907 Marais had visited the remote Waterberg area of the Transvaal, the first of a series of attempts to seek solace for his growing morphine habit; there he observed the behaviour of the chacma baboon, noting 'that the chacma suffers from the same attribute of pain which is such an important ingredient of human mentality . . . suffering inseparable from the new mind which like man the chacma has acquired in the course of its evolution' (p. 204). This pessimistic, post-Darwinist note reappeared in two remarkable accounts of Marais's observations and meditations: *The Soul of the Ape*, which he never completed, but which was finally published in 1969 with an enthusiastic introduction by Robert Ardrey; and *The Soul of the White Ant* (1935) which proposed that the white ant or termite nest was a single organism, an idea widely supposed in South Africa to have been plagiarized by Nobel Prizewinner Maurice Maeterlinck (1862–1949). Despite his celebrity, however, Marais had long become fixed in the downward spiral of addiction, and on 25 July 1936 he shot himself.

According to the original introduction to *The Guest*, Marais was involved

---

[23] Personal interview, London, 13 Mar. 1981.

In a lifelong introspection where the interlocking series of questions that compelled him were: 'What is addiction?' 'Why are humans prone to some form of addiction?' 'Do animals share this propensity?' he developed a theory that explained it all to himself—and perhaps thereby reduced some of his own pain.

This was one of the reasons why we found ourselves attracted to the idea of a film about Eugène Marais. Furthermore, his vision was essentially one which was produced in an interaction with Africa, and we wanted very much to make a film that had its roots here, in the country in which it would be made.[24]

Devenish's film, lucid, unsentimental, bare, and brief, won two prizes at the Locarno International Film Festival the month after its BBC viewing in 1977: for Devenish's direction, and Fugard's performance. The film uses mirrors and windows to great effect, to suggest the splintering of the self: at one point, Marais yells out at us: 'Desdemona lives again, black man!' The only black man (or woman) in the film is the farmworker Stuurie, whose sole task appears to be the provision of Marais's drugs from a distant town; but his race is present to the white unconscious as a sexual threat, linking the film and *Statements*. Like Dimetos, Marais ultimately seeks redemption in vain, lacking any saving grace, as he lacks firm belief. In a thoughtful if severe response, novelist J. M. Coetzee took Fugard to task for stereotyping the Afrikaners, and de-historicizing the Marais of his source-text, Leon Rousseau's biography *Die Groot Verlange* (1974: revised as *The Dark Stream: The Story of Eugène Marais*, 1982). An 'equivocal' product Coetzee called it, which dramatized 'the tragedy of white consciousness in Africa', while 'finally consoling, even flattering, [to] its white South African audience'.[25] Otherwise, the local response was enthusiastic; appearing before the advent of television in the country, it was viewed as a film and, as such, the start of a new, 'local cinema' tradition.

## A Lesson from Aloes

First viewed on television, with its in-built tendency to naturalism,

---

[24] *The Guest: An Episode in the Life of Eugene Marais* (Johannesburg: Ad Donker, 1977), 8.
[25] 'The Burden of Consciousness in Africa', *Speak* (Cape Town), 1/1 (Dec. 1977), 4–7.

*The Guest* has suffered from being interpreted in rather limited, realist terms: viewed as a more symbolic, even Gothic-expressionist piece, it takes its place beside *Dimetos* as a remarkably creative attempt on Fugard's part to reflect inner doubts and promptings about the nature of suffering, and the inevitability of guilt.[26] As if to compensate for the relative obscurity and inexplicitness of these works, Fugard's next project returned to the familiar setting, textures, and accents of his home environment—Port Elizabeth; and to a play he had been contemplating intermittently since the early 1960s. Shot through with didactic symbolism, while naturalistic in character and locale, *A Lesson from Aloes* (1978) seemed designed to counter accusations of failure to act as an artist 'commissioned by society', a phrase he borrowed from Ernst Fischer's *The Necessity of Art: A Marxist Approach*.[27] Nevertheless, Fugard consoled himself, 'our hell (history) is man-made, to that extent it can be unmade by men' (*Notebooks*, Dec. 1968, p. 179).

This optimistic remark becomes a key line in the play, uttered by its central character Piet Bezuidenhout, when he tells his wife Gladys the 'lesson' he learnt from his friend, the political activist Steve Daniels: 'An evil system', says Piet, 'isn't a natural disaster. There's nothing you can do to stop a drought, but bad laws and social injustice are man-made and can be unmade by men. It's as simple as that' (p. 242). Everything about the play contradicts this: Piet is left contemplating his aloes, after having been suspected of informing on the comrades (an earlier title of the play was 'The Informer'); Steve departs for England on a one-way exit permit, after having been broken under interrogation by the security police; and Gladys, violated by the police removal of her intimate diaries, prepares to return to Fort England (a mental hospital in Grahamstown).

*A Lesson from Aloes* is about inner politics, the politics of those reduced to passivity by public events, and the interference of the state. For Gladys, who provides the focus for this dimension of the

[26] For a detailed, enthusiastic account of both *Dimetos* and *The Guest*, see Russell Vandenbroucke, *Truths the Hand Can Touch: The Theatre of Athol Fugard* (New York: Theatre Communications Group, 1985), 148–66.

[27] Harmondsworth: Pelican Books, 1963, 210.

play, 'politics' and 'the black man's misery' are meaningless, she says; yet this is what led to the raid on her home, which she has experienced as a rape. 'I accept, Steven,' she tells Daniels, 'that I am just a white face on the outskirts of your terrible life, but I'm in the middle of mine and yours is just a brown face on the outskirts of that. Do you understand what I'm saying? I've got my own story. I don't need yours. I've discovered hell for myself' (p. 267). Until Fugard realized that her story was the dramatic centre of the play, it did not take off—the earliest references to it begin in February 1961, with notes about a meeting at which 'Solly, bespectacled quiet-spoken leftist', says black people 'must forget about the white, or waiting for them to change', and just 'take' what they want:

Opposed in this opinion by Piet B., red-faced, big-handed Afrikaner. 'We must stand together, man. Together. Together we take the world. They want us. Hell, Solly, when I take my bus out Cadles way at five o'clock, I see them. I see them walking with their backs straight, walking home [the bus strike]. It's the people, Solly. ". . . And they shall inherit the earth."'

His passion was English poetry, and he quoted endlessly, relevantly and with feeling . . . (*Notebooks*, Feb. 1961, p. 23)

But despite trying to help the 'struggle for freedom', standing in a local campaign as the 'Coloured Representative', this man found himself laughed at by those he wished to represent, and having to learn that 'if a coloured could not represent the coloureds, they would rather have no representative at all' (*Notebooks*, Feb. 1961, pp. 23–4).

Then in March 1965, Piet's wife appears in the playwright's notes:

His wife Gladys—English; well-educated by comparison with his J.C. certificate (or Standard 6?). Writes poetry—nothing published. When their house was searched recently by the Special Branch, they found her poems (love?) and read them all—traumatic effect on her (rape?), leading to nervous breakdown . . .

Contrast: Piet's sober sanity—the feeling he gives that he is indestructible, that you'd have to kill him, that you could never drive him mad. And herself—highly-strung, neurotic at her best, really unbuttoned at the worst—the refinements in sensibilities that go with this instability. She is a qualified shorthand-typist but has seldom kept a job for longer than a month because of the recurrent delusion that any new appointment in the office where she is working is a S.B. spy placed to keep an eye on her and Piet . . . Piet is widely suspected here in P.E. of being a police informer. (*Notebooks*, pp. 122–3)

The basic dramatic conflict of the future play has arrived; and by October 1966, we find Fugard adding to Piet and Gladys, 'Steve— a coloured teacher, banned', but struggling with the 'bellyful of clichés' introduced by the 'blatant politics' of his idea, and the 'need to locate Piet, Gladys and Steve in a world of real things, not ideas', seeking 'Brecht's "ease"', finding a defining 'image' in the situation of drought, when a man finds himself 'empty-handed, useless . . . the absurdity of himself, *alone*' (*Notebooks*, pp. 138–40). By September 1967, in the midst of all his other activities (working with Serpent Players, starting to conceive *Boesman and Lena)*, Fugard learns more about 'Steve':

His last story—two days ago in Korsten—of an interview with the S.B. He is convinced they tried to drive him to suicide. After one spell of questioning which lasted an hour, they pushed him into a room and into a chair beside an open window—six storeys up. The policemen with him sat at least fifteen feet away, smiling. Every five minutes or so, the door opened and a captain just stood there, laughing mockingly and gloatingly at him. For Steve, a moment of total despair. This interview took place three weeks after the date on which he had first planned to leave. Pretoria had not yet granted him an exit permit. (*Notebooks*, p. 154)

In his introduction to the first published version of the play, Fugard offered a somewhat different version of these notes, concluding that during 'the next ten years' (from 1961, when he located all the above!) he made several attempts to tell the basic story. 'When the last of these miscarried in 1971 I thought I had finally abandoned the idea.' Then, two years later, 'without any apparent external provocation', memories of the three characters returned 'obsessively', and 'I started working on the play once again. A year later I went into rehearsals in Johannesburg.' Thinking about this 'protracted history' he was conscious of 'one thing: the completion of a work has always depended on a correspondence, a relevance, between the external specifics of the play—the "story" as such—and my sense of myself at the time', which he defined in terms of the search for survival in a country for which drought, 'with its harsh and relentless resonances, is a very apt metaphor'.[28]

'A sombre and disturbing play', remarked Margaret Munro of the Australian production, a production which brought out the 'nuances of domestic routine' in this 'psychological drama'.[29] But despite winning the New York Drama Critics' Circle Award as the best play of the 1980–1 season on Broadway, *Lesson from Aloes* had a mixed reception outside the country: passivity and retreat do not make powerful theatre, perhaps, when viewed in the South African context. 'Diffuse and awkward' was one typical comment; 'Fugard directs his original Johannesburg production in a rather old-fashioned, explicit style which echoes his writing.' In South Africa, the first Market Theatre production elicited enthusiasm for its complexity and subtlety . . . The basic situation is superficially as simple as the symbol of the aloe, but it contains haunting reson-ances, shifts of attitudes, piercing, equivocal insights.'[30] As Munro later pointed out, the real focus of the play is the South African liberal, who is 'not just standing still (implied by the symbolic aloes of the title, dormant in drought, always ready to flower in the right conditions) but is, in fact, regressing daily through the loss of opportunities for interracial brotherhood'. The inadequacy of the liberal position at the time, with its reliance upon 'shared assump-tions and a shared sense of community', is that it finds itself 'willy-nilly acquiescing in racial divisions. Unwittingly, it too becomes a betrayal.'[31] The play's final focus upon Gladys, and her departure for the mental hospital, suggests that she has taken that betrayal upon her own shoulders, in effect.

The white presence in South Africa is what all these plays

---

[28] *A Lesson from Aloes* (Oxford: Oxford University Press, 1981), xiii–xiv.

[29] 'Apartheid's Bitter Symbols', Eastern Edition of *Melbourne Times*, 1 July 1981, 7.

[30] Victoria Radin, 'Letters from Sylvia', *Observer*, 13 July 1980, p. 30; Owen Williams, 'Power, Insight in New Fugard Play', *Argus*, Tonight section, 8 Jan. 1979, 3.

[31] 'The Fertility of Despair', *Meanjin Quarterly*, 40 (1981), 474.

explore and represent: in terms of a reaction to the corruptions engendered by apartheid, but also as a way of exploring the moral dilemmas of life within a repressive society. Symptomatic in their sometimes puzzling and flawed inwardness, they nonetheless raise the issue of how to find freedom from within, when external circumstances apparently render this quest difficult if not absurd. Fugard the playwright is here struggling to invent a theatre which increases our awareness of the nature of subjectivity, without compromising its political implications: a theatre of the interior.

# TEXTUAL NOTE

The texts reprinted here are based on the author's last revised versions, and have been carefully checked against the available manuscript, typescript, and printed versions, currently held in the National English Literary Museum, Grahamstown, South Africa—whose invaluable assistance I wish here to acknowledge, in particular that of Malcolm Hacksley and Ann Torlesse. (The originals have since been purchased by the Lilly Library, Indiana University.) The importance of providing accurate and consistent texts for a major modern playwright, whose work continues to be produced worldwide, should be obvious. But although it has been possible to ensure accuracy and consistency for the texts contained in this and the two accompanying volumes, there remain versions of the plays in circulation which reproduce errors or earlier versions of the plays. Critics and academics, students, performers, and producers should beware.

It has not seemed necessary or appropriate to add detailed textual notes to this edition, but it may be worthwhile here to indicate the kind of change I have felt impelled to make. It may seem a small thing to have corrected Milly's opening 'What are you doing?' to 'What you doing?' although that is how it stands in the author's original manuscript. But Fugard's ear for South African speech forms is one of his greatest assets as a playwright, the rhythms and accents of his characters one of the most engaging aspects of his work, testifying to the reality of his people and his part of the world; and if Milly's way with words—which reflects her reality as a white, lower-middle-class boarding-house landlady in Braamfontein in the late 1950s—matters, then it is something which we should allow to be established by her opening remarks. I suspect that a well-meaning editor corrected her apparent ungrammaticalness for the first printed version of the play, unaware that this is a South Africanism, of a part with such expressions as 'Oupa', 'Native', or 'cool-drink' (which may be found in the Glossary). And the result has continued in print ever since.

On the other hand, the allusion in *Statements after an Arrest* to Julian Huxley's *Principles of Evolution*—a non-existent book, evidently a conflation of Lyell's *Principles of Geology* (also referred to in the play) and Huxley's *Evolution*—has been left standing, on the grounds that this may well have been the character's error, and that it stands thus in all the versions I have seen (although critics and commentators have silently assumed without checking that the book exists). The playwright's interest in evolution, and its relevance as an aspect of the racist ideology explored in these and other plays, suggest it is important to be accurate about such a reference, even if the character is not, and so while leaving the allusion standing in the text, I have supplied further details in one of my notes to the plays, which also refer briefly to such matters as dates and local places, where necessary for understanding by non-South African, as well as local, readers and audiences.

Fugard corrects and revises details for performances directed by him; but since his primary concern is the performance, rather than the printed text, the enacted image, rather than the word (although he is more concerned with his words than is sometimes realized), he does not check everything for the published versions. His current projects are what always absorb his attention. His own spelling and punctuation are occasionally wayward, and these I have corrected, but as lightly as possible, for consistency and sense. In addition, I have supplied revised information about the earliest performances of the plays.

Dennis Walder
*London, 1999*

# PEOPLE ARE LIVING THERE

# CHARACTERS

MILLY, *a Johannesburg landlady*
DON, *one of her lodgers*
SHORTY, *another of her lodgers*
SISSY, *Shorty's wife*

PEOPLE ARE LIVING THERE was first performed at the Close Theatre, Glasgow, on 13 March 1968, directed by Robin Midgley, with the following cast:

| | |
|---|---|
| MILLY | Carmen Silvera |
| DON | Douglas Ditta |
| SHORTY | Ronald Cunliffe |
| SISSY | Rosemary Gerrette |

The South African première took place at the Hofmeyr Theatre, Cape Town, on 14 June 1969, directed by the author, with the following cast:

| | |
|---|---|
| MILLY | Yvonne Bryceland |
| DON | Athol Fugard |
| SHORTY | Ken Leach |
| SISSY | Gillian Garlick |

The first US production took place at The Forum of the Repertory Theater, Lincoln Center, New York, on 18 November 1971, directed by John Berry, with Estelle Parsons as Milly.

# ACT ONE

*The kitchen of an old, double-storeyed house in Braamfontein,\* Johannesburg, one cold Saturday night.*

*Two doors—one leading to the backyard and an outside room where Don lives, the other to a passageway and so to the rest of the house. There is also a window looking out onto a street. Centre stage is a kitchen table and chairs with an electric light hanging above them. For the rest we see, but not too clearly because the light is bad, the walls, a kitchen dresser, shelves and in one corner an old-fashioned gas stove.*

*Curtain-up—early on a cold winter's evening. The room is in darkness except for a little light from the street outside. It is a Saturday night but still too early for the rush of traffic to the city. Only occasionally does the window catch the movement of light as a car drives by.*

*A figure appears in the passage doorway. All we can see is the white blur of a dressing gown. The figure stands motionless, obviously listening, then calls out in a husky woman's voice:*

Hullo! Anybody home? [*Pause.*] Help!

*Silence. A sudden, determined move to the door leading to the backyard. Halfway across the room this is stopped by the frail, silken chimes of a grandfather clock somewhere else in the house. The woman stops and listens. We hear four sets of chimes preceding the hour, then silence. The woman turns and exits back into the passage from which comes the sound of a blow to the grandfather clock which now starts its belated chiming of the hour. At the fourth stroke the woman is back in the doorway. Three more. It is seven o'clock.*

*An arm comes up. The light goes on.*

*We see* Milly. *About fifty years old, dressed in an old candlewick dressing gown, her hair disordered, her face swollen with sleep. She waits expectantly, as if the light and chimes might evoke some response in the silent house.*

MILLY. Shorty!

[*Silence. She directs her attention very obviously to the ceiling and listens. Satisfied that there is no sound of life, Milly moves to the back door and opens it, shivering and clutching her gown against the cold night air.*]

Hey, Don. [ *Louder*] Don! [*She waves*].
Jeez, it's cold hey!

3

VOICE. I'm busy.

MILLY. Winter all right. What you doing?

VOICE. Leave me alone!

[*Pause. Milly shivers.*]

MILLY. Come on over and have some coffee. Warm you up. That room of yours must be like a morgue.

VOICE. No. Go away.

MILLY. Suit yourself. Kettle's on all the same.

[*She closes the door with pretended indifference, then bends down and peeps through the keyhole. Satisfied with what she sees, she straightens up and goes around the kitchen, looking for a cigarette, picking up and discarding several empty packets before she finds the right one. She lights a cigarette and waits, watching the back door.* Don *comes in and moves straight for the passage.*]

DON. Coming!

[*Exit. Milly goes on smoking. Lavatory flushes off—in the passage. Don returns. Plain, almost featureless face with a sallow complexion. Body and movements without virility. He is about twenty years old and is wearing a nondescript grey suit, vaguely ill-fitting. Soft collared shirt, no tie. He stands in the doorway frowning darkly at Milly.*]

What did it look like to you?

MILLY. What?

DON. Me.

MILLY. Bladder-bursting.

DON. No, no. In my room. What did you see?

MILLY. You, on your bed, on your back, looking up at the ceiling.

DON. Nothing out of the ordinary?

MILLY. Hardly call that out of the ordinary.

DON. Purpose was dead in me. When I lay down at four o'clock there were a hundred reasons why I should have got up. When you saw me not one was left. I had systematically abandoned the lot. Sartre calls it Anguish.

MILLY. Still looking for it are you?

DON. I've told you before the expression is 'finding oneself'.

MILLY. What's the difference?

DON. Nothing's lost in the way you make it sound.

MILLY. Well, according to the language I speak, when I want to find something I'm looking for it, and when I'm doing that I can be bloody certain I lost it to begin with.

DON. Well, I never had it to begin with, so I can't lose it.

MILLY. Good Lord!

DON. Look, this is beyond you.

MILLY. You're in trouble, my boy.

DON. Let's talk about something else please.

MILLY. What's all this got to do with Bachelor of Commerce anyway?

[*Don tries to ignore her.*]

Because quite frankly, it doesn't sound like studying to me. For the sake of your poor parents I hope you are going to pass this time.

DON. It's my life.

MILLY. And their money.

DON. In any case I've decided to chuck it up.

MILLY. Just like that! What happened?

DON. Accountancy.

MILLY. Again. How many times does that make?

DON. Only two.

MILLY. I don't think you try hard enough.

DON. Why should I? What's bookkeeping got to do with the dilemma of our age? I need time. I've worked it out. Fifty pounds a month will keep body and soul together, leaving my mind free. The paper is full of jobs.

MILLY. That doesn't sound like a career to me.

DON. An Age of Crisis, and you talk about a career. You're as bad as my parents. You'll be on to pension funds next.

MILLY. Doesn't worry me what happens to you, my boy. As long as I get my rent the lot of you can go down the drain for all I care.

DON. Then it's settled. Where's that coffee?

MILLY [*yawning*]. I've just woken up. Where are the others?

DON. Shorty's at the gym

MILLY. That's right. Saturday. I forgot. And him? [*She indicates the ceiling.*] You see him go out?

DON. No.

MILLY. All quiet on the Western Front. [*Another yawn.*] Hell, my heart is still asleep. Anyway, I think I'll pop out. What's on your programme for tonight?

DON. Nothing. And I want to keep it that way.

MILLY. Well, I want a change in scenery. Get dressed in a mo'. Maybe a walk. Brisk walk. Bit of fresh air. You could do with some too. It's healthy. What about it?

DON. The air outside is not as fresh as you think.

MILLY. Better than the lot in here, thank you very much. You're going all pimply again.

DON. I never said I was good-looking.

MILLY. Maybe you eat too many sweets.

DON. Maybe I do.

MILLY. Well, there's something sickly somewhere.

DON. It's none of your business.

MILLY. Thank you.

DON. That coffee.

MILLY. I feel like a bit of excitement tonight. Movies or something. Been in all day.

DON. Where's that coffee?

MILLY. Coming. [*She doesn't move.*]

DON. So is Christmas.

MILLY [*looking at the ceiling*]. You sure you didn't see him go out?

DON. Why should I lie to you?

MILLY. To spite me. [*Don smiles.*] Yes! Don't think I don't know. There's a spiteful streak in you sometimes.

[*Returns her attention to the ceiling.*]

6

There's no sound of life.

DON. Maybe he's dead.

MILLY. Like hell.

DON. It was meant to be a joke.

MILLY. And I'm not laughing because it's not possible. Must have made a run for it behind my back. He knew I was waiting. Kept to his room all day. Did you notice? Avoiding me. There's proof. Guilty conscience! And then as soon as I closed an eye—the getaway!

[*Stubs out her cigarette viciously and lights another, an automatic gesture.*]

I didn't mean to—close my eye, I mean. I was lying down in wait for him. You know, spring the surprise when he got to the door. But the last thing I remember is Sissy's radio going full blast. Blah-blah-blah! God! I hated it. Get up Mildred, I said, get up and go up and grab it and chuck the bloody thing out! Blah-blah-blah! I must have dropped off then, because the next thing I knew it was cold and dark and . . . I don't know. Empty! Waking up is a cold business in an empty house. Specially old houses. Wherever you look it's just walls. God, it's depressing! Put out the light and you're as good as in your grave.

[*Don takes out a pencil and makes a note on the back of one of the empty cigarette packets. Milly watches him.*]

What did I say?

DON. That bit about the walls. The featureless face of horror.

MILLY. I've got some pictures somewhere. We'll get them up. [*Breaking mood.*] Anyway . . .

DON. Where's that coffee?

MILLY. Give me a chance to get my bearings!

DON [*looking at the stove*]. Isn't it on yet?

MILLY. I'll put it on in a minute.

DON. You told me the kettle was on.

MILLY. I did not.

DON. Milly you distinctly said, 'Kettle's on'.

MILLY. Oh, you're a liar!

DON [*putting away his pencil*]. In that case . . .

MILLY. Give it a rest, man. You won't find yourself tonight.

DON. I came because you said the coffee was ready.

MILLY. Well, I'm going to put the kettle on right now. [*She stands.*]

DON. Call me when it's ready.

MILLY [*stopping his move to get up*]. Sssssh! Activity!

[*Goes quickly to the door, where she listens.*]

It's him! Must have been in the bathroom. So! Togging himself up. Ever known him to have a bath on a Saturday? It's to spite me. God, I wish I knew where he was going!

[*She follows his movements in the room overhead.*]

Bed. Wardrobe. Dressing table. Putting on his hair oil. Ever seen that? If you want to lose your breakfast one morning go up and have a look. It's enough to make any decent person sick. He sort of washes those big paws of his in the stuff, smoothes down the few hairs left on his nut and then smiles at the result. It's revolting. Greenish. Looks like peppermint liqueur.

DON [*standing*]. If you decide to make that coffee, call me.

MILLY. I'm putting it on now—*now*—right this very minute. Satisfied?

[*She goes to the stove.*]

DON. Good. I'll be waiting.

MILLY. Sit down.

DON. Later.

MILLY. Sit down! I want to tell you something.

DON. I've heard enough.

MILLY. You don't know what I'm going to say, so please sit down.

DON. You've got one minute. Well?

MILLY [*looking at the ceiling*]. Him.

DON. I knew it!

MILLY. Do you know what he's done?

DON [*emphatically*]. Yes!

8

MILLY. After ten years, mark you. Ten years!

DON. I know.

MILLY. That's a good piece of anyone's life. Well? isn't it?

DON. It is.

MILLY. You bet it is. Give me back those ten years and he'd never get the smell of them again. [*Pause.*] I'm not finished! [*Pause*]. It was a custom, Don. Every Saturday night. Regular as rent. Beer and sausages for two down at the Phoenix. Until tonight.

DON. Are you finished now?

MILLY. Yes. *No!* Wait. I just want to ask you one question. Is it right? Come on. Answer that. Smearing on his stinking hair oil. Is it right?

DON. It isn't.

MILLY. Then go up and tell him. You call yourself a man, don't you? Go up there and tell him it isn't right. And then hit him. A lady's honour is at stake. Ten years of her life. Hit him for it. [*With intensity.*] All that talk about meeting an old friend from Germany! Old friend, my foot. Where does *he* suddenly come from after ten years and a World War? And last week that new suit. For an old friend? From Germany? I wasn't born yesterday. I can also put one and one together and get two evil-minded birds in the bush.

[Shorty Langeveld *appears in the passage doorway. He is short but stockily built, about twenty-five years old. He is wearing the tunic and trousers of a postman's uniform and carries a small bag, and a pair of boxing gloves.*]

SHORTY. Hey, Milly.

MILLY. Go to hell, I'm busy.

DON [*to Milly*]. Go on.

MILLY [*realizing she has gone too far*]. Oh! So now you're interested.

DON. Two birds in the bush.

MILLY. I'll tell you some other time.

DON. Why not now?

MILLY. This is not the right moment.

9

SHORTY. Hey, chaps. Is Sissy gone?

MILLY. I'm not your wife's nursemaid. Damned good idea to get her one. For both of you. Kids. Man and wife! [*To Don.*] You ever heard such nonsense?

SHORTY. Why you in such a bad mood, Milly?

MILLY [*shaking a finger at him*]. Don't you get impertinent with me, Shorty Langeveld! And take your togs out of here. I've told you before, the kitchen's not a boxing ring.

[*Exit Shorty with bag and gloves.*]

Gutless little whiner. He gets on my nerves.

[*Don, who has been worrying Milly with his intent stare, now laughs at her obvious discomfort.*]

What's so funny?

DON. I'll tell you some other time.

MILLY. Don't bother.

[*Milly lights another cigarette. Shorty returns.*]

SHORTY. What about some coffee to warm us up, Mill?

MILLY. Drop dead!

[*She moves to the door.*]

SHORTY [*in a whisper*]. What's wrong with her?

MILLY [*at the door*]. I heard that.

DON. How did the boxing go?

SHORTY. We was sparring today. Major Jeffries says my defence is weak, but I got a sledge-hammer left, if I try. He's going to pick a team to fight Railways and Harbours in Durban at Christmas.

DON. Think you'll make it?

SHORTY. Well, Don, I'll try my best. Only this afternoon a guy called Jacobs rocked me, man. One-two, one-two, then Dwada! Straight left, straight through. If it was for real, I would be out for the count.

DON. Use that left next time.

SHORTY. Sledge-hammer, he says. If only I could get me a Native* for sparring partner it would be better. Specially Zulus. They is tough, man! You can't just knock them out, you know. Their heads are hard. That's what Toweel* does. I asked Emily if she's got any brothers and she said she will look. What about it sometime, Don? Me and you. A few rounds.

DON. I'm a wrestler.

SHORTY. Judo-jitsu.

DON. Hari-kari, the lot.

SHORTY. You're bluffing! What you doing tonight?

DON. Nothing.

SHORTY. Same here. You seen Sissy? [*Takes out his pay-packet.*] Pay-day!

DON. You're in the money!

SHORTY [*laughing*]. Ja ! There's a guy at work—George—in the Despatch Room. He says: Pay-days is happy days ! We laugh at him, Don. He's always full of sports. But I got worries tonight. One pound ten from ten pound nineteen and six is nine pounds nine and six, right?

MILLY [*joining them at the table*]. And one week's bed and breakfast is four pound ten, please, plus six bob for washing.

SHORTY. Five bob.

MILLY. Six bob. There's a shilling fine. Emily says your socks were very smelly this week.

SHORTY. It's the walking, Milly. I sweat.

MILLY. Six bob!

SHORTY [*handing her the money*]. There's change.

MILLY. Are you accusing me of something?

VOICE [*suddenly and just beyond the passage doorway*]. Shorty!

SHORTY. Sissy!

VOICE. Shorty!

SHORTY. I'm in here, Sissy.

VOICE. Well, I'm waiting.

SHORTY. I'm coming. [*To Don.*] Here goes. Hold your thumbs for me, man. [*Hurries off.*] It was the trams, Siss. I waited . . .

VOICE. You said you would be home by seven. Where's the money?

[*Milly lays out two cups and saucers. Into each cup a teaspoon of instant coffee. Then condensed milk from a tin with two holes.*]

MILLY. She's a little bitch, that one. And he's a little fool.

DON. I have a feeling he knows.

MILLY. That makes it even more disgraceful. He should be ashamed.

DON. But he is.

MILLY. Then why doesn't he do something about it?

DON. Such as?

MILLY. I think that's perfectly obvious. To begin with, he could hit her.

DON. Violence won't solve his problem.

MILLY. Exactly. He's got no guts.

DON. Now there's a word I hate. What's guts?

MILLY. Guts? If you don't know what guts is, my boy, then I feel sorry for you.

[*She adds hot water and sugar to the cups and sits down.*]

'He's got guts.' Let's see. [*Pause.*]

> 'Then up he rose
> With an awful sound
> And smote the bastard down.'

[*Chuckles with deep satisfaction.*] God that's good! And smote the bastard down! Anyway, there you have it. That's guts. If you can't hit out once in a while, you might as well throw in the towel.

[*Don has in the meantime taken out a pipe—new—and is trying to smoke it.*

*Voices of Sissy and Shorty off-stage.*]

SHORTY. Sissy . . .

SISSY. No.

SHORTY. But . . .

SISSY. No!

SHORTY. Please, Sissy.

SISSY [*entering*]. I said *No!*

[*White-faced, about eighteen years old with straight, mouse-coloured hair. Dressed with cheap extravagance. She is barefoot, carrying her shoes and handbag.*]

I'm sick of you and those silkworms! Anyway, you told me you threw them away.

SHORTY [*now also in the room*]. I did, Sissy. Those what you did prick and died.

SISSY. Oh! Hiding the others, are you? From who? From me? That's not very nice, is it? They're mine, you know. Jossie gave them to me.

SHORTY. You didn't want them. You never fed them.

SISSY. I want them now. Where are they? [*Pause.*] Shorty Langeveld, where are my silkworms? [*He doesn't move.*] You know what you are? A bad boy.

SHORTY. If you bring some beetroot leaves for them to eat, I'll . . .

SISSY [*stamping her foot*]. I said N—O spells No! Beetroot leaves! Ask some old Coolie shop for beetroot leaves? On a Saturday night? Are you mad?

SHORTY [*holding out a brown paper bag*]. Only a few, Siss. If you put them in here nobody will see.

SISSY. And what will that make me look like? Going to the movies with a brown paper bag! Full of beetroot leaves. What will Billy think? 'Beetroot leaves, Billy. For Shorty.' Yes. That's what I will say. 'Shorty eats beetroot leaves, Billy.' He'll laugh at you, you know. He'll tell me again I'm married to a poep.

SHORTY [*prepared to suffer this*]. Okay.

SISSY. Ag! Why do I talk to you?

[*Sissy turns away in disgust and goes to the stove where she collects a pair of stockings that have been hanging up to dry. Milly and Don are drinking their coffee, watching the scene between the other two with detached interest.*]

13

MILLY. Since when is my stove your washing line?

SISSY. They got wet. I only got one pair. He's to blame. [*Pointing to Shorty.*] Blame him. He's supposed to earn the living. [*Speaking to Shorty again.*] Jossie's got five pairs, you know. Five. And she hasn't even got a husband.

[*On the point of putting on the stockings she turns to Shorty, who has been standing abashed, watching her.*]

Where's your respect? Look the other way!

[*Shorty turns his back.*]

What I would like to ask you, Shorty Langeveld, is what use is a husband that don't even bring home the living what he's supposed to earn?

SHORTY [*his back turned*]. Please, Sissy.

SISSY. What sort of postman loses his letters! That's what I'd like to know.

SHORTY. Sissy!

SISSY. Ashamed of yourself I hope. [*To Don and Milly.*] I don't suppose he told you. One pound ten taken off because he lost letters again. It's not the first time. There he is. Ask him. You told Ma you could earn me a living. This is no married life.

[*She is finished with her stockings.*]

You can look now!

[*Sissy puts on her shoes, then takes out lipstick, mirror, and powder-compact.*]

You know what I warned you! Well, I mean it. Once more, oh boy! Just you come home once more with your pay short and I'll do it. I swear to God I'll do it. And it won't do you any good to cry.

SHORTY. Stop now, Siss!

SISSY. Yes, he cried. This big boy cried. Whaaa . . . whaa . . . whaa. Real tears. 'Don't, Sissy ! Please, Sissy! I promise, Sissy!'

[*Shorty has not yet turned to face her.*]

I said you can look now. Turn around!

[*He does so. The sight of him provokes her still more.*]

Come here. Let's make you pretty.

SHORTY [*covering his mouth with his hands*]. No, no.

SISSY. Tell Milly and Don what a pretty boy we make you in the room. Red lips, rosy cheeks. [*To Don and Milly.*] He lets me do it upstairs. [*To Shorty.*] Didn't you tell them? You don't seem to tell your friends anything about what goes on. You know what you are?

[*Sissy leans forward suddenly and writes on his forehead with her lipstick.*]

That's what you are!

[*Picks up her bag and flounces out of the room. Shorty stands hanging his head. Milly and Don watch him.*]

MILLY. Shorty! Come here.

[*He moves to Milly. She examines his forehead.*]

'Bad boy.'

[*Don also examines it and then writes on the back of his cigarette packet.*]

Why didn't you hit her? You're a boxer. Why didn't you give her one good wallop?

DON. Who's Billy?

MILLY. She says he's her cousin. Know what I mean?

DON [*to Shorty*]. You know him?

SHORTY. Sort of.

DON. Have you actually met him ?

MILLY. Answer the man!

SHORTY. No.

MILLY. You idiot! Go on. Go and wash your face.

[*Exit Shorty.*]

Satisfied? If that wasn't taking it lying down then I'd like to know what is. And let me assure you that's the only lying down she lets him do when she's around. You heard him. When a woman is stingy that way then she's really stingy. Dammit all, old Shorty's entitled to it.

DON [*looking up from his notes*]. The aggressive female and the submissive male. The loss of male virility and the woman's rebellion. The neurosis of our time.

MILLY. Who?

DON. Shorty and Sissy.

MILLY [*amazed*]. When?

DON. Now. Right here under our nose.

MILLY. This tiff? Come off it.

DON. Undercurrents, Milly. Undercurrents. Didn't you feel them? This room was like a dynamo. I couldn't have taken it much longer.

MILLY. What was going on? In plain language, please.

DON. She was trying to arouse Shorty.

MILLY. Nonsense. It's Billy she's after. I've seen it happen before. Shorty's just too dumb to see it.

DON. He knows all about it.

MILLY. Then why doesn't he do something?

DON. Because the thought of Billy and Sissy arouses him.

MILLY. Where in God's name do you get this rubbish from? Honestly, sometimes you can talk the biggest lot of . . .

DON. I'm not finished. There's something else. She knew I was watching. She was trying to arouse me as well.

MILLY. You sure?

DON. I should know.

MILLY. She's a little bitch, all right.

DON. I wanted to hit her.

MILLY. And where it hurts, I hope.

DON. She aroused a tremendous urge in me to grab hold of her and hit her. The way she put on her stockings? Did you catch that? I saw the suspenders, you know. I think that was deliberate.

MILLY. I seem to have missed a hell of a lot.

DON. There's material here.

[*Turns back to his notes. Shorty returns, his face washed, carrying a large*

16

*pair of black shoes. From a shelf at the back he collects a box containing polish, brush, etc., then settles down on a chair to clean the shoes.*]

MILLY [*to Don*]. Work it out and let me know. There's obviously something going on and I don't know if I like it. I warn you, any high jinks and the lot of you get notice. I won't have it under my roof.

[*She stares idly at Shorty.*]

SHORTY. Spit and polish! Army style.

MILLY [*with sudden suspicion*]. Let me see those?

[*Shorty hands her the shoes.*]

Twelves!

SHORTY. Mr. Ahlers. He wants to see his face in them.

MILLY. You're helping him?

SHORTY [*still unsuspecting*]. He's going out so he asked me to do him a little favour and give his shoes a good shine. He's wearing his new suit.

MILLY. And you're going to? Help my worst enemy?

SHORTY. It's only a little favour.

MILLY. So whose side are you on?

SHORTY. Yours.

MILLY. Sneaking away behind my back to do *him* a little favour! That makes you the enemy.

SHORTY. I didn't know there was anything wrong.

MILLY. The impudence! To sit in front of me, in *my* kitchen, and clean *his* shoes. And think you can get away with it. Wait, my boy. Zero hour is on its way . . . with no holds barred.

[*Milly leaves the table indignantly, but remains in the room.*]

SHORTY [*to Don*]. You think I should polish?

DON. Go ahead. Don't let her bully you.

SHORTY [*polishing*]. It's hell tonight, hey! And I'm trying to say the right things. You know, Don . . . Girls? I give up. What do they want? You try your best but they is still unhappy. Like Sissy. She's unhappy, I know. But what must I do? There's always struggles in life, isn't that so? I tell her. Sissy, I say, there's always struggles in life.

DON. What does she say?

SHORTY. 'Well, struggle harder!' Hey? And I sweat, Don. On my rounds. And at Christmas, when it's three rounds and also parcels. Boy, then I sweat! You know what I think it is? Love takes a long time for a woman. You just got to keep your trap shut and wait.

MILLY [*moving to Shorty at the table*]. Does he look frightened? Ahlers?

SHORTY. No.

MILLY. Well, he'd better be. And when you take back those shoes you can tell him I said so. Before he leaves this house tonight, I want a straight answer to a few simple questions.

SHORTY. I'll tell him, Milly.

[*She moves away again.*]

DON. How long have you been married?

SHORTY. Going on for six months. I met her down by Booysens.*
Her Ma's place. Forty-nine Vereeniging Road. I was still a telegram boy then. Her Oupa died you see. So I gave her Ma the telegram and when she reads it she cries, Don! Hell, man, that old woman cries there on the back stoep. Sissy was in the yard. They got an old tyre hanging from a tree there . . . for a swing, you know. She was swinging. Anyway, her Ma was crying there and Sissy calls out: 'What's wrong, Ma?' So I take off my cap and I go over and tell her. She asked my name. That's how we got friends with each other.

[*He is polishing the shoes all the time.*]

We went like that for maybe six months. Then I reckoned we were ready. I spoke to Sissy and she said it was okay. She wanted to get married for a change. Her Ma asked me if I was making enough money and I said yes. So she said it was certainly okay by her and may God help me.

[*Pause. He puts down the shoes.*]

18

But there's one thing, Don. We wasn't married in a church. It was by Special Licence. She was in a hurry, you see. The man in charge said it was okay and we could now go ahead. Because it's legal, you see. I got the certificate. But it was so quick! Just like seeing somebody for a job. You put on your suit, you get your papers, and your Ma and your Pa, and the bride-to-be. Then there's some questions and more papers . . . and then you got it, you think. But when we got home—we had our honeymoon in the Shamley Boarding House in De Korte Street—well, when we got there, we wasn't so sure we got it. That's the trouble, Don. I think Sissy is still not so sure we got it. She gets scared.

DON. How long do you give yourself?

SHORTY. What?

DON. Your marriage. How long do you think it will last?

SHORTY. For ever.

DON. In the face of all this . . . ! [*Turns to his notes.*]

SHORTY. We do love each other.

DON. Let's discuss this objectively. What do you think love means?

SHORTY. Well, I say to love something is to like it a lot, and more than anything else. And you?

DON. Suppose I say sex.

SHORTY. You mean . . .?

DON. Yes. I put it to you that the heart of love throbs below the belt. Very good! [*Makes a note.*] Yes?

SHORTY [*strongly*]. No!

MILLY [*back at the table*]. For one thing there's that little matter of the fifty pounds which he's so conveniently forgotten about. Well, I haven't. And if he walks through that door tonight I want it back, cash, plus ten years' interest. You can tell him that, too.

Did he say where he was going?

SHORTY. No.

MILLY. Don't just say no! Think.

SHORTY. He just said he was going out.

[*Milly resumes her pacing.*]

[*To Don.*] I would love Sissy even if she only had one leg and eye!

DON. You sure? Picture it.

SHORTY. Yes! Shame, Don!

DON. Aha! Pity. That's something else. It's no good, Shorty, there's only one way out. The womb! A man called Freud discovered it. Do you dream?

SHORTY. Yes.

DON. Give me one.

SHORTY. Well, these days I'm in this building with this letter to deliver. And it's registered, which makes it worse. My bag is weighing like lead. Hell, it's heavy, man! But there's hundreds of postboxes and I can't find the right one and somebody is shouting: 'Hurry up, man! It's urgent!' And I'm looking and sweating and that bag is heavy and then I wake up.

DON. Do you ever find the right box?

SHORTY. No.

DON. Who's the letter addressed to?

SHORTY. I'll look next time.

DON. It's as clear as daylight. The registered letter is phallic, the boxes are female, the bag is your conscience. That's why it's heavy. Mark my words, one night you'll open it and find Sissy inside.

[*A thoughtful Milly is again at the table.*]

MILLY. Shorty. Do you want to wipe out the past with a favour?

SHORTY. Anything, Mill.

MILLY. I want you to do something for me when you take back those shoes. So make them shine! We'll use them as bait. I think I've got it, Don. [*To Shorty.*] But you must be careful.

SHORTY [*polishing industriously*]. Okay.

MILLY. Very careful!

SHORTY [*uneasy*]. What is it?

MILLY. Shorty, my darling, it's a trap.

SHORTY [*now nervous*]. I don't know if I can do that.

MILLY. Of course you can. Polish! I've definitely got it, Don! Now we'll see who gets the last laugh. [*To Shorty.*] Now listen. You're going to take back those shoes. Right?

SHORTY. Right.

MILLY. When you give them back, start talking.

SHORTY. About what?

MILLY. Anything. You were talking to him about something this morning.

SHORTY. Mario Lanza.*

MILLY. So talk about him again, or the shoes, or anything—just get him talking. Then you ask casually: 'Where are you going, Mr. Ahlers?' You got that?

SHORTY. Yes.

MILLY. Casually, you understand. Get his answer, then high-tail it back here.

[*Shorty hesitates.*]

You said you would do me a favour. Anything. Didn't he say anything, Don?

DON. He did.

MILLY. Thank you. Well?

SHORTY. Start talking.

MILLY. Casually.

SHORTY. Where are you going, Mr. Ahlers?

MILLY. But for God's sake casually or else he'll smell a rat. Well, go on!

[*Exit a worried Shorty.*]

MILLY. We've got him, Don. We've got him. Stand by for action.

DON. I haven't volunteered.

MILLY. You'd better, before all hell breaks loose.

DON. I'll stay neutral. Every fight needs a ref.

MILLY. Not this one. It's going to be foul. There's a month's free bed and breakfast in it for you.

DON. What do I have to do?

MILLY. The plan is as follows. Shorty tells us where he is going. Our first move is to get dressed. We tog up to kill the cats. My white costume with matching gloves! You'll see something tonight, my boy. That done we then descend on the enemy. Ha! That will be triumph. He's sitting there, you see, with his so-called friend from Germany, and in we march, sit down and have a good time of our own! And right under his nose where he can see us. Then when he comes crawling to ask if he can join in, I'll have him arrested for molesting.

[*Shorty appears timidly in the doorway.*]

SHORTY. Milly . . .

MILLY [*eagerly*]. Well?

SHORTY. I tried, but he just said thank you and closed the door.

MILLY [hissing]. Then go back there and knock!

SHORTY [*hissing back*]. You didn't say nothing about knock, Milly. Hey, Don? You just said . . .

MILLY. Then listen. Knock! Say you want to borrow a razor blade or something, then Mario Lanza, then where are you going, Mr. Ahlers? But casually!

SHORTY. Where are you going . . . ? [*Exit.*]

MILLY [*with a premonition of disaster*]. I'll murder that little runt if he makes a mess of this.

DON. Suppose it's that place he goes to sometimes . . . the German Club. You've got to be a member.

MILLY. We'll gatecrash. And if they chuck us out, then we'll do it on the pavement outside.

DON. What?

MILLY. Laugh and sing and be happy. So will you. Yes! You're coming! You'll tell me jokes and make me laugh, loudly, so that he can hear.

DON. I've never faced a prospect like this in all my life.

MILLY. You'll survive. It's him I'm after.

[*Shorty is back in the doorway, obviously frightened of Milly. He moves so as to keep the kitchen table between them.*]

SHORTY. I did like you said, Milly.

MILLY. And?

SHORTY [faltering]. And . . . Mr. Ahlers . . . he said . . .

DON. Thank God!

MILLY. Go on.

SHORTY. . . . to tell you that he knows I don't shave and . . .

MILLY. Yes?

SHORTY. . . . and that he is going out to dinner with an old friend from Germany.

MILLY [quietly]. Come here, Shorty.

SHORTY. No.

MILLY. Will you kindly come here.

SHORTY. I did it just the way you said, Milly.

MILLY [*now impotent with anger*]. Shorty Langeveld, come here this very minute.

SHORTY. What are you going to do?

MILLY. I don't know yet . . .

SHORTY. I'll ask him again.

MILLY [*stops and listens*]. Sssssh! [*Moving to the door.*] It's him! [*To Shorty.*] Sit down! [*She lights a cigarette.*] Sit down, I said.

SHORTY. You're not cross with me no more?

MILLY. Sit down. Talk to Don. Pretend nothing's happened. It's him all right.

[*She goes to the door and takes up a pose of studied indifference, her arms folded, smoking. In a loud voice, and heavily sarcastic to start with.*]

As I was saying, chaps, fine feathers making fine birds is one thing but a bald head that can't even speak the English language properly is another. There's not a hope in hell for you know who, even in a new suit. So it's no good anybody trying to get classy ideas around here, because we know all about it! [*Now speaking directly to Alhers, who is in the passage.*] Enjoy yourself . . . with your old friend from Germany. And please don't worry about me. I'll just sit here in the kitchen and twiddle my thumbs. After all, it was only ten years. Why worry about them! [*Her anger and resentment beginning to break through.*] Well, you'd better, because they were mine. Those were ten years of my life and you had them cheap. Just don't think that means I'm hard-up for you. Because I've got a surprise for you, Mr. Big Shot. I'm also going to have a good time tonight. You bet. I'm going to have the best good time of my life. And it won't be beer and sausages at the Phoenix! Put that where the monkey puts his nuts. And when you come home I'll be out and there'll be an account for fifty pounds in your bed. [*Now shouting and gradually moving out of sight into the passage.*] Because if you think this is the end of me you've got another guess coming. I've only started.

[*Front door slams.*]

Yes, go on ! Go on, get the hell out of here, you rotten stinking thief. THIEF!

[*Silence. The clock chimes, then one stroke. The sound of a vicious blow. The clock strikes seven more times. It is eight o'clock. The window reflects heavy traffic in the street outside. Shorty and Don wait. Milly appears quietly in the doorway, standing there for a few seconds before moving to the table for a cigarette.*]

You heard that, I hope? [*Shorty and Don nod.*] Good! I'm glad. I wanted to humiliate him in public, and I think I succeeded. You should have seen him. He crawled through that door like a dog with his tail between his legs. [*Pause. With an edge of suspicion.*] What did you hear?

SHORTY. You told him, Milly.

MILLY. Where to get off! Didn't I?

SHORTY. To get out!

DON. And go to hell.

MILLY. Thank you. Enough! Let's leave it at that. Because I meant it. Every solitary syllable. I *am* going out and I *am* going to have a good time. Because, just between you and me, the old Phoenix was a bit of a flop the last couple of times. Strictly speaking, that makes this a stroke of luck. A chance to really enjoy myself for a change. In fact, why not the three of us? There's an idea! Let's make it a trio.

SHORTY.  What, Mill?

MILLY.  Anything. You're invited.

SHORTY.  I'm game.

MILLY.  Settled. I'll get dressed. [*She sits.*] Where are we going?

DON.  Nowhere.

MILLY.  You promised.

DON.  I did not.

MILLY.  I'm ignoring you. [*To Shorty.*] Your turn. Think. Give us a bright idea.

SHORTY.  There's still time for the second session.

MILLY.  The movies?

SHORTY.  At the Roxy . . .

MILLY.  Seen it.

SHORTY.  What about the Plaza? They is showing . . .

MILLY.  Seen that, too.

SHORTY.  I'll get the paper.

MILLY.  I've seen them all. The movies! Who the hell wants to go to the movies?

SHORTY.  You said . . .

MILLY.  I said, think of a bright idea for a good time. Don't you understand the English language? A good time!

DON.  The movies are all right, Mill.

MILLY.  'The movies are all right, Mill.' [*Turns to the window.*] Look out there. Go on, look! Thousands of them. Millions. Where are they going? They're going to have a good time. Every Saturday night they drive past on their way to have a good time. And don't try to tell me they're going to the movies ! So what I want to know is, where is it?

[*Shorty smiles.*]

25

Don't just sit there grinning like an ape. Go out and ask them.

[*Shorty laughs with embarrassment.*]

What are you laughing at? Go out and ask them.

SHORTY. No, Milly.

MILLY. Yes, Milly! Go out there and stop one of those cars and say 'Milly wants to know where is it? Where do you get this good time every Saturday night? She's stuck in her kitchen with two good-for-nothing nitwits, so can she come?'

DON [*tapping out his pipe.*] You're not going to like this, Milly, but I feel I've got to tell you. Your good time is an illusion.

MILLY. Listen to him!

DON. It doesn't exist.

MILLY. You haven't even looked for it, so stop talking.

DON. Because I know I won't find it. It's not there. It's a hoax.

MILLY. Why don't you dry up! I've had them—good times! And when I walk out of here now, in ten minutes' time, I'll find another.

DON. It's like the sandwiches I took to school. Polony or jam. In a toffee tin. Somebody else had the toffees.

MILLY. What the hell are you talking about now?

DON. Life with a capital F. There's no mystery, Milly. That's what you want to believe. Romance around every corner. Adventure at the bottom of the street. The classic lower-middle-class illusion. I'm telling you it's polony or jam. Will you believe it that in my twenty years I have never yet once been surprised?

MILLY. Well, you had better start! Because it's not like that. [*Indignant.*] There's a hell of a lot of mystery, my boy. Going on all the time. And surprises. Oh yes! I could tell you a thing or two that would surprise you.

DON. Impossible. What?

MILLY. Aha! About me for example. [*Don laughs.*] You think you know all the answers? Well, you don't. Because I could tell you something about me that would make your hair stand on edge.

[*Shorty is busy at a shelf behind Milly's back.*]

DON. Go ahead.

MILLY. It happens to be a secret.

[*Shorty knocks over a pot.*]

What are you doing there?

SHORTY. Nothing.

MILLY. Liar! Come here.

SHORTY [*a shoe-box in his hands*]. Just my silkworms.

MILLY [*in horror*]. And where have you been keeping them?

SHORTY. Sissy doesn't . . .

MILLY. Well, neither do I!

SHORTY. Just that old pot what you never use, Mill.

MILLY. Suppose they escape and crawl into the food?

SHORTY. They was in our room, Milly, but Sissy sticks pins in
them. They don't do nothing. They are nearly all in the silk
already.

MILLY [*vaguely interested*]. Let me see?

DON. Is it something you did?

MILLY. What?

DON. Your secret.

MILLY. I'm not telling.

DON. Something that was done to you?

MILLY. Try again.

[*Shorty puts the shoe-box on the table in front of Milly.*]

SHORTY. I was feeding them. Beetroot leaves.

MILLY [*examining the contents of the box*]. Well, I'll be . . . ! Just look at
that, will you. You seen this, Don?

SHORTY. They was just so small when Jossie gave them to me.

MILLY. Cosy, isn't it. Sort of a pod. Nature is damn marvellous
when you come to think of it.

DON. Simple! An accident of birth.

[*Milly looks at him.*]

Your secret.

MILLY. There were no accidents. I arrived on the dot, head first, six pounds four ounces with everything where it should be. They say I hardly cried.

DON. I mean something before birth. Like your father being the Prince of Wales.

MILLY. There's good blood. But I wouldn't go as far as that. Jenkins is an old Port Elizabeth name.

DON. Then there's nothing. There's no secret. You're just making it up.

MILLY [*with a superior smile*]. Suit yourself. I'm saying nothing.

[*Don is still intrigued. Milly returns her attention to the silkworms.*]

So this is silk. And to think worms do it! Do they . . . how do they do it?

SHORTY. From the back.

MILLY. Their bowels?

SHORTY. Yes.

MILLY [*highly indignant*]. No, they don't! Don, where does the silk come from?

DON. Two glands in the head.

MILLY. That's better. [*To Shorty.*] How could it be precious if you were right?

[*Don now also examines the worms.*]

MILLY. [*to Shorty*]. That's all. [*Shorty smiles.*] You can go now! [*Shorty moves to one side with his shoe-box.*]

DON. Let's get back to your secret.

MILLY. [*delighted*]. Got you guessing, have I? Thought you knew everything.

DON. Be honest with me, Milly. Is there definitely a secret?

MILLY [*simply convincingly*]. Yes, it's there all right. Something happened. I feel it, Don. Nowadays more and more. It gets so bad sometimes I don't want to look or listen any more. Honestly. Because when I do . . . I don't know . . .

DON. Something sad.

MILLY. Sort of.

DON. Pain.

MILLY. It hurts.

DON. You cried.

MILLY. I'll confess to a tear or two, on occasions.

DON. If I said Horror would that be going too far?

MILLY. Horror? Maybe. Horrible? Could be.

DON. Horror, pain, sadness, and you were young.

MILLY. Christ, what a life!

DON. I've got it! You were raped.

MILLY [*indignant*]. By whom?

DON. Wait! Let me give you the picture. I'm good at this. You were on your way to school, a sweet little girl in her gym slip and black stockings . . . garters! . . . when you met this man who'd been hiding behind a tree. You're innocent, you see. So when he offered you toffees you ate one. Then came the suggestions. When you resisted, he forced you down . . .

MILLY. I'd like to see anyone try!

DON. It happens every day.

MILLY. Mind you, there was that old le Roux once, when me and Beryl Conwright were on the swings. But hell! You could hardly call that rape. No! Try again.

DON. What about your mother? She was raped and you're the result.

MILLY. Mommy! I'd have liked to see someone try something with her. She was as strong as an ox.

DON. There's still your father. Why do you never mention him?

MILLY [*promptly*]. Alfred Jenkins, storeman, grade one, on The South African Railways. Retired on pension. You won't find anything there.

DON. Not so fast, not so fast. Let's probe.

MILLY. Dig as deep as you like. Southend Cemetery,* if you want to know. Him and Mommy. Side by side. There's an angel pointing upwards.

DON. Little girls and their daddies! Psychology's got a word for it.

MILLY. What are you getting at?

DON. The realm of the subconscious, Milly. Where lusts and libidos writhe like tormented serpents.

MILLY. Good God!

DON. Yes! So let's have a look at Alfred. Did he drink?

MILLY. Daddy had his pots on a Saturday night with the other ex-servicemen.

DON. That's enough. Too much is anaesthetic. Too little leaves the inhibitions intact.

MILLY. Hurry up! I haven't got all night.

DON. Here's the picture. It's a Saturday night. The pubs have closed. You're in your room, in bed . . . in the dark! Your mother is asleep. She's the ailing sort—psychosomatic. The front door opens and closes. Silence. You think: that must be Daddy. You lie and listen. The footsteps hesitate, then lurch towards *your* room. The door opens, the door closes, and you know he's in the room. You can hear him breathing heavily. Daddy, you say. Silence. Then a few more steps. He's at your bed now. You can smell brandy fumes . . .

MILLY. Stop! [*Don laughs.*] It's disgusting.

DON. Watch it, Milly. Guilt!

MILLY. Alfred Jenkins was a good man. If he could hear what you've just said he'd turn in his grave. And Mommy, too.

DON. It's good enough for a trauma.

MILLY. Well, you're wrong. You're on the wrong track altogether.

DON. Give me a clue.

MILLY. I'll tell you when you get hot.

[*Lights a cigarette, now thoroughly absorbed in the game.*]

DON. Was it something sudden?

MILLY. Give me the picture.

DON. There you are, a young girl in a white dress, full of hope . . .

MILLY. You're getting warm.

DON. Life is peaceful. You are happy. Until suddenly, like a bolt from the blue, it happens. The dream is shattered and you are set on your hopeless journey through dark and dusty rooms. How's that?

MILLY [*emphatic*]. No! It wasn't like that at all.

DON [*still under the momentum of his thought*] An early marriage!

MILLY. No.

DON. A death? A suicide?

MILLY. No.

DON. Then life. Birth! What about a baby?

MILLY [*with sudden vehemence*]. *No!* There was no baby. And I don't care, because I don't want babies. Understood? Finished. Settled. Next one.

DON. So then it took its time.

MILLY. Come again?

DON. Whatever happened to the young girl in the white dress, happened slowly.

MILLY. 'It took its time.' My time ... bit by bit ... yes! That sounds better. Slow, and sly. What I mean is I try to remember when. The Moment When—the way they say: 'And from then on, so and so' ... and so on. But I can't. There doesn't seem to be a day or a date. Once upon a time it wasn't, now it is, but when or where ... ? It's not easy to pin down. Believe me, I've tried.

DON. Milly, do *you* know what it is? [*She smokes.*] You mean you *don't* know?

MILLY [*irritably*]. Wouldn't be much of a secret if I knew, would it?

DON. Just as I thought. You're making it up.

MILLY. I'm not.

DON. This secret is a figment of your imagination. In my opinion you're compensating for a colourless existence by inventing ...

MILLY. Sometimes I could brain you! What do you know about it?

DON. Apparently as much as you. Nothing. Which most likely means there is nothing.

MILLY. Nothing! I said it hurts, didn't I? Can nothing hurt? I'll say it again, as God is my witness, it hurts. And it took its time. Mine. And once upon that time there was a little girl in a white dress, full of hope, and she was happy. But now she's not any more. Is that my imagination? Those are facts.

DON. But not scientific facts. I can't measure them. You tell me it hurts. But what can a scientist do with that? Unless you can be more specific, give it up and suffer in silence.

MILLY. You mean the details?

DON. Call them what you like.

MILLY [stalling]. You're asking for the details?

DON. Yes.

MILLY. Okay.

DON. I'm waiting.

MILLY. Let's see . . . it hurts.

DON. Where?

MILLY. All over.

DON. I give up.

MILLY. Hold your horses. We'll try again. It hurts. An ache. A sort of dull ache.

DON. Go on.

MILLY. Yes, it's coming now. It hurts. There's pain. Sometimes . . . sometimes it's in the colour of things. They go grey. Yes. I'm on to it! Things go grey. Know what I mean? Dull. Dreary. For days on end. And the days too. Sunday, Monday, even Someday . . . all grey. Faces, and calendars and the right time when I look at the kitchen clock and then the taste of the next cigarette—all of them seem to lose their colour. It's enough to make me sick. If you're looking for symptoms, there's one. I get sick. In the afternoons, when I look at the clock and I see it's some old time again, I could vomit. And the way things can suddenly . . . [looking for words] . . . Be! You know, there It Is. Let's just say things get me down.

DON. Don't stop now!

MILLY. Well, I walk into a room—I'm by myself because he's at work and you're somewhere else and it's all quiet so I'm alone—then I walk into a room and I stand still and think about something to do. I look around, you see, for a little task to while away the time. And then it comes. I begin to notice. It's like a plug has been pulled out and something's drained away down a big, black hole, leaving everything stranded. Things stand too still. Chairs and tables. All empty and still . . . and stupid. That's the word! Stupid. Like that chair. I know what it is. I look at it and I say Chair. But it doesn't help. It goes on being empty and useless. Once it got so bad I said: Well, I'll prove it. So I sat down. But that made it even worse.

DON [*eagerly*]. Because then *you* felt stupid!

MILLY. Exactly.

DON. You saw yourself—an object called Milly in an object called chair—but knowing the names didn't help because everything went on being useless, including yourself.

MILLY. You've got it.

DON [*excited*]. For God's sake, Milly, that's Anguish!

MILLY. Let's move on.

DON. Wait ! We've got a situation here. You're in that chair and you think: Enough! Move! or Get Up! . . . one of the commands. But nothing happens. You think about it, but the reasons for moving break like bad string when you try to pull out of your inertia . . .

MILLY. We've already had that!

DON. This is a development. Now you're conscious of what is happening .

MILLY. Well, let's cut it short. I'm conscious. Now I move.

DON. Right. You stand up.

MILLY. That's better. Erect ! I walk again.

DON. Walking consists of picking up one foot, swinging it forward, and putting it down. For a fraction of a second you stand precariously on one leg. Then you remember the other one so up it

33

comes, and again forward and down. While this is going on there's the problem of your arms at your sides, your heart is beating, your chest rising and falling with breathing, your eyeballs swivelling in their sockets . . .

MILLY. Is it as bad as that?

DON. I have a dream. Music is playing, and I'm in a corner and so far no one has seen me. I think it's a party because there's a lot of people, and . . . well, all I know about them really is the noise, because I'm not watching. I'm holding my breath. But the noise is a hubbub—talking and jokes and one very loud voice laughing heartily. Then the music stops. I can't tell you how terrible that is. Just stops. Silence. And sweat. Because I know, I just know that that means *it's my turn*. Don't ask me what. That's the thought. *It's your turn now!* I feel their eyes. Without looking up I know they are staring and waiting and that it is my turn and I must do something. So I move. I walk. One foot up, a second on one leg, then down. Two or three steps, in this silence, safely. Then things start to go wrong. I begin to wobble during that second on one leg, my arms start swinging wildly. There's a feeling that I've got five elbows and they're all sticking out. I'm knocking glasses into people's laps, falling over their legs . . .

MILLY. Wake up!

DON. I always do. The trouble is I wake up too soon. I never reach the end. The terror, you see. My mind protecting itself.

MILLY. It's only a dream. You said so yourself.

DON. But don't you also feel it? How can I put it? The fit. A feeling that things don't fit. Either life is sizes too big or you're too small. Something's wrong somewhere and maybe that is why people stare.

MILLY. At what?

DON. You haven't reached the stage where they stare?

MILLY. At what?

DON. You.

MILLY. No.

DON. It will come. A feeling of being watched, of people waiting,

34

because it's *your* turn. Some pull it off of course. Others make a mess of it, like my dream, and have to leave the party. The failures. You've seen them, those old sticks of skin and bone sitting at the edge of oblivion on park benches. It's happened.

MILLY. Hold on.

DON. Decrepit, decaying . . .

MILLY. Wait!

DON. Neglecting themselves, neglected by others, forgotten . . .

MILLY. *What?*

DON. They've been forgotten. It happens long before you are dead.

MILLY. What do you mean, forgotten?

DON. You lose your place in the mind of man. With a bit of luck once or twice in your life you have it. That warm nest in another mind where 'You' is all wrapped up in their thinking and feeling and worrying about 'You'. But even if you are one of the lucky ones, sooner or later you end up in the cold again. Nothing is for ever. They die, or you get divorced. One way or another they go, they forget, and you end up in your little room with your old age pension and a blind bitch for friendship. From then on it's just a matter of days. When they're good, the two of you crawl out to a bench in the sun where she can hate the pigeons and you can hate the people. When it gets dark, you crawl back to the room. Until one day, one more sunny day with the pigeons flocking and the people passing, you're not there. But who misses you ? Who's to know that inside a room, finally, forgotten by the world . . .

MILLY. Rubbish. That's absolute rubbish. Morbid muck.

DON. Read the papers. There are cases every day.

MILLY. For God's sake, man! This is a civilized country. Nobody gets forgotten like that. One thing I can assure you, it's not happening to me. Oh no! There are limits. [*Pause.*] What were the cases?

DON. A few days ago. An old woman. They had to break down the door. She was found . . .

35

MILLY. I don't want to hear.

DON. Suit yourself. But it's happening . . .

MILLY. I said . . .

DON. Here! Tonight!

MILLY. Who?

DON. You. Him. Me. [*With sudden violence.*] Are you blind? It Happens! Who remembers us? At this moment? Ahlers? Is he thinking about you? With his old friend from Germany? [*Turning to Shorty, who has been following the argument for several minutes.*] Or Sissy? Billy-boy has just made her laugh. She's enjoying herself. She's forgotten she's got a husband, who he is, where he is. And you're waiting. You are waiting for her to remember you, to come back. And when they do, when they walk in and find us again, it will be the way you find something old and forgotten and almost useless. Something in a corner, put away a long time ago, and now there it is again, too broken to mend but too much trouble to throw away. So back it goes, because maybe one day . . . That's us! We're hanging on by a maybe in somebody else's mind. [*Pause.*] I'm finished. [*He sits down and smokes his pipe.*]

SHORTY [*to Milly*]. What's going on?

MILLY. Shut up.

SHORTY [*to Don*]. Sissy misses me. She does, Don. She always comes home.

MILLY. I said shut up! [*Tries to light a cigarette.*] Is it my imagination or is it cold in here? My hands are like ice.

[*Exit Shorty.*]

So who cares?

DON. That's another way of putting it. Who cares?

MILLY. I mean *me*—about *him*. Because it so happens I'm not hard up, you see. You forgot about that. In fact I forget about him sometimes. For hours on end. Pottering around in here, I forget him completely. The other day, playing patience, it was quite a surprise when he walked in because he was clean out of my mind. And tonight. If you think I'm going to spend my night thinking about him you've got another guess coming. I've got plans which will take my mind right off the subject.

[*Shorty returns with his pair of boxing gloves. He offers them to Milly.*]

What's this?

SHORTY.  You said your hands were cold.

MILLY.  But boxing gloves!

SHORTY.  They are warm.

MILLY.  Oh well. Try anything once. But only for a second, you understand. [*She is putting them on.*] I've got to get dressed in a mo', Sssssh!

[*Inside the house the clock begins to chime. They listen. The sixteen chimes end. The clock strikes three.*]

SHORTY.  Three o'clock.

MILLY.  Go and hit it.

[*Exit Shorty. A timid blow. Silence.*]

I said, hit it ! Imagine it's Sissy.

[*A second blow. The clock continues its striking. Milly is obviously counting. After the sixth stroke she relaxes. But the clock strikes once more.*]

Can't be.

DON.  What?

MILLY.  Ten o'clock. I counted nine and then it struck again.

DON.  Then it's ten o'clock.

MILLY.  No. Don.

DON.  All right, so it's eleven.

MILLY.  No, no! It's nine o'clock.

DON.  Never.

MILLY.  The last time that clock struck it was eight.

DON.  We must have been talking and didn't hear it.

MILLY.  Nonsense. Shorty!

DON.  Why get so agitated? Nine, ten, eleven, twelve . . .

MILLY.  Shorty!

DON.  Yesterday, tomorrow . . .

MILLY [*violently*]. *Shorty!*

SHORTY [*off-stage*]. I'm in here!

[*Exit Milly hurriedly into the passage. Don waits, smoking his pipe. Milly returns slowly.*]

DON. Well? [*Milly says nothing.*] It's ten o'clock. I told you. Two left. So much for today.

MILLY. What do you mean by that?

DON. It's ten o'clock, which, when you work it out, means that there are two hours left of today.

MILLY [*in growing agitation*]. So do you think I can't add?

DON. Correction. It's a subtraction sum. A taking away. [*Watching Milly closely.*] More and more. [*Pause.*] Until you've had the lot and then you're dead. Adding never comes into it.

MILLY. Well, just remember, Mr. Donovan Big-brain, it's also happening to you.

DON [*tapping on the table with his pipe*]. The passing seconds. Stop them. [*He taps.*] Go on! The sound of doom, Milly. Seconds becoming minutes, minutes becoming hours, days, months, years . . .

MILLY. All right!

DON. You said ten, didn't you?

MILLY. What?

DON. Years. With Ahlers. That makes a total of three thousand six hundred and fifty-two days, allowing for leap years. Do you want the other statistics?

MILLY. Let's hear them.

DON [*picking up his pencil*]. Was it beer and sausages every Saturday night?

MILLY. Without fail.

DON. How many sausages?

MILLY. Two fat frankfritters each.

DON. One thousand and forty sausages. Beer?

MILLY. Also two bottles each.

DON. Say they hold a pint—exactly one hundred and thirty gallons of beer.

MILLY. Come again?

DON. One thousand and forty sausages and one hundred and thirty gallons of beer, to the nearest belch.

MILLY. Both of us, or just my share?

DON. Just your share.

MILLY [*emphatically, after a moment's reflection*]. It is *not* a lot. Not for ten years, Don. It only sounds a lot. There were three thousand six hundred and fifty-two days, remember!

DON. I can give it to you in hours.

MILLY. Yes! Let's hear that one.

DON [*A pause while he works it out. Shorty returns to the room.*] Eighty-seven thousand six hundred odd.

MILLY. *What!*

DON. Eighty-seven thousand . . .

MILLY. Stop! I don't want to hear. [*Trembling with emotion.*] Jesus Christ, I wish I'd known that when he went out.

DON. For the sake of accuracy we'd better subtract sleeping time. The human being sleeps an average . . .

MILLY. What do you mean subtract? He got that as well. All right! So I've said it. He got the lot. Body and Soul. And me? A pile of sausages and a barrel of beer! You call that a bargain? [*Her mounting anger starts her pacing. She is still wearing the boxing gloves and will keep them on until, as indicated, after the bout with Shorty.*] I must have been off my mind! There he stood ten years ago, on my threshold, with his suitcase of artificial roses—and I could have slammed the door in his face! I only bought a bunch out of pity. He gave me the old song and dance. Down and out, no friends, where's the next meal, and all of this on the verge of tears. So open went the big heart and out came the helping hand. I'm telling you it was pity. That's the only reason why I went out with him to begin with. He looked lonely and as it so happened it was the end of his first week under my roof. 'Dress up', he

said. 'Ve mus haf a celebrashin.' And then they appeared!
Those leather shorts with the bells and braces ! Oh, my God ! I
nearly died of embarrassment. It was his legs! 'You can't', I said.
I'm wearing white. They'll stare.' 'But ve ver dem in da
mountince.' That was him. Da mountince!

SHORTY.  Switzerland.

MILLY.  He's a German.

SHORTY.  No. Milly . . .

MILLY.  I'm telling you he's a German. Look what they did to the
Jews.

SHORTY.  Mr. Ahlers says . . .

MILLY.  Mister? He's just plain Ahlers in this house and what he
says doesn't count because he's a liar, so shut up. Mister! [*Outraged.*] Listen, he was a hobo, an immigrant. He had nothing. If
it wasn't for me he still wouldn't have a penny to scratch his
backside with. I put the firm of Ahlers Artificial Flowers on its
two flat feet that only had one pair of socks when they walked
into my life. I typed the letters to the undertakers, and I'll give
him notice.

DON.  Tonight? When he comes home?

MILLY.  Tonight.

DON.  Want to bet?

SHORTY.  What are you betting?

DON.  Beer and sausages at the Phoenix.

[*Shorty thinks this is very funny.*]

MILLY.  When you're finished laughing, nitwit, I'd just like to
remind you two what I said about somebody being the landlord
around here and getting slowly sick to death. Think about it.

DON [*to Shorty*].  She's threatening us.

MILLY.  I assure you it wouldn't break my heart.

SHORTY.  What?

MILLY.  To kick you out! A change in the faces around here would
be as good as a holiday. Quite frankly, I'd rather do away with
myself than carry on like this.

DON [*picking up his pencil*]. How?

MILLY. Quick, because this is not worth it any more. How many times have I laughed today? Not once. Not even a chuckle. And all the two of you can do is sit there and watch. Look at you now! For God's Sake Do Something!

SHORTY [*Moving across to Milly where he adopts a boxer's stance*]. Put them up. I'll teach you to box.

[*Milly stares at him for a few seconds then lets loose a vicious swipe at his head. He dodges it easily.*]

That's it! Come on!

[*He is now feinting and weaving. Milly tries a second swipe with the full intention of hitting him.*]

No good!

MILLY. I'm warning you.

SHORTY. Okay.

MILLY. I'll knock you out!

SHORTY. Try. Come on. Try!

[*Milly goes after Shorty, swinging wildly. Shorty puts up a great show. Soon Milly is enjoying herself immensely.*]

MILLY. I'll get you. Take that! And that! And that! Wait! Stand still, you little bugger . . . [*etc.*].

[*Eventually Shorty deliberately lets Milly connect. He goes down.*]

You're down! I told you!

[*Laughing freely she turns to Don. The look on his face stops her laughter abruptly. She turns sharply on Shorty who is still lying on the floor.*]

You trying to make me happy?

SHORTY. You was laughing.

MILLY. It was a trick. [*Tearing off the gloves.*] Take them.

SHORTY. Once more.

MILLY. Go to hell.

SHORTY. You did forget your troubles, Mill.

MILLY. Well, I don't want to forget. Not that way! It was ten years.

You think it's quits because you make me laugh for ten seconds.
Ten years! That's what criminals get.

DON. Not again, Milly! . . .

MILLY. Yes, again! And again and again. And you're going to
listen. You're also on the face of this bloody earth. I'll make you
listen. I'll make you say it's all wrong and he's bad and it isn't
fair, because that's what it is.

Go on. Look! You. That. [*Indicating Shorty.*] This. [*Indicating the
room.*] And me here in the middle of the mess while he's out
there spending the profits I helped him earn on some cheap
Jo'burg bitch.

DON. That's right.

MILLY [*outraged*]. Right?

DON. He's having good time and you're forgotten. I told you that
five minutes ago.

MILLY. So?

DON. So full stop. Finished. The end of a sad story.

MILLY. You mean he's going to get away with it?

DON. Why not? He hasn't broken the law. You're not married. He
pays his rent. In the eyes of the law he's an innocent law-
abiding citizen having what you call a good time.

MILLY. And in mine he's a low-down, rotten, stinking bastard,
who has done something dirty and must be punished. And if
nobody else is going to do it, I will. Tonight I will take my
revenge.

DON. You tried once before and it didn't work.

MILLY. This time it will. We'll join forces. [*To Shorty.*] Think!

SHORTY. What?

MILLY. Our plan for revenge.

SHORTY. I don't . . .

MILLY. Don't you want Sissy to be sorry she left you in the lurch?

SHORTY. Yes—

MILLY. And to promise she won't go out with other men?

SHORTY.  Yes.

MILLY.  Then shut up, and think.

SHORTY.  Listen, chaps. I think I'll go to bed.

MILLY.  Stay where you are! You're in this too. Let's work it out. At this moment . . . come on, help me!

DON.  You're forgotten.

MILLY.  Right.

DON.  They're laughing.

MILLY.  Right.

DON.  They're having a wonderful time and you're . . .

MILLY.  All right! We've got the picture. Let's move on. They're going to come home. Expecting to find us at their mercy.

DON.  Most likely.

MILLY.  Waiting patiently.

DON.  Willingly.

MILLY.  Ready to crawl.

DON.  Content with the crumbs.

MILLY.  And that is when we strike. Because instead . . .

DON.  Aha!

MILLY.  And much to their surprise . . .

DON.  It's coming!

MILLY.  Much to their surprise, I repeat . . .

DON.  Wait for it!

MILLY.  I've got it! *They're* forgotten because *we* are having a good time. How's that? They walk in to find that we've forgotten all about them because we are laughing and singing and having a good time.

SHORTY [*with pleasure*].  Hey!

MILLY [*warming to her idea*].  Because guess what's going full swing when they walk in through that front door? A party!

SHORTY.  That don't sound so bad, Milly.

MILLY.  What do you say, Don?

43

DON. You've forgotten one thing. The party. Where does that come from?

MILLY. Us!

DON. You mean you, him, and me . . .

MILLY. Are going to have a party! Let me give you the picture this time. Half a bottle of Muscatel at the bottom of my wardrobe gets the ball rolling. We buy a cake, hang up some decorations. I've got all that stuff left over from Christmas. Let's be carefree, man! Laughing and singing until the cows come home. And them upstairs having to endure it all the time. Let's drive them mad. What do you say, chaps?

SHORTY. That don't sound so bad at all, Mill. I'm game.

DON [*with signs of nervous wariness*]. You can't produce a party just like that, at this hour of the night, and out of thin air.

MILLY. I said we are going to have a party!

DON. To spite them?

MILLY. Yes.

DON. Well, it won't work. Nobody has a party to spite somebody else. Take my advice and drop the idea.

MILLY. *No.*

DON. For God's sake, Milly. Can't you see it? The three of us trying to be happy? We haven't got a reason. Try something else.

MILLY. You want a reason?

DON. Yes. Give me one good reason why the three of us . . .

MILLY. It's my birthday.

[*Pause.*]

DON. I don't believe it.

MILLY. That amounts to calling me a liar.

DON. Let's just say you've made a mistake.

MILLY. And if I prove it? [*Pause.*] If I prove it the party's on. Right?

DON. I'm not saying anything.

MILLY. Well, I'm saying it's my birthday and that I'm going to prove it . . .

DON. I'll buy you a present on Monday.

MILLY. We are going to celebrate my birthday with a party.

DON. Suppose it doesn't work? Suppose we don't have a good time?

MILLY. Leave that side of it to me.

DON. I've tried before.

MILLY. What's the matter with you, for God's sake? We're not going to try to do a miracle. A party! What are you scared of?

DON. I'm not scared of anything.

MILLY. You're trying to get out of it.

DON. Yes!

MILLY. Well, you can't.

DON. There's no law which says I have to, you know. Well, is there? Let's just say I'm not in a party mood tonight. And anyway I'm no good at laughing or singing . . . you won't miss me.

[*Pause. Growing embarrassment.*]

Tell you what, I'll watch.

SHORTY. Hell, Don!

DON. Look, why am I so important? You two go ahead and . . .

MILLY. So this is the thanks I get.

SHORTY. There's nothing wrong with a party, Don.

MILLY. After all the friendship and encouragement I've given you.

SHORTY. Come on, man! Say yes. For her sake.

DON. All right!

SHORTY. Yes?

DON. Yes. But I want it noted that I warned you.

[*He sits.*]

MILLY. It's on. Anybody who backs out now is a deserter. And at

45

the front line you get shot for that. [*To Shorty.*] Get my bag. It's
on my bed.

[*Exit Shorty.*]

She who laughs last, laughs longest, and tonight I'll also make it
loudest. I'll have him down here, on his knees, begging for
mercy before the cock crows thrice. That's my vow. So help me
God.

[*Shorty returns with the bag. Milly takes out her purse.*]

Take that . . . [*in a sudden fit of extravagance*] take the lot. Get us a
cake. The best. Something mouth-watering. Cool-drinks, peanuts and raisins . . .

SHORTY.  Potato crisps?

MILLY.  The lot. It's got to look good. Well? What are you waiting
for? Action stations.

[*Shorty and Milly move to the door, leaving Don at the table.*]

CURTAIN

# ACT TWO

*The room is 'decorated', the table has a cloth, plates, glasses, etc. In the centre of the table is a candle stuck into a bottle.*

*Curtain goes up to the sound of* Milly *and* Don *arguing off-stage.* Don *is the first to appear.*

DON. No.

MILLY [*close on his heels, carrying a long evening gown on a hanger*]. But it's an occasion.

DON. I prefer the one you're wearing.

MILLY. Are you trying to be funny?

DON. Then let's just say the colour doesn't suit you.

MILLY. Apricot.

DON. It's not in the spectrum.

MILLY. Look at the sequins.

DON. Save up and buy a new one.

MILLY. What do you mean? I've only worn this twice.

DON. So now it's out of fashion.

MILLY. Since when?

DON. Donkey's years.

MILLY. Listen to him!

DON. If you want my opinion . . .

MILLY. I don't.

DON. . . . and you did ask for it, that garment is old-fashioned.

MILLY. And I'm telling you it is not!

DON. They stopped wearing those before the war.

MILLY. When you weren't even born yet, hey? [*Derisive laughter.*]

DON. Exactly! My mother had one just like it.

MILLY [*laying it on thick*]. When you weren't even born yet! Ha, ha! So kindly . . .

DON. I warn you if you wear that somebody will laugh.

47

MILLY [*unable to keep up the act*]. So kindly shut up!

DON. I've said what I wanted to. [*His pipe.*]

MILLY. SHUT UP! [*Exit with dress; returns immediately.*] I hope you took the hint and are going to do something about your appearance. You look a disgrace.

[*Exit.*]

DON [*shouting*]. If Shorty doesn't come back soon you had better forget about a birthday party and call it a midnight supper!

[*Milly appears quietly in the doorway. Don doesn't see her. He shouts again.*]

I said if Shorty doesn't return . . .

MILLY. I heard you ! [*Pause.*] We've still got half an hour. As long as we start before twelve it's valid. [*Pause.*] Worse comes to the worst we can start without him. So get ready.

DON. Just the two of us? Are you mad?

[*Pause. Milly stands quite still. So does Don.*]

MILLY. If he gets back too late, I'll kill him. This is a hell of an end to my year. I won't scream, but I think I'm losing my hold.

[*Front door opens.* Shorty *rushes breathless into the room.*]

SHORTY. I've got everything Mill. Hey, this looks good!

MILLY. You know how close you've brought us to disaster?

SHORTY. Disaster?

MILLY. Stop wasting time and give me the grub. Hurry up. It's touch and go now.

[*Shorty puts on the lights, Milly blows out the candle and then sorts out the parcels Shorty has brought back. Out of one she takes a bunch if beetroot leaves.*]

What's this? [*Shorty laughs.*] I'm asking you what is this?

SHORTY. Beetroot leaves, for the silkies. That's why I took a little bit long, Mill. I went to that shop . . .

MILLY. Right! We'll settle that with this.

[*She slaps Shorty's face and then throws the leaves out of the window.*]

SHORTY. Why did you do that?

48

MILLY. Never you mind why. It helped. [*Turning back to the parcels.*] Where's the cake?

[*Shorty hands her a parcel which she opens.*]

And this?

[*She holds up a slab cake.*]

SHORTY. Cake.

MILLY. But it's slab-cake!

[*Shorty examines his purchase.*]

I didn't ask for slab-cake, idiot.

SHORTY. He said it's fruit cake.

MILLY. I wanted a round cake.

SHORTY. You didn't say nothing to me about a round cake, Milly. Did she, Don?

MILLY. Who the hell ever heard of a birthday party with slab-cake? What can I do with this? A few crumby slices. It's supposed to be wedges with icing. [*Throwing the cake onto the table.*] No! That does it.

[*Walks away and lights a cigarette.*]

DON. So what is happening?

SHORTY. Slap me again. Hard as you like.

DON. Are you calling it off?

MILLY [*turning back to the table.*]. Now listen! Both of you! Just once more, you understand. So help me God, either of you just once more and you'll regret the day you were born. [*To Shorty.*] Get a plate. Come on, move! [*Indicating the half-bottle of Muscatel.*] There's only one tot each so don't make pigs of yourselves. Sip it.

DON. I want it noted that I am going into this under protest.

MILLY. And without any improvement in your appearance! [*To Shorty.*] Put off the light.

[*He does so after she has lit the candle.*]

Ready?

[*Each of them is standing behind a chair.*]

49

All together!

[*They sit.*]

No, wait! Stand.

DON. Make up your mind.

[*They stand. Milly exits hurriedly and returns with a few paper hats.*]

MILLY. Last Christmas, but he'll never remember. Take one.

DON. Is this compulsory?

MILLY. Yes.

SHORTY [*singing*]. For she's a jolly good fellow, for she's a jolly good fellow, for she's a jolly good fellow, and so say all of us.

MILLY. All right. Sit. Together.

[*They sit.*]

SHORTY. To Milly, and may she live happily ever after.

[*Glasses are touched, they drink. Pause.*]

MILLY. And now?

DON. You're supposed to make a speech.

MILLY. No.

SHORTY. You must make a speech on your birthday, Milly.

MILLY. A few words then, but no speech. [*She stands.*] Well ... [*Pause.*] No. [*She sits.*]

SHORTY. Come on, Mill.

DON. Reply to the toast.

MILLY. All right. I'm prepared to do that. I'll reply to the toast. [*Stands again.*] God, I feel a fool! [*Pulling herself together.*] Anyway, I'm happy—no, let's not exaggerate—I'm pleased to be here with you. Or rather, to have you here with me. It's my house, remember. It's also my birthday. I'm not an old woman by any manner of means. But I've seen a lot of life. Just don't get any ideas, because there's plenty left. The spirit is willing even though the flesh be weak. I'm not talking about Sin. I mean life, and it's taken its toll. Somebody once said you start to die the moment you are born. The fact remains however that the best years are the middle years, somebody else said. I side with him.

Because the spirit *is* willing even . . . though . . . back to the beginning! Bit of a knot. Anyway, I hope you know what I mean. Which is, there are plenty of kicks left in the old girl!

So what else? No one could call me mean. Share and share alike has always been my motto. I've never begrudged you second helpings or clean sheets. I've tried to make this a home for you boys.

Furthermore, Shorty, I don't hate you. But you do get on my nerves sometimes, quite honestly. Try and behave yourself more. I'm not strict, but I hate fools. Really I do. As for you, Don, for God's sake, man, buck up your ideas a little. Do something. Get a girl or see a skin specialist but do something. I also hate layabouts.

That seems to cover everything. No! One more thing. Let's try and be more cheerful in future. What do you say? Post-boxes and pimples aren't the end of the world, chaps. So let's brighten up with a few more smiles. Let's make that the resolution.

[*Milly sits. Applause from Shorty and Don.*]

SHORTY. Very good, Mill! Very good!

MILLY. Thank you.

SHORTY. Hip hip hooray! [*Still clapping.*] Blow, man! Blow! It's your birthday.

[*Carried away by the flush of success Milly leans forward and blows out the candle, plunging them in darkness. Silence.*]

MILLY. That wasn't very clever of you, was it? [*Pause.*] So find the matches!

[*Fumbling in the dark. A bottle is knocked over, something falls to the floor.*]

Watch out, you clumsy ape!

SHORTY. I got them.

[*Match flares, the candle is lit. Milly examines the table.*]

MILLY. Just look at this mess! No. We'll start again.

DON. Another speech?

MILLY. From scratch.

DON. But the booze is finished. We can't toast you with cool-drink. For better or worse, we've reached the cutting of the cake.

MILLY. Let's at least tidy up.

[*The table is tidied.*]

DON. Cut the cake. I'm hungry.

SHORTY. Same here.

[*Milly cuts the slab of fruit cake, putting a slice on each plate. They begin to eat and drink. Apart from an occasional grunt of satisfaction, not a word is spoken. Milly eats slowly, with affectation. Don and Shorty pile in. They quickly finish their first slice. Milly cuts again. The cool-drinks are opened, the potato crisps disappear, then the peanuts. Not a word is spoken. Don and Shorty hold out their plates for more cake.*]

MILLY. Not so fast!

DON. I'm peckish.

MILLY. You're wolfing.

[*She cuts two more slices. Don and Shorty continue eating. Milly now begins to realize something is going wrong. She eats slower and slower, eventually stopping altogether to watch the other two with growing frustration and disgust. When just about everything has been eaten, Don pushes back his chair and belches.*]

DON. An old Arab custom which means Thank You.

SHORTY. Hear, hear.

MILLY. You mean?

DON. The party. Wasn't as bad as I expected, quite frankly.

MILLY. It's finished? It's over?

DON. Isn't it?

MILLY. No it's not. We haven't even started.

DON. What's left? We've eaten the cake . . .

SHORTY. There's still some cheese-tips here.

MILLY. The fun, for God's sake!

DON. Fun?

MILLY. Don't pretend you know nothing about it. [*Pause. She looks at them.*] The sound of merry laughter.

DON. In here? Us?

MILLY. That was the agreement.

DON. I thought it was too good to be true.

SHORTY. I think we had some fun, Milly.

MILLY. Merry laughter!

SHORTY. I laughed. Ask Don.

MILLY. You smirked once with shame because I caught you with your gob stuffed full of food.

DON [*wearily*]. So there hasn't been any fun. So what!

MILLY. Well, there's going to be. That's what. I'm throwing this party because I want to laugh. Understand? He's going to hear me laughing when he comes back. So this party is not yet over. Nobody goes to bed until I've laughed!

[*She lights a cigarette and smokes.*]

SHORTY. I've got a joke.

DON. No. Don't let's start that.

MILLY. Tell it.

DON. This is courting disaster, Milly. Believe me. Jokes . . .

MILLY. Tell it!

SHORTY. It's rude.

MILLY. We're not babies.

SHORTY. What's the difference between an ostrich egg and an ordinary egg?

MILLY. That's not a joke.

SHORTY. George called it a joke.

MILLY. It's a riddle, you idiot. A riddle doesn't make you laugh.

DON. What's the answer?

SHORTY. An arse-stretch.

MILLY. Apologize! Apologize for that immediately!

SHORTY. Sorry.

DON. Satisfied?

MILLY. Will you stop trying to make me satisfied with nothing.

DON. I think we had a fair run for our money.

MILLY. We've had one dirty riddle, and the spectacle of you gutsing yourself on *my* money.

DON. If I pay you back my share will you call it quits?

MILLY. You'll pay me back your share by making me laugh.

DON. Milly, please! I'm being serious.

MILLY. That makes two of us.

DON. I know, and that's why I'm nervous. It won't work. Take my advice and call it a day. Nothing's happened yet . . .

MILLY. Exactly!

DON [*trying to ignore her*]. We're intact, in shape. We can still retire with grace. But beyond this lies the point of no return.

MILLY. Good! I've always hated going back.

DON. For the last time I'm warning you—this is getting dangerous.

MILLY. Coward!

DON. All right.

MILLY. Yellow belly!

DON [*standing*]. If that's the way you feel about it, I'll leave the two of you . . .

MILLY. Just you try! [*Don stops.*] Just you try!

SHORTY [*trying to pour oil on troubled waters*]. Please, chaps.

MILLY [*to Don*]. So sit down and shut up, because here we go. [*With growing aggression.*] To start off with, there'll be a sing-song.

DON. I flatly refuse.

SHORTY. Don, please, man!

MILLY. We'll start the ball rolling with a sing-song. [*Stubs out her cigarette and lights another. She is now grimly determined.*] What songs do you know, Shorty?

SHORTY. 'Pack up your troubles in your old kit-bag and Smile, Smile, Smile.'

MILLY. One, two, three! [*Singing.*] 'Pack up your troubles in your old kit-bag and smile, boys, that's the stuff . . . [*Shorty joins in.*]

54

What's the use of wor-ree-ying,
It only gets you down,
Sooo—pack up your troubles in your old kit-bag and Smile,
Smile, Smile.'

SHORTY. We did sing that in the lorry going to Military Camp,
Mill!

MILLY. Next one, 'Roll out the barrel.' Sing! [*Shorty and Milly sing.*]
'Roll out the barrel
We'll have a barrel of fun
Roll out the barrel
Ta ta, te ta ta, tum tum . . .' I forget the words.

SHORTY. Same here.

MILLY. 'Jerusalem!' [*Singing.*] 'Ja-roo-sa-lem . . .'

SHORTY. I don't know that one, Mill!

MILLY. What about 'When Irish eyes are smiling'?

SHORTY. I'll try. Come on, Don! [*Shorty and Milly sing.*] 'Sure
the world seems bright and gay . . . for when Irish eyes are
smiling . . .'

[*Don, who has sat tensed through the foregoing, making no attempt to help
the other two, now jumps to his feet. Milly, blinded by determination, does
not see the impending catastrophe. There is from this point on, a growing
momentum to the final chaos, with everybody cutting into or talking over
someone else's words.*]

DON. This is a fiasco!

MILLY. Almost, chaps. Almost!

DON. Officially . . .

MILLY. We're nearly there!

SHORTY. Mario Lanza!

DON. Officially this is now a fiasco . . .

MILLY. Once more and we'll make it!

DON. I can't stand it any longer.

MILLY. Then sit down and sing!

DON. There are fates worse than death.

MILLY [*closing her eyes*]. 'Smiling Through!'

SHORTY. But you isn't even trying, Don.

DON. Because I don't want to.

SHORTY. No, Don. You must sing.

DONO. Are you deaf? I Don't Want To . . . !

SHORTY. Shame on you, Don! It's her birthday.

MILLY [*her eyes still closed*]. I said 'Smiling Through'. On your marks, get set, GO. [*Singing.*] 'There's a little grey road winding over the hill, to a little white house by the sea . . .' [*etc.*]

[*Don and Shorty continue their argument over this.*]

DON. Well, she can have it. Just leave me . . .

SHORTY. No, Don.

DON. Leave me out of it.

SHORTY. No, Don, that's not fair.

DON. I don't care if it's not!

SHORTY. I say you must sing, because . . .

DON. And I'm saying . . .

[*Don and Shorty erupt simultaneously into protestations and accusations. Milly is still singing her song, in her loudest voice, with her eyes tightly closed. Bedlam. At the height of the racket she picks up a spoon and starts banging on the table.*]

MILLY. Order! Order!

[*The argument continues; Milly hammers away.*]

Order, I say!

DON. I warned you this was going to happen. I refuse to take the blame for this fiasco.

SHORTY. Well, it wasn't me, because I was singing.

MILLY. You're out of order. Both of you come to order at once!

[*Silence.*]

We won't get anywhere by shouting. [*She is speaking with a supreme effort at control and deliberation.*]

I know it's serious, but we must keep calm if we hope to get to the bottom of . . . this . . . In fact I think we're already there.

Speaking from experience, I'd say this was rock bottom. I've never known it harder. Keep cool. I'm coming to the point. Hidden in all this confusion is a Crime—a serious criminal offence. I demand Justice! [*Pause.*] I can't show you blood or bruises. The victim isn't even dead. But that won't stop me now from looking at you, and you, and pronouncing you two bastards Guilty!

DON [*held by the accusation*]. And you?

MILLY. Your victim.

SHORTY. What we done this time, Milly?

MILLY. Tonight.

DON. And you're accusing *us*?

MILLY. Yes.

DON. *We're* to blame?

MILLY. I want to say it again . . .

DON. No.

MILLY. Guilty!

DON. No! I tried to stop you. I warned you—every inch of the way. But you wouldn't listen. *You* wanted a party.

MILLY. Yes. A bit of mirth. Sing out the old and laugh in the new. A few chuckles. Is that making impossible demands? This was my birthday.

SHORTY. But what was wrong with it?

MILLY. What do you call this? Slab-cake and pimples, cigarette butts and silkworms, and nothing to do?

SHORTY. It wasn't so bad, Mill.

MILLY. Is this all you want?

SHORTY. I'm happy.

MILLY. You're not.

SHORTY. But I am.

MILLY. Well, you've got no right to be. And if you're too stupid to see why, I'll tell you. And to start off with let me tell you to your face that I don't like you. As true as God is my witness, looking at you now I can say I don't like the sight of you. You nauseate me. He teases you. He's teasing you all the time, and I'm disgusted.

SHORTY. I don't mind a few jokes.

MILLY. There's only one. You. You're the joke. Sissy was right. You're ugly and a joke and I'm filled with shame to find you doing all this to mankind under my roof. Do you understand now. Must I say it again? We find you revolting. Ask him.

[*She smokes violently.*]

SHORTY [*to Don*]. She's joking.

MILLY [*to Don*]. Tell him. [*Pause*] Coward! Funk!

DON. What do you hope to gain from all this?

MILLY. The truth. I want you down here—rock bottom—where you belong. Are you scared?

DON. No.

MILLY. Well, he's waiting to hear it.

DON. I study you, Shorty.

MILLY. He thinks you're a curiosity.

DON. It's in the interest of Science.

MILLY. Get to the point.

DON. You see, you're what they mean by simple-minded.

MILLY. He once called you a perfect specimen of a retarded poor white.

DON. Overseas you'd be a labourer—digging up the streets in London.

MILLY. No you don't! You said he'd be emptying the dirtbins in Birmingham.

DON. Here we have Natives to do the dirty work. You're saved by your white skin. Because, examine the facts. You can just about read and write. You can't carry out the simple duties of a post-man. I don't think you could do anything complicated. You blunder on from day to day with a weak defence—yet you survive. You even have a wife.

58

MILLY. Aha!

DON. I'm amazed at your survival. According to Darwin you should be dead. That's all.

MILLY. No, it's not. You've left out the best bit of the lot. Sissy. Tell him what we whisper.

DON. I don't think she's properly your wife.

MILLY. Don't be clever. He's a simple-minded poor white, remember.

DON. I don't think you know how.

MILLY [to Shorty]. Do you understand? He doesn't think you know how to do it. I think you do, but that Sissy doesn't want it from you, because we *both* think that Billy knows how.

[*They watch Shorty intently.*]

SHORTY. I'll hit you, Don.

MILLY. Bravo!

SHORTY. 'S true's there's a God, I'll hit you.

MILLY. And me? What will you do to me?

SHORTY. If you was a man I'd hit you too.

MILLY. And Billy?

SHORTY. I'll bugger up the lot of you.

MILLY. Now we're getting somewhere. The rock-bottom boxing match! Get out your gloves and hit! But first! . . . Let's tell him if he wants to see a real psychological curiosity, to have a good look in the mirror next time he squeezes his pimples. That's why no decent, clean-living girl will ever stomach the sight of you. Furthermore, you also blow your nose on the sheets, I've seen you use the washbasin in the bathrroom as a W.C., and I've a strong suspicion that, as regards positively filthy habits, that is still not the worst. Sometimes when I think of your hands I want to vomit.

And he's looking for himself! Take my advice—don't! You'll be disgusted when you find it. Who do you think you're fooling? Calling *him* a freak? You're a washout.

DON. You finished?

59

MILLY. If you've hit the bottom with a bump—yes.

DON. Because there's a few things that could be said about you.

MILLY. Go ahead. It's a free-for-all.

DON [*to Shorty*]. Come on. Let's tell her.

MILLY. Christ, you're yellow.

DON. You've started to get old woman odours. You should use scent. It's unpleasant being near you at times. That's why I've got no appetite left. And maybe that's why Ahlers doesn't want to marry you. Yes! You're also not fooling anybody. I guessed it long ago. And quite frankly I don't blame him. Because the thought of living intimately with you for the rest of my life, in the same room . . . !

MILLY. So I'm also ugly. What does that prove?

DON. As much as you've proved against us. Nothing.

MILLY. But I'm accusing you of desertion. That's my charge. That in the hour of need, in the thick of the fight, you deserted a fellow human being who had her back to the wall in a tight corner. Because, I'll say it again . . . I tried!

DON. You won't get a medal for that. I also got out of bed. I also breathed, and walked and scratched myself . . . and all the other heroisms. Shorty, too. We suffered the same fate. We're also victims.

MILLY. Then prove it.

DON. How?

MILLY. By crying. Come on. Shed one tear and I'll believe you.

DON. Have you?

MILLY. Yes! Twice today I went to the W.C., pulled the chain so nobody would hear, and wept! But you two? [*Mimicking them.*] 'It's not so bad, Mill.' 'Let's call it a day.' Is this all we get?

DON [*with sudden vehemence*]. Yes! It's all you get. And what's more you've had it. It's nearly twelve o'clock and then you're a year older. And there's not many more left where that one came from. You're in the home stretch, Milly!

MILLY [*summoniug up all her control to ask the question for the last time*]. You are telling me this is all I get?

DON. Yes!

MILLY [*almost a cry*]. Then somebody's a bloody liar. Because there were promises. The agreement was that it would be worth it. Well, it isn't. I've been cheated. The whole thing was just a trick to get me to go on. Otherwise who would? Who wants to get up tomorrow, if this is it? If this is all? Fifty years! That's a lot of patience. Nobody's so well off that fifty years doesn't leave him hard up for what's left. I am. I'm broke. So I want what I'm owed. Pay up or be damned.

[*Pause. Shorty and Don stare at Milly. Her resolution has reached its climax and now begins to ebb.*]

Why? That's it! That's all. I just want to know why. It's not a silly question. When you lie in the dark and ask, and listen, it sounds like sense, like there should be an answer. Why? Why me? Why this?

[*Don and Shorty are still staring at her.*]

Go on, they said. It's good for you. Go on. Grow up! They all seemed happy with it back in old Pringle Street. So I believed them. I was young. And ... [*Pause, after which she continues softly, her voice charged with amazement.*] I was young! Yes. Come to think of it. Me. Once ... Pringle Street. Number nineteen, near the top. And a time, so young! A day, one special day that was eleven years old in one-way Pringle Street. It was dark. It was Sunday night and getting dark and Basil my best friend was stamping cockroaches under the lamp-post. So I said, 'Shame on you, Basil!' But he said they didn't feel because there wasn't any blood. I was sitting on our wall singing, 'When you wish upon a star, makes no matter what you are.' Usually there was something sad about Sundays because of Monday and School. But this time it was holidays and altogether different. I was thinking about this and then slowly I began to grow happy. The darker it got the happier I grew. So I sang my song again and wanted to cry it was so big. And that night for the first time I beat Basil to the lamp-post when the light went on. He was so busy stamping cockroaches he didn't see. So I ran and touched it first and shouted 'My Wish! My Wish!' Basil got jealous and said wishes didn't come true. But I just laughed at him. Because you know what I wished? Happiness! All those holidays it kept coming. You were right about the dress, Don— white. But you forgot the bell. There was a bell once. It was after Sunday School and I was running home singing 'All things bright and beautiful . . .' and there was this bell. Oh, my God! This bell was ringing, chaps! And I was running in that sun shining the way it should singing, 'All things bright and beautiful, all creatures great and small'! How's that for faith? With all the heart of eleven years old I believed it, that it was mine, and for ever. Because I wished. Every time, every chance—falling stars, black cats, white horses—every wish was Happiness. I had it. That night I mean . . . Happiness. It felt like I was holding it so tight it was for ever and ever. But my hands!

Mildred Constance Jenkins. Fifty years old . . . I'm not a woman any more . . . he says. I never thought of it like that, but he says I'm not a woman any more. Last week it was, one night. He was eating liver sausage in bed and I just told him, you know, in case he started wondering. Then he said, matter-of-fact I'll admit, not meaning to hurt, that therefore strictly speaking I'm not a woman any more. It sounded logical the way he put it. To do with function. The function of a thing, and being a woman, that meant babies. And you see, suddenly he sat up and said he wanted a family! Because of the business and Ahlers being a good name to keep alive through the ages. We better stop now, he said. But we can still be friends.

So you see, it's gone. Or just about. A little left but mostly in the way of time. The rest just gone. Not broken, or stolen, or violated—which might make it sound like there's been no crime, I know. But I did have it and now it's gone and nobody ever gets it back so don't tell me that doesn't make us victims. Don't ask me how! Somehow! Victims of something. Look at us. All flesh and bone, with one face hanging onto your neck until you're dead!

[*Inside the house the clock begins to chime. They listen in silence for a few seconds, then . . .*]

Ignore that! Where were we? Today! What was I saying? Today . . . today . . . Hold on! This one I won't let go! Today, today . . . All right! You win, damn you. Yesterday!

[*The clock mechanism is again at fault. It chimes on and on and on. Exit Shorty. A blow off-stage stops the chiming.*]

MILLY [*softly*]. Mildred Jenkins, you are still alive!

[*Shorty returns.*]

SHORTY. Sunday!

MILLY. So let's sort it out. To begin with don't take what I said too seriously. I got excited—flushed—if you really want to know. Hot and bothered. It's a symptom. We'll survive. Also, if anyone asks, meaning you know who, let's all say we had a good time in the form of a quiet gathering. [*Pause.*] That's all.

[*Shorty goes up to Milly.*]

Well?

SHORTY. You said you hate me.

MILLY. I exaggerated.

SHORTY. So you like me?

MILLY. No need to go to the other extreme. Let's just say you're also human and leave it at that. 'Bury the hatchet on Sunday, dig it up on Monday.'

SHORTY. So we're all friends again. Okay, Don?

DON. Okay, Shorty.

SHORTY. Shake. [*They shake.*] Milly, I got an idea.

MILLY. You keep trying, I'll say that for you.

SHORTY. The zoo.

MILLY. It's cruel to keep living things behind bars.

SHORTY. What about us going tomorrow? It will be fun, man, George says there's a baboon with a blue bum who hates us.

MILLY. I think I remember him.

SHORTY. Everybody laughs, and then he gets cross.

63

MILLY [*in indignation*]. Do you blame him? No, really! I think that's going too far.

SHORTY. What?

MILLY. For God's sake! Blue? How would you feel? Honestly, sometimes, some of the shapes . . . ! I wonder if creation knows what it's up to. I'll have a good look at that poor bastard tomorrow.

DON [*quoting the hymn*]. 'All creatures great and small
The Lord God made them all.'

MILLY. But bright and beautiful! That's how the hymn starts. Blue might be bright, but it's not beautiful *there*. Oh no.

SHORTY. We'll have a good look, Milly.

MILLY. God help you if you laugh.

SHORTY. I won't, I promise.

MILLY. Because it's not funny.

SHORTY. So can I get my leaves?

MILLY. It's pathetic.

SHORTY. Leaves, Milly!

MILLY. Leaves? What leaves? It's winter.

SHORTY. To feed my silkies. You threw them away.

MILLY. So I did. Feed them by all means. I hope they're crisp.

SHORTY. They're still on the pavement. I seen them.

[*Exit.*]

MILLY [*to Don*]. He means well. The heart's good. It's the mentality that's weak.

DON [*standing*]. To bed, to sleep, perchance no dreams.*

MILLY. Not yet. Coffee. Drown our sorrows in the dregs.

DON [*sitting*]. Here we go again.

MILLY [*laughing*]. Into the Valley of Death! Know that one?

DON. 'The Lord is my shepherd. Yea though I walk.'

MILLY. Never! The Charge of the Light Brigade. 'Into the Valley of Death rode the gallant four hundred'.

DON. It's the same valley.

[*Shorty returns and goes to a shelf at the back.*]

SHORTY [*going to the table with his shoe-box*]. Guess what, chaps? They're all in silk. I don't need the leaves now, Milly. Look! One is still spinning.

MILLY [*looking at the shoe-box*]. So that's how they do it! Congratulations, Shorty. Well done! What happens now?

SHORTY. Now?

MILLY. With them.

[*Shorty looks to Don for guidance.*]

The next step.

SHORTY. I don't know. Nothing.

MILLY. But the moths. Moths are going to come out. Isn't that so, Don?

SHORTY. I don't want moths.

MILLY. Well, that's just too bad, because you're going to get them.

SHORTY. Nobody keeps the moths.

MILLY. So tell me what happens to them!

SHORTY. I don't know.

DON. Don't start again.

MILLY. Don, what happens to the moths?

DON. We've had enough questions for one night, Milly!

MILLY. Will somebody kindly tell me what happens to the moths?

DON [*at breaking-point*] I don't know and I don't care and as far as I am concerned . . .

MILLY [*with mounting indignation*]. Now just hang on! There's something wrong here. I smell that rat again. [*To Shorty.*] Why have you been feeding them?

SHORTY. It was Jossie who . . .

MILLY. Why Have You Kept Them Alive?

SHORTY. To see them spin. To see the silk.

MILLY. And now that they've done it, they've had it. Is that it?

65

SHORTY [*desperate*]. I don't know all about this, Milly!

MILLY. You're going to chuck them away.

SHORTY. Okay. I'll keep them and watch the moths.

MILLY. To starve! To die!

DON [*unable to take any more*]. For Christ's sake what do you want?

MILLY [*with equal violence*]. Some other way! Don't you? Must it always be the muck-heap? Isn't there another solution?

DON. Then find it!

MILLY. I will.

SHORTY. Hang on, Don. Look, Milly . . . As God is my witness I'll feed them. They'll get fat.

[*Don gets up. Thinking he is making a move to his room, Milly jumps in front of the back-door and stands there spread-eagled, blocking his exit.*]

MILLY. Where do you think you're going?

DON. Come with. You can hold my hand. Come!

[*Exit into the passage where the lavatory door slams. Milly rushes to the doorway and shouts after him.*]

MILLY. You've got a dirty brain, Donovan Bradshaw!

[*Turning back into the room she finds Shorty staring at her.*]

Feed them!

[*She starts to clear the table. The front door opens. A disconsolate Sissy appears in the passage doorway.*]

SHORTY. Hello, Siss.

SISSY [*noticing the decorations*]. What's going on here?

SHORTY. We had a party.

SISSY. With dancing?

MILLY [*before Shorty can reply*]. Singing, dancing, drinking. The lot.

SISSY. Is it finished?

MILLY. Yes! We had a good time and it's finished. So you missed it.

[*Exit.*]

SISSY. You didn't say nothing to me about a party!

66

SHORTY. It was a surprise party. Even we didn't know. It was Milly's birthday. Say Happy Birthday when she comes back.

SISSY. No.

SHORTY. It's sad, Siss. She's unhappy.

SISSY. Well, so am I.

SHORTY. Wasn't it a good picture?

SISSY. Who all was at the party?

SHORTY. Just us. Me and Don and Milly.

SISSY. That doesn't sound so hot.

SHORTY. It was okay. But ... [*Whispering.*] we didn't dance. [*Pause.*] We discussed. [*Pause.*] Sissy, I don't want you to see Billy any more.

SISSY. Same here.

SHORTY. Why?

SISSY. You men are all the same.

SHORTY. But I'm your husband.

SISSY. That's your look-out.

SHORTY [*pointing to the shoe-box on the table*]. They're all in silk now, Sissy.

SISSY. What do I care?

SHORTY. I'll wait for the moths.

SISSY. I don't want moths in the room. They'll eat my clothes. I only got a few, for your information.

SHORTY. I'll keep them here in the kitchen. Milly likes moths.

SISSY. God help you if you bring them into the room.

SHORTY. I won't, I promise.

SISSY. You always promise but nothing comes true. We been married six months now and just look. You're lucky I didn't know.

SHORTY. Don't say that, Siss.

SISSY. Well then, do something!

SHORTY [*really desperate*]. But what? What must a guy do? I slog.

SISSY. Let's go away from here.

SHORTY. Aren't we happy here?

SISSY. I'm not. They don't like me. You don't protect me, you know. You let them scandal about me.

SHORTY. Where do you want to go?

SISSY. How must I know? [*Pause.*] Somewhere nice.

SHORTY. Shamley Boarding House?

SISSY. Back there! Are you mad? [*Pause.*] Cape Town.

SHORTY. Cape Town? CAPE TOWN.

SISSY. You asked me, so I'm telling you.

SHORTY. But what about my job?

SISSY. Ask them to transfer you.

SHORTY [*with finality*]. I know nothing about transfers, Sissy.

SISSY. Well, ask them. Ask George.

SHORTY. But I don't know the streets down there, Siss! I'll never get the letters right. Please, not Cape Town.

SISSY. So must it be Braamfontein all my life?

SHORTY. Sissy . . . [*Pause.*]

SISSY. Hurry up. I haven't got all night.

SHORTY. Don't be unhappy, because . . . something happens.

SISSY. What?

SHORTY. It's to do with getting old.

SISSY. So?

SHORTY. We get old.

SISSY. What are you talking about?

SHORTY. I don't know. I'm all mixed up. But it was so clear.

SISSY. You're mad.

SHORTY. No. Ask Milly. She told us. Promises don't come true . . .

SISSY. That's not news to me with you around.

SHORTY. And we get old.

SISSY. You've already said that.

SHORTY. But we're young.

SISSY. So what?

68

ACT TWO

SHORTY. You musn't be frightened. S'true's God, I'm your
husband.

SISSY. All right!

SHORTY. So let's go to bed.

SISSY. I'm tired.

SHORTY. Okay. Come.

SISSY. I'm very tired tonight.

SHORTY. But we got it, Sissy. Truly. By Special Licence. It's okay.
They all say it's as good as in a church.

SISSY. Have you been discussing my private life in public?

SHORTY. I just want you to be brave. Let's go.

SISSY. Just remember I'm tired. I want to go to sleep. Understand?

SHORTY. Come.

SISSY. Do you understand?

SHORTY. I'm also tired.

SISSY. Do You Understand? [Pause.]

SHORTY [defeated]. Yes.

SISSY. Because I'm warning you. If you do, I'll call for help again.

[She moves to the door, Shorty following. Before they reach it they are
stopped by Milly's voice, loud and urgent.]

MILLY [off-stage, hammering on the lavatory door]. Don! Hurry up! All
hands on deck. You've got five seconds at the most!

[She now enters the room highly excited, and finds Shorty and Sissy near
the door.]

Get back! Sit down!

SHORTY. What's going on, Mill?

MILLY. Sit down, I say!

[A few seconds of furious activity, during which she piles empty bottles
and plates on the table, rushes out for something and then grabs a glass and
fills it up with cool-drink. In between all this she forces Sissy and Shorty
into chairs, urging them to 'Smile'—'Grab a glass'—'Look Happy', etc.
Don appears in the doorway.]

DON. What's happened?

MILLY. Ahlers! He's coming up the road. Sit down. Now, all together . . .

DON. No.

MILLY. Laugh!

DON. For heaven's sake, Milly!

MILLY. My sake, damn you! Sit down. Laugh you bas—

[*The front door opens.*]

Ha ha ha ha ha! [*Hissing.*] Come on! [*Shorty tries to help.*] Ha ha ha ha ha! Very good! Drink up, chaps! Empty the bottles. Polish off those savouries. Ha ha ha! My God, that's a killer! Ostrich eggs! One of the best jokes I've heard in years! [*Drifting towards the door. Then when she gets there she holds up her hand for silence as if the party was an uproar of merriment and noise.*] Hang on, chaps! Hang on! Come and see what the cat's dragged in. If you asked me, I'd say that a certain old friend from the Fatherland turned out to be a bit of a flop. [*Now speaking directly to Ahlers in the passage.*] What happened? She say you were too old for her? You are, you know. Just don't think that means you can come crawling back to me. Because I had a damn good time without you. Didn't we, boys?

[*Ahlers is now moving up the stairs. Milly shifts her position.*]

So don't start banging on the floor at four o'clock if we're still going strong. This happens to be my house! Let's get that straight. And don't bother to ask if you can join in, because you can't.

[*Milly moves out of sight into the passage.*]

And finally, let me tell you, nothing is finished. I've proved it. You never had anything to do with it anyway. You're not God. You're a parasite. A bloodsucking Hitler!

[*A door slams.*]

That's right, shut your door. But you'll still hear me! [*She is back in the kitchen now and shouting up at the ceiling.*] If it's the last thing I do, I'll make you hear me! [*To the others.*] Sing! Come on! [*Singing.*] 'Why was she born so . . .' COME ON!

[*Shorty is again the only one who tries to help.*]

'Why was she born so beautiful, Why was she born at all!'
[*Silence. Milly lights a cigarette and takes a few draws. To Shorty and Sissy.*] Party's over. Bugger off. [*To Don.*] Not you.

[*Exit Shorty and Sissy.*]

You think he believed it?

DON. Do you want my honest opinion?

MILLY. No! But I bet you anything you like there's doubt. That's even worse. I just hope it gnaws.

DON. You didn't give him notice.

MILLY. I will.

DON. You said tonight. We took a bet.

MILLY. Play my trump card just like that! Don't be a fool!

DON. Milly . . .

MILLY. If you were up in the trenches would you blast off all your ammo at one go?

DON. Milly! Milly! There aren't any trenches. This is Hospital Hill, Braamfontein.

MILLY. Well, if these aren't hostilities, I'd like to know what are.

DON. It can't last for ever, Milly.

MILLY. What?

DON. You and him.

MILLY. For ever! Who said anything about that? I'm halfway there anyway.

DON. So what do you hope to win?

MILLY. Tomorrow.

[*Pause.*]

DON [*helplessly*]. I don't know.

MILLY. That's right.

DON. I'm tired. Declare an armistice.

MILLY. What for?

DON. Then we can sleep in peace tonight.

MILLY. Peace! You can talk about peace in times like these? Are

71

you mad? Some nights when I lie in bed and those ambulances go screaming past and I think: More casualties! . . . I can just about smell the cannon smoke. Anyway, I couldn't sleep with him still stomping around. Last eye open in an old house . . . that's me!

DON. Suppose his doubt gnaws away all night?

MILLY. If that happens, I'm a happy woman.

DON. But if he doesn't go to bed?

MILLY. We hang on. Keep the fort. It's worth waiting for.

DON. We?

MILLY. You're in this up to your neck.

DON. I know. I'm drowning.

MILLY. Then call for help. That'll keep you awake if the coffee doesn't work. No point in going under half asleep.

DON. I can't, Milly.

MILLY. What?

DON. Call for help.

MILLY. [*briskly*]. Go on! [*She moves, but stops after a few steps to stare at Don.*] What's this now?

DON. I'm dumb. When things happen, I watch. Even when it's to myself . . . all I do is watch. I used to think the right word for me was Numb . . . that there wasn't even Feeling. But I think that's wrong. I'm sure if I loved something, and then lost it, or it was killed . . . one of the tragedies . . . I know this is only probability, but I'm sure I would feel. My trouble is I wouldn't protest. [*Pause.*] I'm not too worried. Look at it soberly. Forgetting for the moment my face . . . the damage is not too extensive. The sexual urge is intact; like everyone else, I eat, I sleep, my fingernails grow. The framework is still sound. If it comes to the worst I could always get a job in the Civil Service. The worst that can happen to me is that I'll be forgotten a bit before my time.

MILLY. You still believe that?

DON. If I were to sit down somewhere, unseen, and was quiet for a very long time, and the instinct to return to the herd petered out. All you need is four walls, and a lid.

MILLY [*looking around*]. In here?

DON. It's a likely spot. It's got the feel.

MILLY. But there's a street outside there, Don! All the people! Rush-hour traffic. Right outside that front door!

DON. Yes. But you've got to open it, Milly. [*Pause.*] Did you, today?

MILLY [*suddenly conscious of herself and her predicament*]. I'm still in my nightie. I haven't got dressed . . . yet.

DON. Exactly.

MILLY. You mean . . . it can happen like this? In a dressing gown?

DON. More ways than one.

[*Pause.*]

MILLY. There must be something we can do! Make a noise! . . . Lest they forget, as the monument says. I can still do that. I'll make it loud, make them stop in the street, make them say: People are living there! I'll remind them. Tomorrow. [*Looking at the ceiling.*] And he's gone to sleep. It's always easier when he's asleep even when I was up there with him. I think calmly. Quite honestly, I saw it coming. I still hate him of course. [*Takes out another cigarette.*] Sit out this last fag with me and then you can go.

DON. Promise?

MILLY. Promise. It's hell isn't it? Open your mouth and it starts again . . . The old song and dance.

[*Don is tearing off the backs of the cigarette boxes on which he made his notes during the course of the night. Milly watches him.*]

What's the score for tonight?

DON [*looking at his notes*]. On paper it looks like a draw. But I stopped halfway. It's a pity. You came out with some good things towards the end.

MILLY. I was on form.

DON [*examining his notes*]. Your secret? You and Ahlers?

MILLY. Meant to be. I suppose it's more of a mystery, really. Life.

DON. With a capital F. Remember that? I thought it was rather good.

MILLY. What else?

DON. Let's see. Yes . . . you said you would rather do away with yourself than carry on like this.

MILLY. Did I really?

DON. And quick. The simplest method of course is the brown paper bag. Just put it on and breathe.

MILLY. The old plunge. Head first.

DON. It's supposed to be painless. [*Looks at his notes again.*] Shorty said he'd love Sissy even if she only had one leg and one eye.

MILLY. That's big of him. She'd have to hop, wouldn't she? [*Small chuckle.*] I don't mean to be cruel, Don, but when it comes to sights and sore eyes! My God, you could do something with the lot of us in here if you had a sense of humour. Can you see it? You with your head in a brown paper bag, telling the world it's painless. Sissy jumping around on one leg like a whatsisname . . . that thing with a pouch.

DON. Kangaroo.

MILLY. Chasing Shorty! And him wiping away his tears with his boxing gloves on.

DON. And you in the middle of the mess.

MILLY. As per usual!

DON. Trying not to laugh!

MILLY. Why?

DON. Because we've all got blue bums.

[*Milly's amusement breaks into laughter. Repeating random images from the picture just drawn—kangaroo, boxing gloves, blue bums, etc., etc.—her laughter grows enormous. At its height and with Don watching her . . .* ]

CURTAIN

74

# STATEMENTS AFTER AN ARREST UNDER THE IMMORALITY ACT

# CHARACTERS

A WHITE WOMAN (Frieda Joubert)
A COLOURED MAN (Errol Philander)
A POLICEMAN (Detective-Sergent J. du Preez)

STATEMENTS AFTER AN ARREST UNDER THE IMMORALITY
ACT was first performed on 28 March 1972 as the opening production of
The Space, Cape Town, directed by Athol Fugard with the following cast:

| | |
|---|---|
| FRIEDA JOUBERT | Yvonne Bryceland |
| ERROL PHILANDER | Athol Fugard |
| DETECTIVE-SERGEANT J. DU PREEZ | Percy Sieff |
| POLICEMAN | Christopher Prophet |

The version printed here was given its first performance on 22 January 1974 at
the Royal Court Theatre, London, as part of a 'South African Season' with
*Sizwe Bansi Is Dead* and *The Island*; and was directed by Athol Fugard with the
following cast:

| | |
|---|---|
| FRIEDA JOUBERT | Yvonne Bryceland |
| ERROL PHILANDER | Ben Kingsley |
| DETECTIVE-SERGEANT J. DU PREEZ | Wilson Dunster |

The first US production took place at the Manhattan Theater Club on
5 February 1978, directed by Thomas Bullard, with Veronica Costang and
Robert Christian.

# STATEMENTS AFTER AN ARREST UNDER
# THE IMMORALITY ACT

A man *and* a woman *on a blanket on the floor. Both of them are naked. He is caressing her hair.*
*Dim light.*

WOMAN [*shyly*]. I dried it in the sun. Just sat there, on a chair in the backyard, feeling the warmth of it on my head. Every strand felt separate and my head very light. . . . The texture of the hair changes as it dries. And then the smell of it when it falls over my face . . . the smell of clean hair and shampoo. The warmer it gets the more you smell it. And if there's a breeze, even a small one, the way it lifts and floats. Also . . . the colour of the strands, specially when they hang close to your eyes. . . . The colour seems to pulse. [*Pause.*] There's no sense of time. Everything very still. Just the sounds of a warm afternoon . . . warm sounds, warm smells . . . specially the fig tree. A lot of the fruit has fallen now and burst, rotting on the ground . . . almost like wine! The leaves also have a very strong smell when it's hot. [*Pause.*] What else? . . . Doves . . . a locust flying suddenly . . . bees . . . Just sat there. . . . Quiet Saturday afternoon . . . hearing and smelling it all quietly, being very lazy and thinking all sorts of things.

[*Turning to the man.*]

And you?

MAN. Oh . . . another day. Nothing special . . . until now.

WOMAN. I don't care. Tell me.

MAN. There's nothing to tell. I did a bit of work at the school. . . . No! Of course! I know what happened today.

WOMAN. Tell me.

MAN. I built a five-roomed house. [*She laughs.*] I did! Lunch-time. On the way home I passed a little boy . . . Izak . . . his older brother Henry started school this year . . . Izak Tobias . . . anyway Izak was playing there in the sand with some old bricks and things. I stopped and watched him. Building himself a house, he said. Told me all about it. His mother and his father and his baby brother sleep in one room, and he and his sister and his granny in the other. Two rooms. It's the house he lives in. I know. I've been in it. It's a Bontrug house.* [*Pause.*] You know what I made him do? Build a separate room for his granny. Then I explained that when his sister got big she would need a room for herself. So he built another one for her. When I left him he had a five-roomed house and a garage. . . . That's what it's all about, hey.

WOMAN. Yes.

MAN. If you're going to dream, give yourself five rooms, man.

[*Silence.*]

WOMAN. I love you. [*Pause.*] What's the matter? What are you doing?

[*A match flares in the darkness. She scrambles away.*]

WOMAN. No!

MAN. Please.

WOMAN. No!!

[*The match dies. Darkness.*]

MAN. Is it me or you?

WOMAN. You don't understand.

MAN. Understand what? There is seeing, and being seen. Which one are you frightened of? Me or you?

WOMAN. It's not as simple as that!

MAN. Yes, it is! It's got to be . . . sometimes.

That last book you lent me ends off a chapter with a paragraph, and the paragraph ends off his speculation about the origin of life . . . conclusions . . . vague. Nobody will ever know. . . . 'These questions cannot be answered at this point and are perhaps unanswerable.' But we do know that the differences between life and even the most complex of chemical processes are four-fold . . . metabolic processes of a wide but not unlimited variety; a degree of independence from the environment; sexual reproduction; and, finally, a susceptibility to death. Because life lives, life must die. Simple. [*Pause.*] Moon's nearly full out there tonight, you know. Toringberg will be splendid when I walk back. Hell, Frieda, if we could have opened those curtains . . . !

WOMAN. Don't! Please . . .

MAN. Why? What about me? I want to be seen. I want you to see me. [*Moves suddenly into a faint patch of light from the curtained window.*] The brightest spot in our world. Here I am. Me. Can you see me?

WOMAN. Yes.

MAN. And?

WOMAN. I see you.

MAN. Frieda! Frieda! Life . . . is three billion years old. Fact. This little piece of the earth, the few miserable square feet of this room . . . this stupid little town, this desert . . . was a sea, millions and millions of years ago. Dinosaurs wallowed here! Truly. That last book mentions us: 'The richest deposits . . . Permian and Triassic periods . . . are to be found in the Graaff Reinet district of the Cape Province of South Africa.'* Us. Our world. Are you listening?

WOMAN. Yes.

MAN. You *can* see me?

WOMAN. Yes.

MAN. You want to hear more?

WOMAN. Yes.

MAN. [*thinks . . . then*]. There was a point a billion or so years after the beginning of the earth, when the surface cooled sufficiently to permit water to accumulate in liquid form. Up until then it had just been gaseous, remember. But when this stage was reached . . . [*Pause.*] It rained continuously for millions of years. Rain . . . water . . . on and on . . . [*Pause.*] Frieda? [*Holds out his hand. She moves to him, but remains shy and reticent.*] What are you frightened of?

WOMAN. Everything. Me . . . you . . . them . . .

MAN. Them?

WOMAN. No. That as well, of course. But I wasn't thinking about them now. [*Pause.*] The dinosaurs and those hairy . . . missing links . . . that look like baboons, stand like men, and could almost smile.

MAN. Australopithecus. Fossilized skull in a limestone quarry in Taung, Bechuanaland. Raymond Dart. 1930.*

WOMAN. Is that the one . . . ?

MAN. Yes. That's the one you don't like.

WOMAN. With the females and their babies . . . looking so . . .

MAN. Yes. [*Laughing.*] You're frightened of him! You know who I am frightened of? Bishop Ussher.* God created the world . . . the act of creation took place on October the twenty-sixth, four thousand and four B.C., at nine a.m.

WOMAN. You shouldn't . . .

MAN. He worked it out. From the Bible. [*Pause.*] Come.

WOMAN. Try . . . please try to understand.

MAN. No. You understand. Do you think I just want to *see* you? Do you think I just want to look? [*Pause.*] I do. [*Pause.*] Listen to this one: ' . . . no vestige of a beginning and no prospect of an end . . .'. Did you hear that?

WOMAN. Yes.

MAN. And? Listen again. '. . . no vestige of a beginning and no prospect of an end'. The conclusion of Charles Lyell after a good look at what was happening on the surface of the earth. *Principles of Geology*, 1830.* What does that do to you?

WOMAN. Nothing.

[*Pause. He laughs quietly.*]

MAN. You're wrong. You're so wrong. If it wasn't for that sentence . . . I don't think we should have ever met. Hey, when did . . . ?

WOMAN. Almost a year ago. January the twenty-sixth;

MAN. Then it was the night of January the twenty-fifth. My family were already asleep. It was quiet . . . the best time to read or study. . . . The lamp on the table, me, one of Bontrug's mongrels barking outside in the dark. . . . Anyway, I was reading,

understanding everything clearly . . . fact after fact . . . the time
it all took. . . . So slow . . . God is so lazy, Frieda! . . . and then
suddenly those words: '. . . no vestige of a beginning, no prospect of an end . . .'. I stopped. I had to. I couldn't go further.
They weren't just words, it wasn't just that I understood that
somebody had said . . . I'm expressing myself badly. It's hard to
describe. It was almost like having a . . . No! . . . it was a
'comprehension'—*ja*, of life and time . . . and there in the
middle of it . . . at that precise moment . . . in Bontrug, was me.
Being me, just being me there in that little room was . . . [*choosing
his words carefully*] . . . the most exciting thing that had ever happened to me. I wanted that moment to last forever! It was so
intense it almost hurt. I couldn't sit still.

I just left the book . . . didn't look at it again . . . I didn't want to
see another word, read another fact. . . . *Ja!* It wasn't a question
of facts any more, something else, something bigger. I went
outside. Walking round Bontrug. I looked at the Bontrug *braks*
with their tails between their legs. . . . Dogs . . . I stopped in
front of old Tobias' little place with the five of them inside at
that moment sleeping on the floor. . . . I looked at it and said
'House' . . . at the stars. . . . My hands were cold . . . but ten
fingers, Frieda. . . . If I was the first man I could have started to
count the stars.

There was nothing I was frightened to see.

WOMAN. You've never told me about that before.

   [*Pause.*]

MAN [*as if he hadn't heard her*]. So, the next morning there I was, on
   . . . what did you say it was . . . the twenty-sixth . . . January the
   twenty-sixth . . . asking if you had—

WOMAN. Julian Huxley's *Principles of Evolution.** [*Pause.*] Why . . .
   why have you waited, almost a year . . . to tell me about that?

MAN. I've told no one.

WOMAN. I'm not no one. I'm also me. I'm the other person on the
   floor. With you. [*Pause.*] I'm jealous. You can make me so jealous. And I'm frightened. Yes. And there are things I don't want

81

to see. . . . They found two snakes in my neighbour's backyard yesterday . . . Mr. van Wyk . . .

MAN. What were they?

WOMAN. Somebody said they were rinkhals.

MAN. Rinkhals, the drought's bringing them out. We've had no trouble in Bontrug.

WOMAN. They killed them.

MAN. Well, if they were rinkhals . . . old people say, if they sit up in your footpath, they can spit you blind.

WOMAN. Mr. van Wyk . . . said they were mating at the time. Their . . . the pieces kept moving . . . for a long time afterwards.

MAN. *Ja* . . . it's the nervous system. . . . I think they die later, or something.

[*Pause. He feels around in the darkness for his trousers.*]

What's the time?

WOMAN. No . . . not yet. I'm sorry. Please. Say it again.

MAN. What?

WOMAN. Those words . . . that sentence . . .

MAN. '. . . no vestige of a beginning and no prospect of an end.'

WOMAN. Did it work?

MAN. *Ja.*

WOMAN. Good. [*She draws closer to him out of the darkness.*] It's so quiet. Just those dogs.

[*Pause. He listens.*]

MAN. Town dogs.

WOMAN. What makes you so sure?

MAN. I've walked past them.

[*He has removed a few coins from his trouser pocket and is idly trying to count them in the dark.*]

Which ones have got the ridges round them?

WOMAN. What?

MAN. Coins. Which ones have got those little ridges?

WOMAN. Two cents and one cent.

MAN. [*counting*]. Five . . . seven . . . seventeen.

WOMAN. About two years ago I thought of leaving here. Going back to Cradock.*

MAN. Why didn't you?

WOMAN. Too much bother I suppose.

MAN. What was it like?

WOMAN. Cradock?

MAN. Yes.

WOMAN. You've been there.

MAN. I mean . . . were you happy there?

WOMAN [*after a pause*]. My first memory is being very small and sitting on the floor of the long passageway in our house. The shutters must have been closed, because it was all dark and quiet. Then somebody opened the front door at the other end and suddenly I saw all the sunlight and noise of the street outside. I started to walk towards it, but before I could get there the door closed. I was so upset! I sat down and cried and cried. [*Pause.*] My last memory of Cradock is locking that same door from the outside, and taking the keys to the estate agent.

MAN. You sold the house.

WOMAN. Yes . . . after my mother died, and I got the job here.

MAN. What else?

WOMAN. That's all.

MAN [*the coins in his hand*]. Forty-three.

WOMAN. What?

MAN. Forty-three cents.

WOMAN. Are you sure you are happy?

MAN. Of course. [*Pause*] It was good, man. Wasn't it?

WOMAN. Yes.

MAN. Do you ever do that? Imagine that what you've got in your pockets is all you've got, but really all you've got. No family, no place to go, nothing to do, just standing suddenly in Church

Street with forty-three cents . . . and then try to work out what you would do with it.

WOMAN. No.

MAN. Ten cents for bread . . . that would last the whole day . . . ten cents for cooldrink.

WOMAN. Buy milk.

MAN. No. When *we're* thirsty we drink cooldrink. Twenty-three cents left. What would you do? What do you think you'd want? You got something to eat, you're not thirsty.

WOMAN. Save something for tomorrow.

MAN. No. There's no tomorrow. Just today.

WOMAN. Why not?

MAN. Just part of the game.

WOMAN. I don't like the game.

MAN [*in vacant fascination with the thought of himself, one day, and twenty-three cents*].

Could buy a newspaper. Read what happened in the world yesterday. Seventeen cents left. Place like Cape Town, that could be bus fare. Go and look at the sea. Here you could only spend it in the shops.

Buy a stamp, post a letter!

WOMAN. Envelope and writing-paper?

MAN. That's true.

Could you send a telegram for twenty-three cents?

WOMAN. If the address and message was short enough.

MAN. How short?

WOMAN. I don't know.

MAN. Let's say ten words. [*Counting them on his fingers.*] 'Give us this day our daily bread.' Three left for my name and His address. What's your message?

WOMAN. 'Forgive us our trespasses as we forgive those who . . .'*

MAN. You haven't even got enough for the message! I still haven't spent the twenty-three cents. Shops close at six. *Ja!* That's what

84

would do it. Twenty-three cents and the shops closing. That's how I'd make my mistake. I'd be too late for anything except twenty-three cents of sweets, or six stale cakes. Eat them all and be sick. What would you do?

WOMAN. Am I alone?

MAN. What do you mean?

WOMAN. Do I have you?

MAN. No. I haven't got you. You haven't got me. All you've got is forty-three cents, and one day. [*Feels for her hand in the dark and gives her the money.*] What would you do with it?

WOMAN. Nothing.

MAN. Nothing! You wouldn't . . .

WOMAN. No, I wouldn't. I wouldn't even have bought bread. [*Pause.*]

MAN. The only reason I bought it was because . . .

WOMAN. You had nothing except forty-three cents and one day.

MAN. *Ja.* I'm a *brak*, hey!

WOMAN. No.

MAN. It's true. I'm hungry enough to make every mistake . . . even bark. [*Pause.*] But if that one day also had a real chance to start again—you know, to make everything different—and forty-three cents would buy me even just the first brick for a five-roomed house . . . I'd spend it on that and go hungry. [*Pause.*] Anyway listen. I'm going to try hard now to look after things. Okay? Give me one more chance, man.

WOMAN. Don't ask for that. You are my chance. I don't want to lose it.

MAN. It all goes wrong because I don't! Like my correspondence course.* Three assignments unopened. In my drawer. Twenty-five rand. That's no good. I must finish it. I've got all the time until school starts. And this year . . . I'm really going to teach. You watch.

And stop hurting you. I don't do it on purpose. I don't want to hurt you. I love you. But hell, it's just so useless, at times I can't help it. And then that makes me feel even worse Some of those walks back have been hard. Specially when I wanted to turn round and come back and say I'm sorry . . . but you know you can't.

[*Pause.*]

Hey. You know what I was thinking coming here? I must try and buy a car this year. Good second-hand car.

[*A sudden noise startles them. They scramble apart, the woman grabbing the blanket and covering herself.*]

Ssssh!! [*Pause.*] Sure you locked it?

WOMAN [*nodding*]. Back door?

MAN. Yes. [*Tense, motionless pause as they listen in silence for a few seconds longer. The man moves to his clothes on the floor.*] Hot tonight, hey.

WOMAN. Do you want the towel?

MAN. *Ja*, okay. I'm sweating. [*The woman finds a towel, takes it to him.*] There's no water left in Bontrug.

WOMAN. We're going to have prayers for rain next week. Wednesday.

MAN. The location dam is empty. Little mud left for the goats. They're going to start bringing in for us on Monday. Got to be ready with our buckets at twelve. Two for each house.

WOMAN. Then why won't you let me send you some of mine? The borehole is still very strong. Please! It would be so easy.

MAN. Thanks, but I'll go along with Bontrug.

WOMAN. Don't thank me for something you won't take.

MAN. For the thought, then.

WOMAN. To hell with the thought! I'm not trying to be kind. It's only water, and you need it.

MAN. We all do.

WOMAN. Exactly! So your family must suffer because of your pride.

MAN [*disbelief*]. Pride?

WOMAN. It sounds like it.

MAN. Pride doesn't use back doors!

WOMAN. Sssh, please!

MAN. Or wait until it's dark. You don't walk the way I do between the location and town with pride.

WOMAN. Please don't let's argue tonight.

MAN. Okay. [*Defeated by her apparent lack of understanding, he turns away from her to his clothes. For a few seconds he tries to sort them out, then stops. He confronts her again.*] Water. Water, man. You know . . . water! I wanted to wash before I came here tonight.

*Your* water. You want to send me some of *your* water. Is it so hard to understand? Because if you can't . . . ! Why do you think it's easy? Is that what I look like? Is that why they're so nice to me out there? Because I'm easy? But when for once I get so . . . I feel so buggered-up inside that I say 'No' instead of 'Yes' . . . I'm proud! Proud! I teach children how to spell that word. I say to them: 'Proud as a Peacock!' Me? Holding my breath and sweating, really sweating, man, because suddenly we heard something and I thought: 'They've found us! Run!' Coming here tonight I heard a car coming, from the location. . . . I hid under that little bridge over the *spruit* . . . people relieve themselves there! . . . I was on my hands and knees among the shit, waiting for that car to pass, so that Bontrug won't start asking, 'Why is the Meester walking into town every night?' [*Stopping her from moving away.*] No! Please listen. I must talk. When I take that same walk just now . . . back . . . out there in the dark where the tar and the light ends, where the stones start. I'm going to sit down and say to myself: 'Back home again!' . . . and hate it. *Ja.* Hate it! Bontrug. The *braks* that run out at me when I get there. My school. The children I teach. My home. The same world I looked at that night a year ago and said 'Mine!!' and was excited that I was there, in it! Easy to hate, man, when you suddenly find you're always walking back to it . . . and I am. Whatever happens I'm going to be there walking back to it. So I say to myself: 'Careful, Philander. It's yours. It's all you can ever really have. Love it. You've got to.' Sometimes that's easy too.

87

But you see, even when I do . . . there's still you. I'm in the shit, hey. That's how I walk now between Bontrug and the town . . . one way guilty, back with . . .

[*Pause.*] I'll tell you something else. Coming here once . . . in the 'old' days . . . I passed a man and a woman and their child . . . little boy . . . going back to the location. They got names, but it doesn't matter. You don't know them. They had stopped half-way up the hill to rest. It's hard walking up there with the sun on your back. All three of them . . . hot and unwashed. They smell. Because I was coming to you, you know what I saw? Rags. I don't mean their clothes. The people inside looked like rags. The man drinks too much, he's a useless rag. The woman's an old rag. Their child is going to be somebody's good rag, until . . . What do you do with yours? I was looking at my feet when I walked past them. Frieda! . . . [*shaking his head*] . . . when I realized that . . . when I realized what I . . . I wanted to call them and bring them with me to the library. I wanted to knock on that back door and stand there with them when you opened it. I wanted you to see me with them! What would you have done? Asked them in? Called them Meester and Miesies? Would you have given them tea in your cups? How long before you would have started waiting for them to go? You understand now. The reason I don't want your water is just because Bontrug is thirsty.

WOMAN. And that is not pride.

MAN. No. Exactly the opposite. Shame.

WOMAN. I don't understand . . . anything.

MAN. Then you can't. Don't even try. [*He turns away from her, back to his clothes and puts on his vest.*]

WOMAN. It really would be better if you could wait until it's darker. [*He stops. Pause.*] Old Mrs. Buys is still staring and being strange. She changed her books again today. I might be wrong but . . . She's taken out more books this month than she did the whole of last year.

MAN. And you think I'm proud.

WOMAN. You should be . . . of some things. [*Pause.*] I didn't think you were going to come.

MAN. I couldn't help myself.

WOMAN. Didn't you want to?

MAN. No, I wanted to. But I thought maybe you'd had enough of me for a while. . . .

WOMAN. That's not true.

MAN. I haven't been cheerful company lately.

[*Pause.*]

WOMAN. What must I do? Please tell me.

MAN. Don't say that.

WOMAN. I've got to. What will make you happy?

MAN. Something that doesn't hurt anybody.

WOMAN. We do?

MAN. Yes.

WOMAN. Your family?

MAN. Not we. I do.

WOMAN. It's the holiday, isn't it?

MAN. That's one thing;

WOMAN. Listen. Stop worrying about it. Take your family. I promise I'll understand.

We won't talk about it again.

MAN. I don't want to go. I decided to settle it last night after supper. Be firm with them, I said to myself. Explain you need the time for the course. Before I could bring up the subject, they started talking. When must they start packing? How much they were looking forward to it! Selina hasn't seen her mother for three years. I couldn't even open my mouth. I'm so bloody sick of my lies.

WOMAN. How much do you think your wife . . . ?

MAN. I don't know. I can't tell. I can't see or do anything properly any more, except come here, and even that I do thinking it's a mistake. [*Pause.*] No, she knows nothing. How can she? She

89

doesn't have tea with your old Mrs. Buys. She thinks I'm tired! Been studying too hard. All I need is a good holiday. Jesus, they're so innocent.

WOMAN. Even if you could, you would never leave them.

MAN. I don't know.

WOMAN. No! Tell the truth, please.

Even if you could you would never leave them.

[*Pause.*]

MAN. No. I would never leave them. I'm not . . . strong enough to hurt them, for something I wanted.

What would happen to them if I did?

WOMAN. Go home. Take your conscience and your guilt and go back to Bontrug and look after your family. I've also got problems. I can't add your adultery to them. If you haven't got the courage to say No . . . to anybody . . . me or her . . . I'll do it for you. Go home.

MAN [*viciously*]. It would be better if I waited until it's dark . . . remember! [*Pause.*] My adultery? And yours? *Ja*. Yours! If that's true of me because of you and my wife, then just as much for you because of me and your white skin. Maybe you are married to that the way I am to Bontrug.

You sneak out of it the way I sneak out of my house to come here. Let me see you choose!!

WOMAN. I will. Take me with you. Now.

[*Silence.*]

MAN. You're right. I'm a coward.

WOMAN. Is there nothing we can do any more except hurt each other?

MAN. One day when I was a boy, my father came home after work to our hut on the farm; He brought with him a jackal's foot. The animal had escaped that way . . . chewed off the foot caught in the trap. For a long time I waited for the story of the dogs that had caught and killed a jackal with only three legs. You see, I could only think about how much it must have hurt to do that. I didn't know anything yet about being so frightened of something else, that you would do that to yourself. [*Pause.*] That's what we're doing . . . chewing away, chewing away. And if we're frightened enough . . . we'll escape . . . but . . . [*Pause.*] What's the time?

WOMAN. Too dark. I can't see the clock. Or you.

MAN. I'm here.

WOMAN. What are you doing?

MAN. Nothing.

And you?

WOMAN. Waiting. . . .

[*Pause.*]

MAN. For what?

WOMAN. I don't know. I suppose the dogs.

MAN. Frieda. [*Holding out a hand in the dark.*] Frieda!

[*A moment's hesitation and then they impulsively come together and embrace. Against this image of the two lovers,* a plain-clothes policeman, Detective Sergeant J. du Preez, *walks on. He carries a police dossier and notebook. His statement is dictated to the audience.*]

POLICEMAN. Frieda Joubert. Ten, Conradie Street. European.

Errol Philander. Bontrug Location. Coloured.

Charge: Immorality Act.*

Joubert runs the library in the town. Been living here for six years. Unmarried. No previous convictions.

Errol Philander is Principal of the location school. Born here. Wife and one child. No previous convictions.

My suspicions were first aroused by a report from Mrs. Tienie Buys.

[*Abandoning 'dictation' . . . he takes a statement out of the police dossier and reads it aloud.*]

Statement to Detective Sergeant J. du Preez at the Noupoort* Police Station on December the seventeenth: 'My attention was first drawn to the behaviour of Joubert and Philander on a night in June last year. Late that afternoon I was down at the bottom of my garden when I saw Philander arrive at the back door of the library and without knocking, go in. A few moments later, the light in the back room of the library was put on. Some time later, Joubert herself came out and emptied some rubbish in the dirt bin. At about eight o'clock that night I was down at the bottom of my garden again and I noticed that the light was still on. I'd no sooner noticed this when it was switched off. No other lights were on in the library. I waited to see what would happen next. After some time—about forty-five minutes of darkness—the back door opened and Philander came out.

He closed the door behind him, locked it with a key which he put in his trouser pocket, and walked away. This pattern of events—Philander's arrival followed by a period of darkness until he left—was repeated on many occasions between that night and today . . . December the seventeenth. I also noticed that his movements became more and more secretive over the six months. I am prepared to repeat this statement under oath in Court.

Signed: Mrs. Tienie Buys, 2 Riebeeck Street, Noupoort.'

[*Replaces the statement in the dossier. He continues his 'dictation' to the audience.*]

Mrs. Buys's back garden is immediately behind the library. On her side there is a row of quince trees. The back entrance to the library—which leads directly into the room Joubert uses as an office, and in which the two of them were arrested tonight—can be clearly seen from under these trees. I asked Mrs. Buys to contact me the next time Philander arrived at the library. She did this the very next afternoon, the twenty-ninth. I watched the library back entrance from under the trees at the bottom of Mrs. Buys's garden. After at least an hour of darkness, Philander came out of the back door, locked it behind him, put the key in his pocket, and walked away. I went round quickly to the corner of Church and Conradie Streets. I was just in time to see Joubert leaving by the front door. I decided that these events warranted a thorough investigation of the whole matter. The library was kept under observation. Philander visited it every day. On a further three occasions the pattern of events was suspicious. After discussion with Warrant Officer Pieterse it was decided that Joubert and Philander should be apprehended at the next opportunity. It was also decided that a camera should be used to obtain photographic evidence of the suspected offence. On the twelfth of January, Constable Harvey, who had been keeping a watch on the library, reported in the late afternoon that Philander had arrived and was in the building with Joubert. Together with Harvey and Sergeant Smit, we went to Mrs. Buys's back garden. We waited from six o'clock to eight o'clock. Constable Harvey reported that nobody had left through the front door. We climbed over the fence, and in the dark made our way to the back door. Even though it and the window was closed, we could clearly hear voices whispering inside. On a sign from me the window was forced open, and a torch shone into the room. I saw Joubert and Philander lying side by side on a blanket on the floor. She was naked and he appeared to be wearing a vest. Sergeant Smit started to take photographs.

[*A blackout, during which the policeman exits. A sequence of camera flashes in the darkness exposes the man and the woman tearing apart from their embrace; the man then scrambling for his trousers, finding them, and tying to put them on; the woman, naked, crawling around on the floor, looking for the man. As she finds him, and tries to hide behind his back, the flashes stop and torches are shone on them. The woman scrambles away, finds the blanket, and covers herself. The torches are relentless, but we never see anything of the men behind them. These 'flash-sequences' are nightmare excursions into the split second of exposure and must be approached as 'sub-text' rather than 'reality'.*]

MAN [*terrified. Covering his genitals with his trousers he talks desperately to the torch shining on him.*] Look . . . look—before you make up your mind let me tell you something. . . . I'm . . . I'm Principal. . . . I . . . I won't do it again. . . . I'm frightened. *Ja*, I'm frightened.

[*Blinking back at the torch with terror he tries to get into his trousers without exposing himself. He can't manage it. The operation becomes a nightmare. For a few seconds the woman watches him with vacant horror.*

*Then she scrambles forward and, using her blanket, tries to shield him while she talks compulsively to the torches. Her first words are an almost incoherent babble. As she moves around, the torches follow her. Finding himself in darkness, the man gets slowly to his feet, retrieves his hat, and then tries—carefully and quietly—to get away.*]

WOMAN. Tennis biscuits! Only one. In the afternoons I have my tea at four. I like to make it myself. The tea things are kept in my office, nice and neat on a tray under a clean drying-up cloth. I can see the library clock from my desk. I was [*Pause.*] I was waiting for him. I was always waiting for him. I tried as long as I could to think he might still come. Then at half-past five I thought to myself . . . No, he's not going to . . . and suddenly . . . nothing. There was . . . nothing. Just lock up and go home, have supper, go to bed, try to sleep so that tomorrow and its chance of seeing him would come.

I locked the library door—I was hating myself for having waited—walked back into the office, and there he was. He looked tired, hot, his shoes were dusty. We talked a bit. But I didn't really listen to him because . . . he wasn't really talking to me. I could see something was wrong, that he was still unhappy, so I went to the desk—I was carrying a pile of books. . . . The new books have come! . . .

I was trying to work out what I could expect. I knew he was going to hurt me . . . I mean, not on purpose, but it just seems we can't avoid it. So I waited for it. It came. He said he supposed he shouldn't have come.

[*Pause.*]

I didn't want to stay there then, in the office I mean, so I took the books I had sorted out and went into the library. But I didn't want to be there either! I had to go back because I couldn't leave it like that. When I did he said he was sorry and that he hadn't meant it. I was at the desk again stamping books and just wishing he would stop saying and doing all the things that always made him feel so sorry! It was getting dark and I had that hopeless feeling inside. He tried to explain, again. Said it was because of the way he was neglecting things—me, his

94

family, his correspondence course, his school—all the things that really mattered in his life because they all still did, only he felt he'd become so useless at looking after them. I told him . . . I said, he wasn't neglecting me and that even if he did I would understand so he shouldn't worry about it, but he said he did, because he loved us all—me, his family, his school. . . . [*Pause.*] I was feeling terribly lonely again. We seemed so far away from each other and I didn't know why, or what to do. It was dark. I couldn't see properly where to stamp the books any more. I should have put on the light. But I just went on stamping and wishing it would get still darker so that everything would disappear—him, me, the room, what I was feeling—just disappear. . . . [*Frightened of what she has just said; very loudly . . .*] No. No!

[*One of the torches leaves her abruptly and picks up the man still trying to get away. He drops his trousers with fright and shields his genitals with his hat. He listens carefully to what the woman is saying.*]

He stopped talking suddenly, and stood up. I had given him a fright. He asked me what was wrong. I just said . . . 'Nothing.' We were whispering. Whispering makes you sweat. He loosened his tie and said . . .

[*The man realizes he must stop, and correct, this vein of intimate confession. With a sign to the torch he puts his hat on, then steps forward and faces her, and then takes his hat off in the correct and respectful manner.*]

MAN. Miss Frieda Joubert?

[*The woman stops talking, turns, and looks at him. She can't believe what she sees. She laughs with bewildered innocence. The man accepts her amusement. He handles his hat with a suggestion of nervousness as he starts to talk, respectfully.*]

There's no water left in Bontrug. The dam's empty. Little mud left for the goats. They're going to start bringing in for us on Monday. We've been told to be ready with our buckets at twelve. Two for each house.

[*The woman has watched his performance with growing bewilderment. At the end of it she tries to cope with the situation with another laugh. Pause. The man, under pressure, tries again, now more desperately.*]

Miss Frieda Joubert! There's no water left. . . .

WOMAN. I know.

MAN. There's no water left in Bontrug. Dam's empty.

WOMAN. I know! You told me.

MAN. Little mud left for the goats. They're going to start bringing in for us on Monday. We've got to be ready with our buckets at twelve. Two for each . . .

WOMAN. You've already told me!! Don't you remember . . . ?

[*Her desperation now growing. A move to him. He backs away from it. He is hanging on.*]

MAN. Miss Frieda Joubert. There's no water left in . . .

WOMAN. Why are you . . . ?

MAN. There's no water left in Bontrug!

WOMAN. What are you doing?

[*Her bewilderment now edged by anxiety. Equivalently, his performance degenerates more and more.*]

MAN. Please listen, Miss Frieda! There's no water left in Bontrug, man. Dam's empty. Little mud left. For the goats. They're going to start bringing in for us. . . .

WOMAN [*her desperation mounting*]. You've already said that!

MAN. Miss Frieda . . . they going to start bring for us. . . .

WOMAN [*hanging on to herself*]. And I said . . . I said I'd send you some of mine and you . . .

MAN. I got to be ready with my buckets at twelve.

WOMAN. You got angry!

MAN. Two buckets, lady. Got to be ready with my buckets at twelve. 'Cause they sending to us . . . me and my buckets . . . two for each . . .

[*The woman now starts to lose control. The man's 'performance' has now degenerated into a grotesque parody of the servile, cringing 'Coloured'.*]

WOMAN. Sit down!

MAN. Bontrug's dry. Little mud in the dam.

WOMAN. Come!

MAN. Water, Miesies. Please, Miesies . . . water. . . .

WOMAN. The way you . . .

MAN. Just a little. . . . We're thirsty . . . please, Miesies. . . .

[*The woman, now almost hysterical, looks around wildly for an affirmative action.*]

WOMAN. Sit down . . . here . . . and read. . . .

MAN. Water, Miesies, water, Miesies.

WOMAN. No, no . . . stop it . . . [*knocking the hat out of his hand.*] STOP IT!

MAN. I'll . . . I'll just go. I'll use the back door.

[*Camera flashes and finally torches as in the previous sequence. This time, however, the torches trap the man against a wall and the woman on the floor looking down at the man's jumbled pile of clothing. To start with, she is completely unaware of the torch shining on her.*]

WOMAN. I don't understand. . . . You can't. Don't even try. [*Carefully examines one of his shoes.*] Dust on his shoes. Him. His feet. His thoughts. A man . . . walking, from Bontrug to here, the town, to me . . . and then back again. [*Pause.*] One night I watched him through the window, walk away, quietly, quickly, and disappear down the street. I tried to imagine. . . . [*Pause.*] I can't. [*Very carefully replaces the shoe as she found it. His clothes. She is trying hard to understand.*] There is no water in Bontrug! . . . I'm not thirsty. . . . I don't understand. . . . He uses the back door. He can't come to me any other way. When I heard the knock and opened it, the first time, wondering who it was . . . and saw him. . . . No! I didn't. I saw a Coloured man. . . . I was not surprised. Because it was the back door.

MAN. I needed a book. I knew I couldn't be a subscriber. But it was my third assignment. . . .

WOMAN. . . . Julian Huxley's . . . *Principles of Evolution* . . .

MAN. . . . and I didn't have any of the books on their list. It had happened with the first two as well.

[*Both talk to the torches, and each other, in a frank and eager manner.*]

WOMAN. He was very serious about it. Explained what he was doing.

MAN. You were interested, hey.

WOMAN. Oh yes! Very. I could see it was important to him. I didn't have any of the books he mentioned . . . but I knew what he wanted and I found something else that I thought would help him. I said if there was anything I could do to help he must just tell me.

MAN. I could see she really meant it. So I didn't worry too much about going back again.

WOMAN. He always used my office. It started to seem so silly. Nobody was reading the books he needed. Only a few people ever went to that side of the library.

MAN. It made a big difference . . . being able to go there and use the encyclopedias, and read.

WOMAN. I found myself seeing books and articles in newspapers which I thought would help him. He's a very fast reader . . . and shy . . . at first . . . but once we started talking it was almost hard to keep up with him. And exciting. For me too. Even going home after I'd closed the library, began to be different. I had something to do, and think about at night. You see, the library is not very busy . . . there's not all that much to look after.

MAN. We talked about lots of things, didn't we?

WOMAN. Oh yes! Not just the course. That's how we came to know each other. [*Pause as they both wait innocently and eagerly for a response to what they have said. Nothing. The silence slowly becomes a threat.*] Say something. [*Mounting hysteria.*] SAY SOMETHING! . . . Yes, we have made love. I switched off the light. Yes. Yes. Guilty. No doubt about it. Guilty of taking my chance and finding him. Hands, eyes, ears, nose, tongue . . . totally guilty. Nothing is innocent.

MAN. *Ja*, she put off the light. I mean . . . suppose I had made a mistake. Hey? And she wasn't feeling the way I did. Or even thinking about it. You know what I'm saying? I couldn't move. Just sat there looking at what I was thinking, and I couldn't

98

move. It wasn't the first time I realized what was happening to us. We knew all right what we were doing. But that night I knew, it can happen now! If I was right about her, and did the right thing, it was going to happen. But suppose I was wrong? Suppose she screamed?

[*Camera flashes and finally torches as in the previous sequences. This time the torches trap the woman alone, naked. Once again she is unaware of the light shining on her. She studies herself quietly, privately.*]

WOMAN. Ugly feet. The soles have got hard patches. My legs are bandy. Good calf muscles . . . probably got them riding to school on my bicycle up a very steep hill each day. Skin around my knees is just starting to get a little slack. I enjoy making the muscles in my thighs move. Hair is very mousy . . . very sparse. . . . I think the area around my waist is quite nice.* Few soft and feminine contours around my hips. My breasts are slacker than I would like them to be. My neck is unattractive. My face is quite interesting but can be very plain sometimes. Lines around my mouth are starting to worry me. Hair causes me concern. I think it's going off. Ashamed of my hands. Nail-polish has come off in patches. Skin looks very old.

I think there is a lot of me in my hands somehow.

My favourite colour is blue. . . .

My favourite flower is . . .

You say you have no previous experience of men. That you were a virgin, and yet you took the initiative. What would you have done if Philander had rejected you?*

Hated him.

Would the fact that a Coloured man had rejected you have humiliated you more than if a white man had done so?

By the time it happened his colour did not mean anything to me any more.

Did you encourage Philander?

Yes.

Why?

I wanted him.

Would you say that you encouraged him against his will?

No. I think that he felt almost as strongly about me as I did about him.

Did it ever occur to you that he might have accepted a physical relationship with you out of respect for your feelings?

Yes. It did occur to me sometimes.

You are older than Philander?

Yes.

By how many years?

Six.

Do you think it possible that Philander thought you provided him with an easy opportunity to have intercourse with a white woman? Because as a Coloured man the law forbids it.

No.

What makes you so sure?

He was a man who had too strong a feeling of responsibility towards his family to take that chance for that reason.

Did you feel any responsibilities towards his family?

I did think about them for a time.

After you put out the light did he then initiate the physical encounter?

No.

What did you do? Describe what happened until you are told to stop.

I . . . I put off the light. . . .

Well. . . .

Yes . . . *ja* . . . I stood there. . . . I knew why I had put off the light. . . . But once I had put it off . . . I was . . . hesitant . . . I was nervous . . . I wasn't sure what to do next. . . . Well . . . he . . . he didn't move or do or say anything. . . . I knew it was so hard for him that if I didn't do something . . . nothing would happen . . . so I . . .

[*Pause.*]

I knew where he was. . . . So I took a few . . . paces . . . towards him. . . . My hand came in contact with his . . . coat or jacket. . . . There was another moment of hesitation. . . . I had found him. And then . . .

[*Pause.*]

I moved in close to him. I knew that the response coming from him was the same. I wouldn't have had the courage if I didn't know that he felt . . . that he . . . So I leant against him . . . his shoulder. . . .

[*Pause.*]

He put his arms around me. . . . It felt like he . . . there was . . . his lips . . . yes. Then his lips touched the top of my head . . . it's very hard to remember anything.

[*Pause.*]

I know that we finally did kiss each other. Please, do I have to . . . please, it's very hard for me.

[*Pause.*]

So . . . so then . . . yes. . . . So then we made love. . . . I don't know how . . . but we were on the floor . . . the floor of the library. . . . And he . . . And me . . . We . . .

[*Another sequence of flashes during which the woman scrambles around looking for the man and finally finds him—standing against a wall, protecting his genitals with his hands. This time the sequence does not end with torches, but harsh, directionless, white light. The image is suggestive of one of the photographs handed in to the Court as evidence, and it is with this as a background that the policeman finally completes his statement.*]

MAN. There was nothing left to say. I had thought there would be. That if it ever happened, and we had known it could, that there would be something left to say, to her, to myself. Something to say to them. But when the light went on, it burnt out all the words I had left. Nothing to say. Nothing to do.

[*The policeman, still carrying his dossier and notebook, enters and completes his statement.*]

POLICEMAN. Exhibit A. We gained entry to the room by forcing the door, and put on the light. By this time Joubert had covered herself with a blanket. Exhibit B. I immediately arrested them, and asked them whether they wished to make a statement, warning them, at the same time, that anything they said would be taken down in writing and could be used in evidence against them. Full stop. Joubert's response to this was: quote 'I'm not ashamed of myself' unquote. I asked her if she was prepared to repeat the statement in front of a magistrate. She said quote 'Anyone' unquote. She then turned to Philander and said quote 'I'm sorry' unquote. Philander said nothing. On being searched, a key was found in Philander's trouser pocket. I asked him to identify it, and he said it was a key to the back door of the library. When I asked him where he had got it, he did not reply. Joubert then interrupted and said quote 'I gave it to him' unquote. The key is attached to the statement as exhibit C. I finally asked them to get dressed and to accompany me to the police station, where they were formally charged.

Signed: Detective Sergeant J. du Preez . . . South African Police. Noupoort.

[*Exit. A short pause and then the man leaves the pool of light in which he and the woman have been standing. The woman is totally isolated in her last speech, as will also be the case with the man.*]

WOMAN. I am here. You are not here. I know that without even trying to find you, as I did once, because nothing can be here except me. That doesn't mean I don't want you. But you are gone from other places. The pain will come. I'm holding it far away. But just now I will have to let it go and it will come. It will not take any time to find me. Because it's mine. That pain is going to be me. I don't want to see myself. But I know that will also happen. I must be my hands again, my eyes, my ears . . . all of me but now, without you. All of me that found you must now lose you. My hands still have the sweat of your body on them, but I'll have to wash them . . . sometime. If I don't, they will. Nothing can stop me losing that little bit of you. In every corner of being myself there is a little of you left and now I must start to lose it. I must be very still, because if I do anything, except think nothing, it will all start to happen, I won't be able to stop it.

MAN.   Frieda! [*He discovers himself alone . . . with his clothes.*]

Now I must understand it.
If they take away your eyes you can't see.
If they take away your tongue you can't taste.
If they take away your hands you can't feel.
If they take away your nose you can't smell.
If they take away your ears you can't hear.
I can see.
I can taste.
I can feel.
I can smell.
I can hear.

   [*Pause.*]

I can't love.
I must understand it.
If they take away your legs you can't walk.
If they take away your arms you can't work.
If they take away your head you can't think.
I can walk.
I can work.
I can think.

   [*Pause.*]

I can't love.
I must understand it.
When you are hungry you eat.
When you are thirsty you drink.
When you are tired you sleep.
I will eat.
I will drink.
I will sleep.

   [*Pause.*]

I won't love.

I must understand it again.

If they take away your soul, you can't go to Heaven.

I can go to Heaven.

[*Pause.*]

I can't love.

And then I'm running away very fast, from everything but especially God, because he mustn't know. But the street doesn't work any more. Because when I reach the end where the stones and the darkness should start, the light goes on, and I come out of the back door of the library and I've got to start running again. But I can't run very fast. My hands get in the way because I don't want them to see. So I'm crawling instead and she is not surprised. Nobody is surprised. They still greet me.

But I know you see.

An arm without a hand.

A leg without a foot.

A head without a body.

A man without his name.

And I'm terribly frightened they will find out. That the dogs will tell them. Because they can see. And then I'm sitting just past the lamp-post where my shadow always turn into the night and she asks me, 'What do you want?'

I don't know.

Yes, you do.

Everything.

You can't have it. Choose.

I can't.

You're a coward.

I know.

You realize it's useless.

Yes.

What will you do if they find out about us?

I don't know. So she tells me.

Nothing. You do nothing. They do it all.

Trust them. They know what to do.

They find you.

They put on the light.

They take the picture.

They take your name.

And then they take you.

And then they take your belt and your tie and your shoelaces.

They lock the door.

They will ask the questions.

They will try you.

And then at the end as at the beginning, they will find you again.

Guilty.

That frightens me. I get up and I start running. And I can't understand why she doesn't call me back, because I'm only running home.

And then I'm in Bontrug. And the dogs don't bark at me, they laugh. They're all standing up and walking around on their back legs to show me theirs.

And then I reach my house. But I don't find anyone there, only God, waiting in the dark. And now I'm too tired to run away any more. I just think he must have driven there by car because otherwise how could he have got there before me. He lives in the town.

And it's a court case. That on the night of January the twelfth 1966, I . . . who had been made in his image . . . did lose a part of me. They did it I say. They dug a hole and buried it. Ask the dogs. And then Frieda comes in to give evidence. It's very dark. God shines a torch to see what she looks like. Did he have it, he asks her. Yes, she says. Then he asks me: 'Why did you let them do it?'

So I tell God I don't smoke and I don't drink and I know the price of bread. But he says it makes no difference and that he wants back what is left. And then I start to give him the other parts. I give him my feet and my legs, I give him my head and body, I give him my arms, until at last there is nothing left, just my hands, and they are empty. But he takes them back too. And then there is only the emptiness left. But he doesn't want that. Because it's me. It's all that is left of me.

STATEMENTS AFTER AN ARREST

They arrest it all the same.
Now I'm here.
There is nothing here.
They can't interfere with God any more.

**THE END**

# DIMETOS

# FOR LISA

. . . May God us keep
From Single vision & Newton's sleep!
(William Blake)*

# CHARACTERS

DIMETOS, *an engineer*
LYDIA, *his orphaned niece*
SOPHIA, *his housekeeper*
DANILO, *a young man from the city*

DIMETOS was commissioned by the Edinburgh Festival and was given its first performance at the Church Hill Theatre in Edinburgh on 27 August 1975 with the following cast directed by Athol Fugard:

| | |
|---|---|
| DIMETOS | Carel Trichardt |
| LYDIA | Vanessa Cooke |
| SOPHIA | Yvonne Bryceland |
| DANILO | Wilson Dunster |

In 1976 it was produced in a modified version (printed here) in Nottingham (Playhouse, 26 April) and London (Comedy Theatre, 24 May) with the following cast, again directed by the author:

| | |
|---|---|
| DIMETOS | Paul Scofield |
| LYDIA | Celia Quicke |
| SOPHIA | Yvonne Bryceland |
| DANILO | Ben Kingsley |

DIMETOS was revived for its first local production at The People's Space Theatre, Cape Town, on 23 December 1981, directed by Dieter Reible, with the following cast:

| | |
|---|---|
| DIMETOS | Marius Weyers |
| LYDIA | Mitzi Booysen |
| SOPHIA | Trix Pienaar |
| DANILO | Blaise Koch |

Act One—*In a remote Province**
Act Two—*Beside the Ocean**

# ACT ONE

## Scene 1

Lydia *is lowered to the bottom of a well to tie ropes around a horse that has fallen down.*

LYDIA [*calling up*].  I'm on his back, Dimetos! What must I do?

DIMETOS'S VOICE.  How is he?

LYDIA.  Frightened.

VOICE.  Keep calm. Make sure you are comfortable.

LYDIA.  I am.

VOICE.  The two slings . . . can you hear me clearly?

LYDIA.  Yes.

VOICE.  The first one, as I explained up here, behind his front legs
  . . . knotted above the withers . . .

  [*She follows the instructions. Lying prostrate on the horse's back she
  slowly positions the first sling. It is very dark; she works by touch, making
  comforting noises all the time.*]

Take your time. Shout when you are ready.

LYDIA.  Ready.

VOICE.  The second one . . . in front of his hindquarters, around
  his flanks . . . take your time. [*She positions the second sling.*]

LYDIA.  Ready.

VOICE.  Now the ropes around you . . . untie one but don't let it go
  . . . only one. Give a hard pull when it's free.

  [*Straddling the horse she unties one of the ropes around her waist and gives
  it a hard pull.*]

Right . . . now listen carefully . . . you have got to tie the knot I
showed you. I can't see your hands clearly enough to stop you if
you make a mistake . . . so listen carefully. Thread a good length
through the two rings.

LYDIA.  Ready.

VOICE.  Take the loose end . . . loop it twice around the other . . .
  now take it under itself . . . loop it around the other end

again . . . and again under itself. Now tighten it. Does it slip?

LYDIA. No.

VOICE. The second sling . . . untie the second rope . . . the same knot . . . listen carefully again . . . the loose end through the two rings . . . [*She repeats the knot.*] Do you want to rest?

LYDIA. No.

VOICE. I am going to slacken the rope you've just tied. Make a loop the way I showed you and put your foot into it.

LYDIA. Ready.

VOICE. Hold on tight. We are going to pull you up.

## Scene 2

*Beside a pool. Evening.* Dimetos, *unknotting and coiling a length of rope, and* Lydia.

LYDIA. I did it! He's free!

DIMETOS. Come out now, Lydia. Sophia will start worrying if we are not home soon.

[*Lydia, clean and wet after a swim, dries herself with her dress and then throws it impulsively into the air.*]

LYDIA. I'm too happy to be shy. And I can't stop laughing! I can still see him standing there, his legs shivering while you untied the ropes, and then galloping away . . . No! He walked first, didn't he? A few steps. And then . . . [*She starts laughing again, as she relives the horse's moment of liberation.*] He looked so splendid. Why did we have to leave? I could have stayed there and watched him until it was dark.

DIMETOS. It will certainly be that by the time we get home. Sophia wouldn't have been too pleased if we'd arrived back with you covered from head to foot in mud. Did you get it all out of your hair?

LYDIA. I'll wash it properly when we get home. I think he was also laughing. And the way he kept shaking his head, as if he couldn't believe it was true. Everybody was laughing! Except you. If I didn't know you I would have thought you weren't glad that we had got him out.

DIMETOS. Was it as bad as that?

LYDIA. Yes. But you were, weren't you?

DIMETOS. Of course.

LYDIA. Then why do you do that?

DIMETOS. What?

LYDIA. Hide your feelings.

DIMETOS. There wasn't that much to hide. All I saw galloping away was an obviously stupid animal that we had hauled out of a deep hole. I'm not even sure that he will have learnt a lesson. You must make allowances, little one. I've seen more accidents than you. Not all of them had happy endings.

LYDIA. All the more reason for laughing when one does. How do you think it happened?

DIMETOS. At a critical moment he found nothing under hoof and became a helpless victim of that force which attracts masses to each other. He fell in.

LYDIA. Stop joking.

DIMETOS. I'm not. It's a fact . . . mysterious! . . . but still a fact. 'Every particle of matter in the Universe attracts every other particle with a force whose direction is that of the line joining the two . . .' It's called Gravity. The potential in all bodies to move or be moved.

LYDIA. I don't want any of your old facts now!

DIMETOS. They're not mine, and they're not old. And what's more you should. They are all that really matter. They'll help you understand a lot more than falling horses, little one. That law holds the universe together. But I think I know what you do want. 'Once upon a time there was a horse. He was a very happy horse until the day he noticed that the grass in his field was not as green . . .'

LYDIA. Don't tease me! I was just wondering how it happened.

DIMETOS. We'll never know. But even if we did, it wouldn't have helped us get him out. All I needed was a reasonably accurate estimate of his weight and the breaking strength of these ropes. I'm an engineer, Lydia, not a story teller. An artisan, not an artist.

LYDIA. Well he has got a story even if you don't care what it is, and you did give it a happy ending.

DIMETOS. That happy ending was made by a system of pulleys with a mechanical advantage of five to one. Anybody who knew how to use them could have done what I did.

LYDIA. But it was *you*. You also don't want people to be grateful to you.

DIMETOS. I don't think that's true.

LYDIA. Oh, yes! When they started to thank you for what you had done, you just turned your back and walked away.

DIMETOS. Their stupidity annoyed me. In any case it was you they should have thanked. Were you frightened?

LYDIA. Yes.

DIMETOS. I wouldn't have let you go down if I wasn't sure I could get you up.

LYDIA. I know that! I meant helping him. It's the first time I've tried to help something that was in real trouble. I was frightened I'd make a mistake.

[*Sitting with her chin on her knees, wide-eyed and clutching her dress. Dimetos takes up an end of the dress and dries her back while she talks.*]

I didn't have time to think about it until you started to lower me. We had been so busy digging, putting up the poles and everything. When I had to take off my dress I just felt shy with all the men staring. I was anxious to go down, to get away from them. But when I stepped off the edge and started to swing . . . and that one rope got stuck! I thought I'd never reach the bottom. I smelt him first, you know. That's when I opened my eyes. It was so terrible finding him down there in the dark . . . feeling him . . . living and warm and frightened. I don't ever want to be as frightened as that. I didn't care about anything then, except him, and listening carefully when you started calling down to me.

DIMETOS. You called first.

LYDIA. Did I?

DIMETOS. Yes. 'I'm on his back, Dimetos! What must I do?'

LYDIA [*laughing with embarrassment*]. Uncle.

DIMETOS. No! I liked it. You've earned the right to call me Dimetos now. It was the voice, the demand of a colleague, and equal. Dimetos and Lydia. Come. We must go.

LYDIA [*singing as she puts on her dress*].

> 'Over fences and ditches he jumped like a stag,
> His silken tail streaming behind like a flag . . .'

[*Dimetos leaves.*]

Hey! Wait for me!

# Scene 3

*Dimetos's house. A large table with tools.* Sophia *and* Danilo.

SOPHIA. He and his niece have gone to help a farmer. A horse has fallen down a well. I don't know when they'll be back.

DANILO. You don't mind if I wait, though?

SOPHIA. Of course not.

[*She starts working. Danilo goes to the table.*]

DANILO. This is where he works.

SOPHIA. Yes.

[*Danilo picks up a tool and examines it. He smiles to himself. Sophia looks at him enquiringly.*]

DANILO. On my way here I couldn't help wondering what I would find. None of my guesses were right.

SOPHIA. I'm not sure I understand.

DANILO. I tried to picture this village, his life here.

SOPHIA. I see. We've surprised you, have we?

DANILO. Yes. I didn't expect it to be so isolated, so remote. I'm not

just thinking about the day's travelling it took me to get here.
That mountain pass puts more than a few miles between you
and the rest of the world. Horses at the bottom of wells! Tools
that could go into a museum . . . and Dimetos using them!
There's a sense of having travelled back in time. I felt it very
strongly when I stopped at a farmhouse to ask the way. The old
man treated me with a formal suspicion that made me very
conscious of being a stranger.

SOPHIA. They are like that. It took a long time before they
accepted us. But once they do they are quite hospitable. You are
from the city?

DANILO. Yes.

SOPHIA. It does seem very far away . . . and a long time ago.

DANILO. Nearly five years now.

[*Pause. Sophia smiles.*]

SOPHIA. That's right. Five years. Said like that it doesn't sound
long, does it?

DANILO. Do you miss it?

SOPHIA. The city? No. Life is much slower and simpler here, but
once you get used to it, the days are as full as they were
anywhere.

DANILO. And Dimetos?

SOPHIA. Miss the city? I don't think so. It would be simple enough
to return if he did.

DANILO. He's kept busy then, is he?

SOPHIA. I wouldn't say that either. It's not every day that we have
a horse at the bottom of a well.

DANILO. Don't the people around here know who he is?

SOPHIA. Yes.

DANILO. They're fools not to use him.

SOPHIA. City reputations don't count for much in these parts. But
when the need arises they come to him for help, as you can see.

DANILO. Dimetos not busy! Another surprise.

SOPHIA. You knew him well?

DANILO. No. We met once a long time ago. He won't even remember. But I'd heard about him like everyone else, and from what I'd heard I wouldn't have believed he could be happy if he wasn't working.

SOPHIA. I didn't say he was happy . . . [*She smiles easily at Danilo.*] I'm not saying he's unhappy. Our life here is also without extremes. The climate has enough of those.

DANILO. Is it always as dry as this?

SOPHIA. This summer has been particularly bad. They've already started praying for rain.

DANILO. They might do better asking Dimetos to build them a dam.

SOPHIA. Don't let them hear you say that. They take their religion very seriously. If there is one respect in which they haven't accepted the three of us, it is our seeming negligence in that direction.

DANILO. Dimetos, Lydia . . . and you of course are Sophia.

SOPHIA. His housekeeper.

DANILO. You've been with him a long time, haven't you?

SOPHIA. I started working for his mother when I was seventeen. He was ten. But I'm sure you knew that as well.

DANILO. Yes, I did. I tried to find out as much as I could before I came here.

SOPHIA [*stops working*]. What do you want?

DANILO. That's obvious surely.

SOPHIA. Dimetos.

DANILO. We need him. It's as simple and selfish as that. We've woken up to realize what should have been obvious years ago: that unless a few things are done very quickly our 'bustling little metropolis' is going to be in very serious trouble. My particular responsibility is one he knows all about—water, thirsty people . . .

SOPHIA. Is there a shortage of engineers?

DANILO. His sort, yes. There are plenty of others who know as

much, a few who are even as experienced. Dimetos is remembered and talked about by men because he had something else
as well . . . a quality we're running dangerously short of. Vision.
That's why I'm here. What chance do I have persuading him to
return? He can dictate his own terms.

SOPHIA [*reflectively*]. I don't know. [*Danilo is watching her.*] I don't. All
I can suggest is that you try, and find out.

DANILO. You are pessimistic about my chances.

SOPHIA. I don't know enough to be pessimistic or optimistic. He's
a very private man. He never talks about going back.

DANILO. But he can't mean to spend the rest of his life here.

SOPHIA. Why not?

DANILO. It doesn't make sense. No more than his departure did.

SOPHIA [*speaking easily enough, but with a sensed undercurrent*]. What is
so strange in a man retiring to the peace and quiet?

DANILO. Retire? It wasn't an old man that suddenly packed up
and left us. I don't doubt that it's peaceful and quiet here but for
a man like him that's as pointless as a grave.

SOPHIA. Choose your words carefully in talking to him.

DANILO. Forgive me. My bad manners and impatience are a
measure of how much we need him.

SOPHIA. There are men here as well. He's helping one at this
moment.

DANILO. I admitted to being selfish. Cities have no morality
except their own survival. [*He tries again.*] I know it will be pointless asking him to come back if he doesn't want to. But I'm
hoping he does. That our selfish need will coincide with what he
wants.

SOPHIA. You'll know the answer to that soon enough. They
shouldn't be long now. Will you excuse me? [*Exit.*]

DANILO [*alone*]. Prayers for rain. 'On your knees, sinners. You've
done it again.' Nothing as good as a little human misery to
highlight the mysterious workings of His will being done on
Our earth. Dimetos! What are you doing here! [*He thinks.*] They

showed me a stone wall . . . three miles long, shoulder height.
The stones were hewn from the local rock. Every one shaped
. . . chisel and hammer of course . . . to interlock perfectly with
the next. There's not a trowel of mortar in its entire length. It
really is beautiful. A mosaic with cellular depth, as if living
tissue had been its inspiration. And strong. It no longer serves
any purpose, yet it defies dereliction. You could walk the length
of it comfortably in . . . an hour? It was built a long time ago by
two slaves and it took them their entire lifetimes. 'Men don't
build like that anymore!' I was told proudly. [*Pause.*] No they
don't. It costs too much. That wall isn't made of stone. Fear.
That's why it's still there. A monument to man's capacity to
stand still.

# Scene 4

Dimetos, *hanging ropes and pulleys from a roofbeam above the table, and*
Danilo.

DIMETOS. What do you mean? 'Hard to find'? The only red tiled
roof in the village, two cypresses in front and an old mulberry
tree next to the house. What could be simpler?

DANILO. Looking for a prophet in the wilderness. To start with,
this village isn't even marked on the map I was using. And when
I did find it—well, the locals even seem to resent their neighbour having a name. A lesser man than you could easily be lost
to the world out here. What made you choose it?

DIMETOS. I had a workman once, from this valley. A strange
man. He handled a tool as if he had personally declared war
on matter. So I put him charge of the quarries. He assaulted
that rock as if nothing short of its total obliteration would
satisfy him. It was a clever move. He produced stone faster
than we could use it. He was very typical of this region. Without that dour tenacity of purpose, survival here wouldn't be
possible.

DANILO. I suppose that's the most that can be hoped for out here.

DIMETOS. Don't be too hard on them. They get a little living done as well. It's a harsh environment, but not impossible.

DANILO. It depresses me. It seems to invite the brutal response you described in your workman.

Who do you talk to, Dimetos?

DIMETOS. Talk! I didn't come here for that.

DANILO. Obviously. I can't help wondering what did bring you here.

DIMETOS. They might be simple around here, Danilo—how else will you describe them when you get back? Primitive? Uncultured?—but their needs are real. If anything, more so, just because life is basic. When a man needs water here he doesn't look for a tap, he digs a well. And having dug that well he must get the water to the top, and having got it there he must get it to his lands. It might all seem very obvious to you, but that is exactly what fascinates me. Problems your citizens have forgotten about, solutions to those problems which I had taken for granted, are again very real issues. It's refreshing, Danilo. Stimulating.

That's not to mention the further challenge of getting a new idea past the barriers of habit and prejudice. Their tools, techniques, are crude and inefficient. But they're the ones their fathers put into their hands and taught them how to use. To suggest modifying them not only demands a new dexterity of the wrist, but also of the soul. It's almost sacrilege. I haven't been all that successful, but they're learning to trust me. They've started to knock on my door when the need arises.

DANILO. That's what I'm doing.

DIMETOS. You've come a long way to do that.

DANILO. It's a big need. Didn't Sophia tell you why I'm here?

DIMETOS. No.

DANILO. But you can guess.

DIMETOS. Yes. Don't waste your time, Danilo.

DANILO. I owe it to more than just myself to try.

DIMETOS. I don't want to waste mine either.

DANILO. But you haven't even heard what I've got to say?

DIMETOS. Because there's nothing you could that would make me want to return.

DANILO. The city doesn't mean anything to you any more?

DIMETOS. Nothing.

[*Pause.*]

DANILO [*not knowing what to say*]. Well . . .

DIMETOS. I've shocked you.

DANILO. Yes, you have. I came prepared to argue about a lot of things, but not that.

DIMETOS. What should it 'mean' to me, Danilo? Do I owe it something?

DANILO. That wasn't what I was going to say.

DIMETOS. All right . . . what were you going to?

DANILO. I don't think there is any point to it now.

DIMETOS. Your city is simply more people in one place than any-where else. And if it's to people I owe something—which I don't think I do—there are enough of them here for me to repay my debt in full. You must understand, Danilo. If I'd wanted to engineer another project for your citizens, I'd be back among them. I wasn't forced to leave and I'm not being kept here against my will. Both were choices. Eat with us before you go. The news you take back mustn't be that I have also aban-doned my manners.

[*Exit Danilo. After a few seconds alone, Dimetos is joined by* Sophia. *He looks up expectantly as she enters.*]

Where's Lydia?

SOPHIA. Washing mud out of her hair, and singing. I don't think I've seen her so happy.

DIMETOS. She's got every reason to be. If it wasn't for her, that horse would still be down there. None of the men was prepared to do it.

SOPHIA. Did she really take off her clothes in front of them?

DIMETOS. It would have been impossible otherwise. She wouldn't have been able to move.

SOPHIA. That will give them something to talk about in the village. I go cold every time I think of her at the end of that rope.

DIMETOS. I knew what I was doing.

SOPHIA. I don't doubt that.

DIMETOS. I've asked Danilo to eat with us.

SOPHIA. I thought you might. I've prepared enough. [*Watching him.*] He's upset you, hasn't he?

DIMETOS. Is it that obvious?

SOPHIA. I would have been surprised if he hadn't. He told me what he had come to see you about. Asked me what I thought of his chances.

DIMETOS. And?

SOPHIA. And what?

DIMETOS. What did you say to him?

SOPHIA. The truth. That I didn't know.

DIMETOS. Why do you smile?

SOPHIA. I think it's the first time I couldn't guess what your response would be . . . not that I would have told him if I had.

DIMETOS. The answer was 'No'.

SOPHIA. So I gathered. Then why does he still bother you? Didn't he accept it?

DIMETOS. He had no choice. I have no intention of going back. Even when I've disagreed, or haven't understood, I've always respected other men's decisions as to how they wanted to live their lives. Is that asking too much for myself?

SOPHIA. Wasn't he respectful? I thought there was more than enough of that for Dimetos the Engineer. He came a long way to see you.

DIMETOS. He should have spared himself the trouble.

SOPHIA [*quietly*]. I'm not persuading you to return.

[*Pause.*]

DIMETOS. I'm sorry, Sophia. I'm not even angry with him. It's myself. I lied to him.

SOPHIA. I know. [*He looks at her.*] I couldn't help hearing. I wouldn't worry too much about it though. I don't think he realized.

DIMETOS. Of course he didn't. It was a very convincing performance. I almost believed it myself 'Dimetos is working! And his inspiration? Another man's need.'

SOPHIA. That was certainly true once.

DIMETOS. I'm not even sure of that any more. [*She is watching him.*] Desertion does more than just terminate a loyalty, Sophia. It makes a lie of whatever loyalty there had been.

SOPHIA. Those are strong words.

DIMETOS. I am sure that is how Danilo sees it.

SOPHIA. Is he right? [*Dimetos makes a vague gesture.*] That's how you see it.

DIMETOS. Sometimes. I know you are very patient, Sophia, but have you ever felt provoked into asking me 'What are you doing here?'

SOPHIA. Have you been waiting for me to?

DIMETOS. I would have thought it an obvious question by now.

SOPHIA. I did ask it . . . a long time ago and not here, but it was the same question. The day you came home and told me you were leaving. I was surprised. I'd been expecting something but nothing quite as abrupt and final as that. I asked you, why? Only once . . . I didn't need to a second time because you never stopped answering me. You were tired, you needed a change, the stimulus of fresh challenges . . . Are you saying none of that was true?

DIMETOS. It wasn't as simple or as blatant as that. I *was* tired at the time. No, I'm saying that I used that to hide, from myself, something else.

[*Pause. She waits.*]

SOPHIA. Do I have to ask?

DIMETOS. No. It's not easy to know where or how to start. This afternoon at the well. Lydia had secured the ropes and was safely up. Everyone stood around waiting. I checked everything for the last time—the tripod, pulleys—all were fine. There was nothing left to do except try. So we tensed the rope, just enough to feel the weight of the animal at the other end. We dug in our heels . . . Lydia joined us . . . made sure of our hold on the rope. Then I gave the word and we pulled. It was remarkable. At that precise moment, when we all strained in unison, it was as if our faces and names disappeared. All that mattered was what each of us, trying his utmost, could contribute. And our individual efforts brought to a simple focus by that rope. It worked. Hand over hand we brought him up, a few inches at a time. It's been long since I experienced the excitement I felt at that moment. It used to be like that all the time. Do you realize there must have been an actual moment in history, one specific place and time when something on two legs picked up a stone and used it for the first time—smashed a bone so that he could get at the marrow? We've come a long way since then, but that moment this afternoon was part of the campaign that started with that first blow. [*He indicates his table and tools.*] The armoury—six mechanical powers—lever, pulley, inclined plane, wedge, screw and wheel. That's what they are. The tools and machines I've used or put into other men's hands . . . extensions to those hands, giving them new powers in their defiance of a universe that resists us. The battle cry: Help men Defy!

There is nothing more beautiful than a man making something and making it well, than a pair of hands urgent and quick with a need, and behind those a guiding intelligence. Do you know what bridges that mysterious distance between head and hands, bringing them so close together that they are almost one? Caring. Not the most exciting of words is it? Almost as humble as a tool. But that is the Alchemist's Stone of human endeavour. I know what I'm talking about, Sophia, because mine were like that, head and hands fused, alloyed to a point where you couldn't separate the action of the one from the intention of the other. And they were like that because I 'cared'. Not about the city, but about people.

[*He pauses. Sophia is listening carefully.*]

SOPHIA [*before he can continue*]. Don't say anything you are going to regret.

DIMETOS. It would only be a question of hearing the words aloud. I've already said it to myself. I don't care any more. Don't ask me why, because I don't know. But something eroded away the habit of caring. I carried on behaving as if I still did, until the lie became intolerable. [*He picks up a tool from the table.*] Usage blunts a tool, but when that happens you sharpen it, when it wears out you replace it. It's not as simple as that with . . .

SOPHIA. The heart, Dimetos.

DIMETOS. Head, hands, and heart. It's easier here only because I don't have to lie to myself, or others. I do what little work comes my way, dispense what little help I can because it's a civilized habit, not a passion. And even then . . . ! If I'd been myself this morning I might well have left that horse and those squabbling idiots to their predicament.

SOPHIA. Lydia.

DIMETOS. Yes. She was very upset when she saw the animal.

SOPHIA. Your caring hasn't stopped completely then.

DIMETOS. I don't 'care' about Lydia . . . [*Sophia waits.*] I love her as if she were my own child.

[*Exit Dimetos. Sophia is alone and thoughtful for a few seconds before* Lydia *enters.*]

LYDIA. Sophia, it's dry now. [*She sits and hands Sophia her hairbrush.*] Who is the visitor?

SOPHIA. A young man from the city. [*Tapping Lydia on the head with the brush.*] Come on. [*She brushes Lydia's hair while they play their 'game'.*]

LYDIA [*closing her eyes and thinking*]. Yes! The sunlight when I came out of the well.

SOPHIA. One.

LYDIA. The horse galloping away from me.

SOPHIA. Two.

LYDIA. I saw a pig.

SOPHIA. What's beautiful about a pig?

LYDIA. He had two big pink ears.

[*They laugh.*]

SOPHIA. Three.

LYDIA. I found a beautiful stone by the pool.

SOPHIA. Four.

LYDIA. I heard someone whistling.

SOPHIA. Five.

LYDIA. I saw a small cloud far away.

SOPHIA. Six.

LYDIA. I looked at that big tree in the meadow again. It is still beautiful.

SOPHIA. Seven.

LYDIA. The sunset on our way home.

SOPHIA. Eight.

LYDIA. Our house as we came over the hill.

SOPHIA. Nine.

LYDIA [*pausing to think, then quietly*]. Your hands when you brush my hair.

SOPHIA. Ten. [*She embraces Lydia.*]


# Scene 5

*The garden.* Lydia *and* Danilo.

LYDIA. It was more than thirty foot deep. We measured it afterwards. When we got there they were all just standing around arguing about whose fault it was. The old man who owned the horse said that the man who owned the well was to blame because the fence around it was rotten, but the man who owned the well said the man who owned the horse . . .

DANILO. . . . said that the man who owned the well said that the man who owned the horse said that the man who owned the well . . .

LYDIA [*laughing*]. That's right! Nobody was trying to do anything. There's a saying here that whoever throws the first stone must take responsibility for the last . . . only it wasn't stones they were offering each other, but big rocks. They were going to kill him. We just listened at first. Then my uncle got very angry. I've never seen him like that before. 'Use your hands, you bloody idiots, not your tongues.' He just pushed them aside and went to work. While he was putting up the ropes and pulleys he made them dig a slope down into it—he called it a ramp—so that the horse could climb out when we got him half way up. I could see none of them thought it was going to work but they were too frightened of him to argue.

DANILO. And you?

LYDIA. Frightened of my uncle?

DANILO. No. Did you think it was going to work?

LYDIA. Of course. He doesn't do anything unless it will work. And it did. The first time, with all of them pulling.

DANILO. You're a loyal apprentice. One way or another it has certainly been a day of surprises. None of the young women I know spend their time pulling horses out of wells.

LYDIA. It's the first time I've really helped him. I usually just get in the way.

DANILO. I'm sure that's not true.

LYDIA. Yes, it is. He's very patient, though. Always pretends I've been a big help.

DANILO. What else do you do?

LYDIA. Help Sophia in the house. I think I get in the way there too, sometimes.

DANILO. Dimetos and Sophia. Anybody else?

LYDIA. Not really.

DANILO. It must be lonely for you.

LYDIA. I'm used to it now. Just when I really start getting bored something happens . . . last year there were floods, today it was the horse. That makes up for everything.

DANILO. You might have to wait a long time before that happens again.

LYDIA. No! I'd rather have nothing to do.

What did you come to see my uncle about?

DANILO. I was hoping to persuade him to return to the city. Help us to rescue some of our horses. [*Lydia smiles.*] I wish it was a joke. But the truth is, we also just stand around looking at our disasters, arguing whose fault it was and doing nothing. The only difference is that it is not horses who are in trouble but people.

LYDIA. He'll help you if he can.

DANILO. Oh he certainly can, but he won't.

LYDIA. Why do you say that?

DANILO. Because he told me. Life here is far too exciting and challenging for him to think of leaving.

LYDIA. My uncle said that?

DANILO. Words to that effect. Didn't you know it? You look as surprised as I was.

LYDIA [*confused*]. He . . . we never talk about it. I've always just taken it for granted that . . .

DANILO. This was home?

LYDIA. Yes.

DANILO. You'd like to go back, wouldn't you?

LYDIA. Yes.

DANILO. At last! Somebody on my side. Sophia was also indifferent to the prospect.

LYDIA. She'll go wherever Dimetos goes.

DANILO. So I gathered.

LYDIA [*with a defiant note in her voice*]. So will I!

DANILO. I'm not arguing with you. I'm disappointed, that's all. We really could use your uncle.

LYDIA. Did you try very hard?

DANILO. No. I got off to a bad start by antagonizing Sophia. And when it came to Dimetos . . . well, he wouldn't even let me speak. It was almost as if . . . [*Pause.*]

LYDIA. What?

DANILO. You'll get angry with me if I say it.

LYDIA. I can't be your friend if you don't like him.

DANILO. I respect him, Lydia. I wouldn't have come all this way if I didn't.

LYDIA. I know I should be happy here. We've got everything we need.

DANILO. Maybe you haven't. There's no disloyalty in that. I'm sure they'd be the first to admit it. You're younger than them, that's all. And the city's got more to offer someone with a life still to be lived.

LYDIA. I think I've forgotten what it looks like.

DANILO. You'll find it changed. Five years is a long time in a city's life.

LYDIA. Bigger?

DANILO. Much.

LYDIA. More people?

DANILO. Too many!

LYDIA. And happy people!

   [*They laugh.*]

DANILO. Your villagers certainly are a serious lot.

LYDIA. I didn't mind it when we first came here. Everything was different and strange. I'm sure my uncle felt that way too. We had all sorts of plans and schemes. We built the footbridge across the river in that first year. None of them would use it at first. I used to run up and down it to prove it was safe. But some of the old people are still waiting for it to fall. [*Pause.*]

DANILO. What's the matter?

LYDIA. Just thinking . . . it was good to have something to do again today. [*Turning to Danilo.*] I think you gave up too easily. Everybody does that with him.

DANILO. He's a very formidable man.

LYDIA. Not really. Why don't you try again?

DANILO. I wouldn't know where to start.

LYDIA. I'll help you. I'll tell him I want to go back. Sometimes he does things for me when he's already said no to others.

DANILO. I can understand why. All right.

# Scene 6

*The meal.* Dimetos, Danilo, Sophia *and* Lydia *are sitting round the table.*

DIMETOS [*to Danilo*]. They've left the old fort intact?

DANILO. Intact? It's become impregnable. A wave of historical necrophilia swept through us a few years ago. We dug up the bones of every hero we could find and reburied them inside its walls. Reverence as well as history now protects it.

DIMETOS. I remember sitting up there one day, looking down. You could see a lot of the city from up there—the road through the valley, all the way down to the harbour. From that height the people were no bigger than ants, the traffic a child's game with little toys. I wondered what the correct analogy was for what I was looking at. Organic or mechanical? The complexity of it! That system of roads, like arteries, with life flowing along them. Was the city finally an organism, something more than just the sum total of all the individual lives it contained . . . or was it still only a machine, a system of forces that could be controlled?

DANILO. What did you decide?

DIMETOS. I didn't. Because a third possibility occurred to me. That I was looking at the creation of a modern Daedalus into which Theseus has gone without his ball of twine.*

DANILO. That image could be read as either pessimistic or a challenge to us to get out of our mess but this time without any help from the gods.

DIMETOS. That depends on how clever our unaided Theseus is, doesn't it?

DANILO. I think he stands a chance. After all, the labyrinth, for all its intricacies, remains man-made. In fact that little part of it you looked down on, has now been unmade. Most of it has been demolished and cleared for re-development.

DIMETOS. I suppose that was inevitable.

DANILO. It was long overdue. I don't share your affection for it. I've also stood up there and looked down, but all I saw was a slum. People crowded together in conditions that made a decent life impossible, and our efforts to give them that frustrated by prejudice and sentiment. I'm cast in the role of the Villain these days, Dimetos. Progress has become a dirty word.

SOPHIA. I'm one of those who are suspicious of it.

DANILO. Why?

SOPHIA. The schemes get bigger and and bigger, the people smaller. It's become so soulless, Danilo, like the masses of concrete it always entails.

DANILO. Concrete is a mixture of sand and cement. It's the architects who are supposed to have the souls, and I'll be the first to admit that a lot of them design as if they didn't. Why reduce what we are trying to do, what we have *got* to do, to that one, very useful material?

SOPHIA. There is so much of it.

DANILO. Because there are a lot of people, Sophia! We haven't got the luxury of time any more. Maybe we never had it. There might be a definition there. Man is the only animal to be trapped by time. That's the real labyrinth and to get out of it we have got to plan and build very fast, and bigger than before. [*Turning to Lydia.*] Are you frightened of progress?

SOPHIA. I said I was 'suspicious'.

LYDIA [*uncertainly*]. I don't know.

DANILO. It's only a word. It means to move forward . . . to try and live your life in the only direction it has got—tomorrow! How do you feel about tomorrow?

LYDIA. Good.

DANILO. Why?

LYDIA. I don't know . . . No, I do! Because today was good.

DANILO. And if it had been bad?

LYDIA. I'd try very hard to make tomorrow better.

DANILO. So one way or another, you want tomorrow.

LYDIA. Oh, yes!

DANILO. You believe in progress.

LYDIA. Do I?

DANILO. Oh, yes.

LYDIA. But I also agree with Sophia. I don't like concrete. I prefer bricks.

DANILO. Then build with bricks. We use them as well. Get Dimetos to build you a house of real bricks down in the valley. Would you like that?

LYDIA. Yes.

[*She looks at Dimetos. He has been watching the exchange between her and Danilo, quietly. Sophia has been watching him. He speaks easily enough in reply to Lydia's look.*]

DIMETOS. Not in the valley. I spent too much of my youth in those streets. There are ghosts waiting for me there.

LYDIA. Good or bad?

DIMETOS. They were good men.

LYDIA. Then they'll be good ghosts! Who are they?

DIMETOS. The people who lived there.

LYDIA. You've never mentioned them before.

DIMETOS. Haven't I? I used to walk around down there . . . watch them live and work. [*Lydia is waiting expectantly.*] A man called Jerome . . . a potter. Yes! His hands would certainly be a ghost in those streets if I ever went back there. [*Remembering.*] Slender, but surprisingly firm and strong. The clay hadn't softened them.

I can still see him wiping them on his apron before greeting me
. . . and then giving them back to work. I used to watch them
while we talked. And we did, without interrupting them at all.
In those hands the clay became something that combined the
virtues of both liquid and solid. It flowed or stayed just as he
wanted.

Or Daniel! There was a different pair of hands. The difference
between clay and metal, between finger tips and the impact of a
four-pound hammer wielded by an arm as thick as a man's
thigh. But they also knew their business. The last time I saw him
he was at work on a chain—for one of the ships in the
harbour—forging each link as if it was the one destined for
Prometheus.*

The pair I think I'll remember longest, though, did not belong
to a worker. They were also very accomplished in their business,
as sure in their grasp as Daniel's and as effortless in their action
as Jerome's. But they produced nothing, unless you can count
the gasp of a throng of spectators as produce. A juggler! A
circus pitched its tent in one of those vacant lots one year. A sad
little show—a few flea-bitten goats who could spell their
names—but they also had a juggler. In explaining his trade to
me he posed a paradox: 'Learn to give and take with the same
action.'

DANILO. What about a beggar's hands?

DIMETOS. Beggars take, what do they give? I have no patience
with that bloodless ethic that elevates beggary to a state of
Grace.

DANILO. Almost your exact words! About ten years ago. My first
and only meeting with you before today. You don't remember.

DIMETOS. No.

DANILO. The market square. The storm-water system. You were
very busy, irritable . . . you hadn't been given enough workmen,
the equipment was inadequate . . . [*He smiles at the memory of
himself.*] A very junior official added to your irritation by asking
for an inventory of the materials you had on site. You told me
exactly what you thought about inventories, turned your back

133

on me and stumbled over a beggar. Your anger was magnificent! 'What do you give men back for their charity! Blessings won't hold bricks together. Your hands can still work. You blaspheme them by begging.'

DIMETOS. You've got a good memory, Danilo.

DANILO. It's a moment I don't want to forget, as you haven't forgotten yours. Those few words made me realize what it meant to be a man among other men. A reciprocity, not of tears, but sweat.

DIMETOS. A stirring vision.

DANILO. It is, isn't it? At times we come close to making it our reality.

DIMETOS. They were rare occasions when I was there. Most of what passed as 'vision' could be better summed up in the word profit.

DANILO. That is still very much the case, but there are exceptions . . . as you were.

DIMETOS. You flatter me, Danilo. All I ever did . . .

DANILO [*cutting him short*]. No! We're playing games with each other, Dimetos. I respect you too much to 'waste your time' yet again and in that fashion. I am going to risk your anger. I don't believe what you said to me about being here. I don't know whether you are lying to me or yourself, but I cannot believe that pulling old plough horses out of wells or being an odd-job man to a crowd of peasants satisfies you. Do you know what you're keeping company with here? An abject and servile dependence on superstition and religion that reduces man and denies history. That's what I'm really asking you to leave . . .

LYDIA [*moving impulsively towards Dimetos*]. Please listen to him.

DIMETOS. I have. Very carefully.

LYDIA. That's what I mean . . . don't be angry. Yes, you are! But don't be. Maybe it is time for us to return.

DIMETOS [*smiling at her then moving away*]. I think I do remember that beggar. If those were my words they certainly didn't have any effect on him. He was still sitting around in the sun when we finished there. I wouldn't be surprised if he was still. Yes, those empty hands always angered me. They seemed to betray the 'vision' more significantly than your profiteers ever will. It's not pleasant to see a man end up that useless. [*Turning to Danilo.*] Don't go tomorrow. Give me time to think.

DANILO. As much time as you need.

SOPHIA. It's late, Lydia.

LYDIA. Not yet. [*She looks at Dimetos.*] Just a little longer.

SOPHIA [*to Danilo*]. I'll show you to your room.

DANILO [*to Dimetos*]. Goodnight. [*To Lydia.*] . . . and thank you.

[*Exeunt Sophia and Danilo.*]

LYDIA. This is the happiest day of my life. I don't want it to end. First the horse, then a visitor, and now . . .

DIMETOS. All I said . . .

LYDIA. I know! But please think hard . . . Dimetos.

DIMETOS. The two of you left me no choice.

LYDIA. Are you cross with me?

DIMETOS. For what reason?

LYDIA. Being on his side. He told me what he'd come to see you about. I made him try again.

DIMETOS. I see. So that is what inspired our young visionary. You like him?

LYDIA. Yes. [*She pulls down an end of rope hanging from the roofbeam and ties a knot.*] And you?

DIMETOS. Yes.

LYDIA. He does respect you. I'd like him for that alone.

DIMETOS. But he's also handsome, he made you laugh and now the thought of him is making you blush. Don't be embarrassed. I've thought of you as the little one for too long. You're a young woman and Danilo is a young man. It's as simple as that.

LYDIA [*finishing the knot*]. Now pull it tight . . . and it doesn't slip. That's right, isn't it—the knot we used this morning?

DEMITOS. Yes. Perfect.

LYDIA. I didn't even have to think. My hands will never forget how to tie it.

DIMETOS. The Fisherman's Bend. It can't slip because the knot will tighten and bite into itself when subjected to strain.

LYDIA. Teach me another. [*He sits beside her.*] Slowly . . .

DIMETOS [*ties a knot*]. There. Figure of eight.

LYDIA. Let me try.

DIMETOS [*watching*]. That's not what a young woman should be applying her hands to. Let me see them. [*Looks at her hands.*] The ones that worked for me were calloused and rough with biographies of hard work and tools. Men's hands. These . . . have a different purpose waiting for them.

What would you like to do with them?

LYDIA. Use them the way I did today.

DIMETOS. No. We don't want any callouses on these. They're meant for other skills than pulling old plough horses out of wells.

LYDIA. He's not a plough horse. You know that.

DIMETOS. That's what Danilo called him. And what was I? Handyman to a crowd of peasants! He wasn't exactly the model of tact in his persuasion was he?

[*Lydia watches Dimetos in silence for a few seconds.*]

LYDIA. You don't like him.

DIMETOS. I don't dislike him. He's given me a lot to think about, that's all.

LYDIA. And you are still cross with me.

DIMETOS. Don't be silly.

[*Lydia goes up to him and faces him with simple and total honesty.*]

LYDIA. I owe you everything. If I thought you were happy here, I wouldn't have interfered.

DIMETOS. What makes you think I'll be happy back in the city?

LYDIA. Work. He was right. People need you.

DIMETOS. I'm tired of other men's needs, other men's disasters.

LYDIA. I don't believe that. You wouldn't have saved the horse this morning if that was true.

DIMETOS. I saved that horse for you! [*Looks at her.*] You understand and see so much, and yet you're so blind to other things. [*Pause.*] Yes, I saved that horse for you. I knotted those ropes around your waist and lowered you because I had sworn to myself I was going to pull your pain out of the world. But what started off with such grim determination then became the most remarkable thing I've ever seen. He succumbed to you! Stood absolutely still while you straddled him and went to work. There was one moment when you were prostrate on his back, your cheek resting on his powerful neck, your hands working away quietly underneath him as you placed the slings ... both of you covered in mud! Yes, that was it! Two bodies separate, and yet mysteriously at one with each other. I wonder what memory the animal has of that moment ... at the bottom of a dark hole, too stupid to believe in the possibility of help ... frightened ... and then something so light and beautiful coming to your rescue. If I was an artist I'd turn my hand to modelling that. Try to capture the contrast between the powerful contours of his help-lessness and the delicacy of your determination.

[*Pause. Exit abruptly.*]

## Scene 7

*The garden.* Dimetos *and* Sophia.

SOPHIA. More wine?

DIMETOS. No. I've had too much already.

SOPHIA. Have you got work to do?

DIMETOS. Yes. But my head is not very clear.

SOPHIA. I hope it was when you asked him to stay on. You changed your mind very quickly.

DIMETOS. I didn't change my mind, Sophia! All I said ...

SOPHIA. I know ... you are going to think about it. [*Something in her tone makes Dimetos look at her.*] Please work. I enjoy watching your hands.

DIMETOS. I don't know that I can trust them tonight.

[*Pause.*]

SOPHIA. The dogs are very noisy.

DIMETOS. I haven't noticed.

SOPHIA. Listen. They make the night sound full of trouble, don't they? When we first came here I use to lie and listen and wonder what mischief there could be in a place like this to keep them so busy.

DIMETOS. Shadows.

SOPHIA. But of what? Shadows aren't things in themselves. There's always something else, isn't there, something more real . . . even if it's only a thought. It's all we know about them sometimes; and then, like dogs, raise our hackles and bark.

DIMETOS. You're in a strange mood, Sophia.

SOPHIA. I suppose I am. Must be the heat. These summers have never got any easier. I'll be glad when the cooler weather comes.

DIMETOS. A few more days to the solstice.

SOPHIA. You haven't been sleeping too well either, have you? I've heard you moving around the house at night.

DIMETOS. Like you I find this weather very uncomfortable.

[*Pause. He looks up to find Sophia staring at him.*]

SPOHIA. You don't trust me, do you?

DIMETOS. What makes you say that?

SOPHIA. Because you don't.

DIMETOS. I don't know what you're talking about, Sophia.

SOPHIA. Maybe I've also had too much wine. Lydia will sleep soundly, though, won't she . . . after her busy day. The sleep of the innocent.

DIMETOS. What are we guilty of?

SOPHIA. Our lives, if nothing else.

DIMETOS. All we've done is live them.

SOPHIA. Speak for yourself. A dedicated servant ends up without
a life of her own.

DIMETOS. Where does that word come from suddenly?

SOPHIA. Which one?

DIMETOS. You know the one I mean. I've never called you or
thought of you as that.

SOPHIA. But it's true, isn't it? If I'm not a servant what am I?
Mother? Sister? I'm not old enough for the first and I've never
thought of myself as the second. There's also 'friend', 'companion' . . . if the others are too personal. How do *you* see me,
Dimetos? Who am I?

DIMETOS. Sophia.

SOPHIA. Faithful, loyal, trustworthy Sophia!

DIMETOS. You have been all of those.

SOPHIA. They are the virtues of a good servant.

# Scene 8

Lydia *wakes with a scream.*

LYDIA. DIMETOS! [*Pause. Then softly.*] Sophia! Sophia!
[Sophia *enters and starts brushing her hair. The mood between the two
of them is muted and in strong contrast to their first scene together.*]
Your turn.

SOPHIA [*hollowly*]. The first light in our room this morning.

LYDIA. One.

SOPHIA. The fire in the stove.

LYDIA. Two.

SOPHIA. Water . . .
[*Lydia shakes her head. Sophia abandons the game.*]

LYDIA. What's happening?

SOPHIA. I don't understand.

LYDIA. Something is happening to us.

SOPHIA. We're waiting for Dimetos to make up his mind. While he is doing that you are entertaining Danilo and doing it very well.

LYDIA. Is that all?

SOPHIA. Isn't that enough for you?

[*Pause.*]

LYDIA. Your hands seem different, Sophia.

SOPHIA. In what way?

LYDIA. It's hard to imagine you when I feel them.

SOPHIA. I'm doing it as I've always done it.

LYDIA. You're not hurting . . . but it's as if I don't know them, and they don't know me.

Let me look at you?

SOPHIA [*avoiding her eyes*]. You're very strange, Lydia. Let me finish. I have work waiting.

LYDIA. Look at me. Smile.

SOPHIA. I don't feel like smiling today.

[*Pause.*]

LYDIA. Uncle is also avoiding me.

SOPHIA. What do you mean?

LYDIA. He just . . .

SOPHIA. What do you mean?

LYDIA. I don't know.

[*Pause.*]

SOPHIA. You're still hoping he will decide to go back.

LYDIA. Of course. Why do you say it like that? Aren't you?

SOPHIA. It's not important to me . . . and if it was, I would quickly stop it being so. Because he won't.

LYDIA. Did he tell you that?

SOPHIA. No.

LYDIA. Then what makes you so sure?

SOPHIA. I've been with him longer than you. Sometimes I know his mind even before he does.

LYDIA. Is this one of those times?

SOPHIA. Yes.

[*Pause.*]

LYDIA. You're saying he's lying.

SOPHIA. Yes. Didn't you think he could?

LYDIA. Why is he?

SOPHIA. That's his business.

LYDIA. Don't you know that as well?

SOPHIA. I don't want to know.

[*Pause.*]

LYDIA. It's still your turn.

SOPHIA [*mechanically*]. Butterfly . . . bird . . . rainbow . . .

LYDIA [*shaking her head*]. No . . .

SOPHIA. I saw a dead dog.

LYDIA. That's enough Sophia. Thank you.

SOPHIA [*stops brushing Lydia's hair*]. Be careful, little one. [*Exit.*]

# Scene 9

*Beside the pool.* Lydia *and* Danilo.

DANILO [*off-stage*]. Lydia! Lydia! [*He enters. He has obviously had too much to drink.*] Why did you run away?

LYDIA. I didn't run, I walked.

DANILO. You know what I mean. One moment you were there and when I looked again . . .

LYDIA. I wasn't enjoying myself.

DANILO. It wasn't that bad. In fact, I was pleasantly surprised to see what a few glasses of wine could do for these 'stern sons of the soil'. One of them even had a joke. You believe that? 'What's the difference between a duck?' Well?

LYDIA. I don't know.

DANILO. One of its legs is both the same! [*He laughs at himself*] Danilo . . . you're a long way from home.

LYDIA. Have a swim. You'll feel better.

DANILO [*laughing*]. Better? That is absolutely impossible. I feel better than I have ever felt. You look clean and fresh and I . . .

LYDIA. You have had too much wine.

DANILO. That . . . is putting it mildly. [*Pause.*] How long have I been here now?

LYDIA. Five days.

DANILO. You sure?

LYDIA. Yes. Does it seem longer or shorter?

DANILO. I don't know. I honestly don't know. That's a bad sign, isn't it? No sense of time! That's how it starts.

LYDIA. What?

DANILO [*stops himself in time*]. Nothing. This little valley of yours is a dangerous place. I felt it the day I arrived. A man's sense of purpose could end up as stunted as the thorn trees out there if he stayed here too long.

LYDIA. Like my uncle.

DANILO [*making a vague gesture*]. We'll water his purposes back to life. [*Lydia moves*] What's the matter?

LYDIA. I thought I saw someone.

DANILO. Where?

LYDIA. Among those lemon trees.

DANILO. So?

LYDIA. So I thought I saw someone.

DANILO [*finally registering her depressed mood*]. What's wrong?

LYDIA. Nothing.

DANILO. I'm not that drunk, little one. Or are you saying it's none of my business?

LYDIA. No. It is. You must go, Danilo. You are wasting your time. Dimetos won't go back.

DANILO. You certainly are down. Don't be such a pessimist. I had a word with him back there. He's promised to give me his decision tonight.

LYDIA. That is what he will tell you.

DANILO. What?

LYDIA. Please listen, Danilo. He is not going back to the city.

DANILO. Don't make me think, Lydia. This sun is very hot. [*Pause.*] When did he tell you?

LYDIA. He didn't. It was Sophia.

DANILO. He told her?

LYDIA. No.

DANILO. That's her guess.

LYDIA. It's not just a guess. She . . .

DANILO. What makes you think she's right?

LYDIA. Please Danilo! Dimetos is not going back.

DANILO. All right! Well . . . that's rather abrupt and sobering. I thought I had succeeded. Mission accomplished! He put up a damned good performance of having not yet decided. 'We'll thrash out the whole matter tonight.' Come to think of it, he did get away from me in a hurry. Well? Aren't you going to make me try again?

LYDIA. No.

DANILO. Sorry, Lydia. The sarcasm was really directed at myself.

LYDIA. I should never have interfered.

DANILO. Interfered?

LYDIA. If I hadn't persuaded you to talk to him again you would have gone and we would have carried on as before.

DANILO. That's exactly what is going to happen.

[*She shakes her head. Pause.*]

LYDIA. It won't ever be the same . . . Dimetos, Sophia, and myself. Something has happened.

DANILO. What?

LYDIA. I don't know . . . but it's suddenly like we've all got secrets from each other.

DANILO. That's bad. And I'm the cause.

LYDIA. I wish you were. I wish there was just one person or thing to blame. But I know you aren't . . . not in that way.

I'm not making sense.

DANILO. You are sure you are not just depressed because . . . well, the possibility of getting away from here seems to have been lost?

LYDIA [*with absolute sincerity*]. I'd give up any chance of ever going back to the city if the three of us could go back to what it was like . . . five days ago. It's changed so suddenly!

There's an old man who lives at the bottom of the road past our house. I used to think he was mad because no matter what I would say to him, he just shrugged his shoulders and answered 'Tomorrow was yesterday.' I know what he means now, and I wish it was true.

DANILO [*Shaking his head angrily*]. No! That is not good enough.

LYDIA. I'd be happy if it was true.

DANILO. Don't say that! You've let them frighten you. Don't argue with me. Answer me honestly . . . are you frightened?

LYDIA. Yes.

[*The admission leaves Danilo almost speechless.*]

DANILO [*quietly, sincerely*]. Leave them, Lydia. No . . . you listen to me now. When the time comes, and it can't be far off . . . you leave them. Even if you were his daughter, I'd say as much.

LYDIA. No.

DANILO. All you owe him is gratitude, and you've obviously paid that debt in full. You don't owe him your life. No! I haven't finished. I want to tell you about an old man *I* know. Strangely enough he also lives at the bottom of a road. In a funny little house made of 'real bricks'. A little boy carries out a chair first thing in the morning, puts it down on the pavement . . . and a little later the old man comes slowly out, sits down and watches—the people passing on the pavement, the traffic in the street, encounters between friends, arguments between neighbours, accidents . . . Life! He'd been watching it for a long time when finally one day I plucked up enough courage to stop and talk to him. I wasn't much older than you and . . . I had a question. 'Excuse me, sir', I said, 'But can you help me . . .' [*Pause.*] Before I could go any further he shook his head sadly and said 'No. I'm too old. Help yourself.'

LYDIA [*laughing*]. You've just made that up.

DANILO. That's right. Don't you think it was good?

LYDIA. Until you couldn't think of a question to ask him.

DANILO. Can you?

LYDIA. Why is nothing forever?

DANILO [*shaking his head*]. No. You want to feel sorry for yourself. Forever? What does that mean? Museums try to make things 'forever'. Do you want to do that to yourself? Stick a pin through your 'five days ago' and still be there in a hundred years of time? You've lost faith in tomorrow, Lydia . . . and I'm going to give it back to you.

LYDIA. How?

DANILO. Oh, God, I wish I knew.

[*He kisses her gently. At first Lydia responds but as Danilo goes further she begins to resist him. He can't control himself. The struggle becomes violent. Her dress gets torn. She eventually manages to break free and runs away. Danilo is left alone.*]

Danilo? Danilo?

## Scene 10

Lydia, *her dress torn, alone.* Sophia *enters.*

SOPHIA [*terrified of her question and its possible answer, but unable to resist asking it*]. Who . . . who was it?

I saw a most beautiful bird.

Lydia who was it?

I saw a marvellous dragonfly . . .

Lydia please . . . Who was it?

Remember our funny little chicken . . .

Lydia, who was it!

I saw a pretty little blue egg . . .

[*Sinking to her knees beside Lydia.*] Lydia, please help me. Who was it? [*Her pain turns to violence. She scrambles to her feet and assaults Lydia physically.*] For God's sake, tell me. Who was it?

LYDIA. Danilo.

[*Pause.*]

SOPHIA. Danilo. [*She starts laughing, finally uncontrollably.*] Don't let it upset you too much. A pretty little thing like you will have to cope with a lot more passion before she's old. But in your prayers tonight make sure you ask that it be the other person's and not your own. To love is a position of weakness, to be loved a position of power. I was careless about my prayers when I was your age. [*Pause.*] I did warn you. Now I'm going to leave you. [*Exit.*]

## Scene 11

Lydia, *alone and very frightened.* Dimetos *enters. He is breathless, his manner wild and disturbed. He is frightened of his hands.*

DIMETOS. Did he . . . hurt you? There . . . there . . . it's . . . it's all over now. And so, very nearly, is today. You must go to bed . . . sleep . . . and when you wake up . . . all that happened will already be yesterday. Time is not always our enemy, Lydia. What shall we do tomorrow? You decide. Something . . . something impossible. My hands want to work.

LYDIA. Your hands smell of lemons. You were the man in the orchard. You were watching us. You didn't stop him.

[*Pause.*]

DIMETOS. You ran away before I needed to. I wouldn't have let him hurt you. [*Looking at his hands.*] It was so hot. The blossom made me giddy. I remember holding onto a branch . . . I must have crushed the leaves. Do you know what day this is? The solstice. The longest day of the year. This was the longest day of the year. From *sol*, meaning sun, and *sistere*, to stand still. The day the sun stood still. So did I. I never knew I had that much stillness in me. Only my shadow moved. And then at a moment, together with the sun, that seemed to stop as well. I thought I was going to faint. You were so long in coming. I closed my eyes, and then, as if I was dreaming, I saw you again beside the well waiting to go down, modest and beautiful. I saw you on the horse and then afterwards in the pool. I heard your laugh again . . . but that wasn't my dream. I opened my eyes and there you were. He kissed you. [*Pause.*] This will be the shortest night. The year has turned on its side. We've so much time left, Lydia. Don't be frightened. We'll save all the stray horses that fall into wells.

LYDIA [*quietly*]. Go.

　[*Exit Dimetos. Lydia is alone.*]

I know your story now.

You didn't know that men make holes in the world. You thought it was safe. So you trusted it. Grass is green . . . water is sweet . . . the shade of big trees is cool . . . and you walked and galloped as if it was all there just for you. But one day, without any warning . . . down, down, down to the bottom where it was cold and dark and you were alone and you were frightened. Horses are stupid. Stupid, stupid horses. Stray and fall. For all its holes the world is still worth it—because Dimetos makes happy endings.

　[*She climbs on to the table, pulls down a rope hanging from the ceiling. Speaking with authority.*]

We need a knot that won't slip. The rope must bite into itself and tighten when subjected to strain. I can do it with my eyes closed. [*She ties the knot, puts the noose around her neck, and hangs herself.*]

# ACT TWO

## Scene 1

*Beside the Ocean. Many years later.* Dimetos, *older, on the beach.*

DIMETOS. Sea. Sand. Sun. Sky. Elemental. There could be a beginning here, as easily as an end. The footprints leading across the wet sand to this moment, suggest a purpose.

The tide has pulled out so far I despair of its return. The sand underfoot is loose and heavy and when I try to erase the weight of my emptiness with handfulls of it, it spills out between my fingers as if my fists were lunatic hour-glasses, impatient to measure out what's left of my time. There are no landmarks. You walk until you've had enough.

## Scene 2

*A small cottage.* Dimetos *and* Sophia *at a window.*

SOPHIA. What is it?

DIMETOS. I'm not sure. I can't get close enough. It looks like one of the Cetaceans.

SOPHIA. Speak English.

DIMETOS. One of the sea mammals . . . maybe a walrus. It was very frustrating. That rock is so close. But even with the tide as low as it is, I couldn't reach it.

SOPHIA. Why did you throw stones?

DIMETOS. To see if it was dead.

SOPHIA. Is it?

DIMETOS. I think so. It didn't move. Must have crawled onto that rock during the night and died. It wasn't there yesterday. I wouldn't have noticed it if it wasn't for a bad smell on the way back. At first I thought it was something in one of the pools. Then I saw the gulls.

SOPHIA. Your stones disturbed them.

DIMETOS. I know. Didn't take them long to settle down again though, did it? There's a good meal for them there.

SOPHIA. I see.

DIMETOS [*moving away from the window*]. Yes . . . they're essentially scavengers.

SOPHIA. Just lie there and rot. It's going to stink.

DIMETOS. Unfortunately yes. When the wind turns we will know all about it.

[*He empties his pockets of a collection of stones and shells onto a small table already cluttered with similar debris. Sophia leaves the window.*]

SOPHIA. A good walk?

DIMETOS. Yes. Almost too pleasant. I'm getting a little tired of this perfect weather now. It's beginning to feel as if there is nothing left to happen except a blue sky and calm water. I don't think I've ever seen the sea so still in the . . . time we've been here.

SOPHIA. Here? This one? Three years now.

DIMETOS. You say that as if you've counted the days.

SOPHIA. Not deliberately.

DIMETOS. Three years. As long as that.

SOPHIA. Is it time to move again?

DIMETOS. I don't think so.

SOPHIA. That's good. Because I don't know what you would do if it was. We can't go any further, you know. This is the limit. There is nowhere from here except back.

DIMETOS. I'm content here. Aren't you?

SOPHIA [*She is staring at him.*] What do you shout at the sea? You were standing at the edge of the water, looking out over the waves. You put your hands to your mouth and shouted something. I couldn't hear.

DIMETOS. Oh that! Just a game. The little waves were lively, full of surprise. Almost as if the sea wanted to play. I thought maybe that *that* innocence was still possible. So I threw it my name. The waves will break it up and tomorrow, after high tide, I'll pick up the pieces.

SOPHIA. So that is what they are.

DIMETOS. The pieces of my name.

SOPHIA. Is the sea obliging, Dimetos? Does it always let you win? As a little boy you would never play if there was a chance of losing.

DIMETOS. It's not one of those games. There's no winning or losing. We play just for the fun of it.

SOPHIA. Throwing stones and playing games. You know what that sounds like, don't you? Dimetos's hands have come to an end. That's a lament worthy of a poet. It was strange seeing you so helpless you had to resort to throwing a stone. For a moment I almost saw the little boy I was led to a long time ago. Do you remember? 'Dimetos, this is Sophia. She will look after you.'

DIMETOS [holding up a round beach-rolled stone]. Look, nearly perfect. I couldn't do better if I tried. And this almost perfect shape is without a purpose. Form without a function. The sea is a clever but mad craftsman, Sophia. His is the ultimate mockery. You should relax. He ridicules my hands and all they did more than you ever will. A colossal and totally absurd energy. I imagine there is more in one tide pushing up that beach than a man uses in a life-time. The energy in one wave could build a wall. But what does it do instead? . . . polish stones until they disappear.

SOPHIA. It also makes you skip sometimes. You never tell me about the waves you don't see coming. Preserving your dignity? One caught you this afternoon. [She laughs.]

DIMETOS. Yes, one did. You watch me very carefully, Sophia, don't you?

SOPHIA. Yes.

DIMETOS. Are you frightened I might leave you?

SOPHIA. Yes. I'm frightened of that. Have you ever tried?

DIMETOS. No.

SOPHIA. I find that hard to believe.

DIMETOS. Do you? In all the years since . . . Have I ever walked too fast for you?

SOPHIA.  No, you haven't. But why? You must have surely thought about it?

DIMETOS.  Not even that. I have no argument left, Sophia . . . least of all with my fate.

SOPHIA.  So I've finally got an identity. Not mother, sister, companion or friend . . . but your fate.*

DIMETOS.  Part of it.

SOPHIA.  Not all?

DIMETOS.  No. You'd like to be, though, wouldn't you?

SOPHIA.  I'll tell you something you don't know. I've tried to leave you, and not just thought about it. Physically started walking away. Several times. You never noticed because no attempt lasted very long and do you know why? The thought of you alive—seeing, hearing, doing, and eventually forgetting . . . without me, the thought that there might be even just one moment's happiness for you, without me—was a hell I couldn't endure. [*She goes to the window.*] The wind has turned. You're right. I can smell it now. [*As she leaves the room*] Your socks must be wet. Take them off.

# Scene 3

Danilo. *Like Dimetos and Sophia, he has aged.*

DANILO.  And that is more or less how it was when I found him again. A sense of it all being over . . . all the adventures and misadventures finally parcelled up and packed away to gather dust . . . which of course was true for all of us. He was down on the beach, staring vacantly out to sea. There's a sense of retribution in the image, isn't there? Behind him land and a world of men he would never return to, who didn't want him any more, had in fact finally forgotten him. And ahead of him the ocean, a world he could not enter . . . unless he was tempted to act out a fanciful metaphor for the last adventure of all. That didn't appear to be likely, however. To all intents and purposes he had come to terms with himself in that no-man's land

between the tides, collecting his sea shells. If there was something more at work I saw no evidence of it.


## Scene 4

Danilo *finds* Dimetos *on the beach, sieving shell-grit.*

DANILO [*calling*]. Dimetos! You've forgotten!

DIMETOS. No, I haven't. Danilo.

DANILO. That's right! You're not surprised to see me?

DIMETOS. No. I half-expected you to try and find me again!
    [*They meet.*]

DANILO. It was hard enough the first time. This time it was almost
    impossible. You have a talent, Dimetos, for the remote and
    inaccessible.

DIMETOS. And you for proving they are not that.

DANILO. Did you move here directly?

DIMETOS. No. We wandered around for quite a long time, before
    ending up here.

DANILO. You covered your tracks very well.

DIMETOS. Not deliberately. Word of what had happened spread.
    Nobody would have anything to do with us.

DANILO. [*A deep breath of the sea air.*] It's at least healthy here.

DIMETOS. And quiet.

DANILO. Yes. I hardly passed a soul on the last day's travelling.

DIMETOS. A few fishermen come this way occasionally.

DANILO. It is as I expected.
    I've never forgotten the feeling I had, when I found you in that
    village, of having travelled back in time. Heaven knows that was
    primitive enough . . . but this!

DIMETOS. Shell-grit. That little bay has a rocky bottom. Waves
    and tides have reduced the shells to this. I sell it inland to the
    farmers. They feed it to their poultry.

DANILO. A very basic operation.

DIMETOS. Yes. My last apprenticeship, Danilo. To the sea. My Master's only tool is time.

[*He works. Danilo watches him.*]

DANILO. Are you alone?

DIMETOS. Haven't you seen Sophia?

DANILO. No. At the cottage?

DIMETOS. Yes.

DANILO. She must have been out. I knocked and called but no one answered.

[*They walk.*]

DIMETOS. And the city?

DANILO. In trouble as usual. But I'm resigned to that now. Crisis is obviously its permanent environment.

DIMETOS. You had a vision once, Danilo.

DANILO. Don't embarrass me. Vision. No, Dimetos. A few old cranks and their young followers still keep that word alive. The rest of us muddle along as best we can. I came across a theory the other day which struck a responsive chord. The City of the Living—our metropolis—has its origins in the City of the Dead—the necropolis. That is how it all started, apparently, with burial grounds . . . a permanent place not for the living, but the dead. Sometimes I think it's on its way back to being that. But tell me more about yourself. I suppose you left the village immediately after . . .

DIMETOS. Yes.

DANILO. I didn't imagine you would stay on.

DIMETOS. Superstition gained the upper hand. They feared bad crops. Threatened to stone us. They wouldn't let me bury her there.

DANILO. So what did you do?

DIMETOS. Nothing. We just . . . left . . . What have you come for this time, Danilo?

DANILO. To see you.

DIMETOS. About what?

DANILO. Nothing. I literally meant . . . just see you. When I got back to the city and time passed without any news of you reaching us, I assumed something had happened, that you were dead. It came as quite a shock to hear that you were in fact still alive. Because you see, Dimetos, I eventually worked out what had really happened during those five days with you. You do understand, don't you, that her death was on *my* conscience. She committed suicide because of what *I* had done. When I eventually realized that it belonged on yours . . . ! [*Pause.*] You had a guilty love for her, didn't you? When I discovered that, everything fell into place. The endless flow of wine; the frequency with which I found myself, as I thought, alone with her. Because you were watching all the time. All your sober and serious thinking about returning to the city was just a ploy to keep me on.

Those five days must rank as one of your more ingenious pieces of engineering. You used us like tools and with such consummate mastery because of your passion for your niece. She was your only real mistake . . . a miscalculation of the stress that little soul could take. So there it was. Dimetos's last piece of ingenuity. I'm sorry to rake up the past like this, but do you know what it did to me? I went back to the city, my life, despising myself. Because of that I started despising others. When I eventually stumbled on your responsibility for all that happened, and realized that mine was that measure smaller . . . it was too late. I despised myself more . . . to the extent that when I heard you were alive I couldn't even think of revenging myself for what you had done. I am here simply out of morbid curiosity to see what you have also done to yourself.

DIMETOS. What have you found, Danilo?

DANILO. Dimetos older, quieter, but tanned and healthy. Looking at you it would seem as if your actions have run dry of consequences in your life. Because you did know what you were doing, didn't you?

DIMETOS. Yes.

DANILO. And you did try to stop yourself?

DIMETOS. Yes.

DANILO. So did I. Why couldn't we? This rational intelligence of ours, our special human capacity for anticipating, predicting pain . . . our own or another's . . . as the consequence of an action, was useless, wasn't it?

DIMETOS. What are you trying to say, Danilo? What do you want?

DANILO. Punishment. Not just for you specifically, but as a fundamental law of the universe, and of a magnitude on a par with your gravity. Because without it our notions of justice manmade or natural, of good and evil, are the most pathetic illusions we have ever entertained. Maybe I came too soon. After all, you're still alive. Who knows? Who knows anything? [*Danilo goes.*]

[*Dimetos alone.*]

DIMETOS. Tide's turning. Mustn't get my feet wet again.

'. . . That flowing and swelling of the sea, or its alternate rising and falling, twice in each lunar day, due to the attraction of the moon and to a lesser degree of the sun . . . the space of time between two successive points of High Water . . .'

# Scene 5

*The cottage.* Dimetos *and* Sophia.

SOPHIA. Who was the man on the beach?

DIMETOS. Didn't you recognize him?

SOPHIA. Danilo.

DIMETOS. Yes. Where were you?

SOPHIA. Here.

DIMETOS. You didn't answer when he knocked.

SOPHIA. There are no doors left to open . . . least of all to him. What did he want?

DIMETOS. We talked about. . . the past.

SOPHIA. My God, are we still frightened of her name? So you talked about 'the past'. Did you finally confess to him?

DIMETOS. I didn't have to.

SOPHIA. He knew, did he? Had he worked it out?

DIMETOS. Yes.

SOPHIA. Everything?

DIMETOS. Just about.

SOPHIA. What did he say about me?

DIMETOS. Nothing.

SOPHIA. What did you tell him?

DIMETOS. About you? Nothing.

SOPHIA. I wasn't important, was I? Yours is unquestionably the most selfish soul I have ever known. Your life, your passion and now *your* guilt. You want to take all of that as well, don't you? [*Confronting him.*] You understand nothing. She could have been my child, you know. We were the right ages. When she first came to us I was frightened of her . . . I don't know why, but I was more frightened of her than I had been of anything before, or since. One day I found her alone, somewhere . . . her room I think . . . and I just knew, just realized that she was also frightened of me. An impulse made me tell her. When I did we just laughed, and laughed . . . and at the end of it we had adopted each other.

Do you know how to go to heaven? We worked out a way. Ten beautiful . . .

[*She speaks with sombre passion.*]

No, Dimetos. NO! She would still be alive today if I hadn't abandoned her to . . . You are not God! If I had so much as put my arm around her when she sat there wilting . . . one gentle touch, and I had it in my soul. But I was jealous and I knew, that left to your own devices, you were going to hurt her. So I went for a walk, for a long walk. [*Pause.*] A long time ago I committed myself to your life. That was a mistake, and in making it I wrecked mine utterly. That knowledge is all I'm left with. You are not going to take that away.

[*She goes to the window.*] It's really starting to stink now. Good night. [*She goes.*]

[*Dimetos is alone.*]

DIMETOS. Tides . . . Tides . . .

Let E and M be the centres of the earth and moon respectively; let R be the radius of the earth which will be assumed to be a sphere. Let ME and MM be the centres of the earth and the moon respectively. Expressed in the same units . . . Lydia . . .

. . . the attractive force of the earth on a unit mass on its surface is G, where G is the force of Gravity on the earth's surface . . . Lydia. . .

. . . since the attractive force varies directly as the mass and inversely as the square of the distance . . . Lydia . . .

. . . since the attractive force varies directly as the mass and inversely as the square of the distance . . . Lydia.

. . . at new and full moons when these times and tides coincide, the crest would be under the moon, and at the quadrature, the solar wave crest and trough combining symmetrically with the lunar wave crest and trough respectively, produce merely a difference in height and not in displacement . . . LYDIA!

[*Pause.*]

Don't look, Dimetos. Don't look.

Lydia . . .

The silence chokes on your name, as if that knot will never let another sound into the world. I am going to try to let you down. That won't be easy . . . because there is no measure to the distance between your feet and the earth they never reached. But I've got hands . . . all I need to do . . . is use them . . .

## Scene 6

Dimetos *and* Sophia. *Sophia holds a handkerchief to her nose. Dimetos is at the table fiddling compulsively with his beach debris.*

SOPHIA. All the windows are closed but that only seems to have made it worse. It's trapped in here now. The smell of decay has itself started to decay. [*She is at the window. She laughs.*] The birds are so gorged they can't leave that rock. The wind is bowling

them off it like ten-pins. There goes another one! [*She prowls.*]
You said it wouldn't last long.

DIMETOS. It's only been blowing for three days.

SOPHIA. And done nothing but get stronger.

DIMETOS. Once it's reached its peak it will start to abate.

SOPHIA. That better be soon. I can't stand it much longer.

DIMETOS. If you find it so intolerable . . .

SOPHIA. Don't you?

DIMETOS [*trying to ignore the interruption*]. . . . if you find it so intolerable go away until it's all over.

SOPHIA. Go away.

   [*Pause.*]

DIMETOS. You're free to do so.

SOPHIA. Very clever, Dimetos. If I didn't know otherwise I could
believe that you'd hauled that bloody thing onto the rock deliberately. Stink her out! You'd try anything, wouldn't you? No.
You won't get rid of me that easily. [*Watching him.*] And if you
want to do something with your hands why don't you try hauling it off. You've done nothing but fidget and fiddle for days. A
rotting carcass can't surely defeat a great engineer.

DIMETOS. Stop it, Sophia!

SOPHIA. Or put them in your pockets since your toys don't make
them happy any more. That's what naughty boys do. I had to
smack yours once or twice for that, remember? Is that when you
fell in love with your hands?

   [*He ignores her. She sits down at her end of the table, where there is a
small heap of lemon leaves. She starts crushing them in her hands and
smelling them.*]

These are the last few left. I've stripped the tree bare. Didn't
help anyway . . . or if anything only made it worse . . . like
making filth palatable. It's permeating everything . . . even
thinking makes me want to vomit. What should we try next? Go
for a nice long walk Dimetos, and find us a sweet-smelling herb
native to these parts* to spice the prevailing odour of death and
decay. You haven't been out for days.

DIMETOS. The weather outside is not very inviting . . .

SOPHIA [*cutting him*]. Nor for that matter the weather inside! First time I've known that to stop you though. I thought you liked your playmate in his unruly moods. You should see him. He's throwing everything around on that beach except . . . A moment's respite from you would also be a relief. I used to enjoy watching your hands work, but their present idiocy is driving me mad. What are you trying to do!

DIMETOS. [*His compulsive fiddling with his shells and stones has now become obsessive. His hands seem to have a life of their own.*] Nothing . . . just . . .

SOPHIA. Playing another game.

DIMETOS. Yes. It's like a puzzle. I can't believe that these don't somehow . . . fit together . . . that a human intelligence can't make sense of them . . .

SOPHIA. But they do?

DIMETOS [*desperate innocence*]. They do . . . ?

SOPHIA. Yes . . . your name. Don't you remember. They spell D-I-M-E-T-O-S . . .

DIMETOS. NO.

SOPHIA. What's the matter?

DIMETOS. Nothing.

SOPHIA. What was that thought? [*Dimetos shakes his head. Sophia is watching him carefully.*] I'll find out . . . unless this wind doesn't turn and we die of suffocation.

What an end. They survived their own consciences and other men's stoning, but were suffocated to death by the stench of a carcass. [*Violently.*] Don't you also smell the damned thing!

DIMETOS. Stop talking about it!

SOPHIA. Silence only makes it worse. I refuse to surrender to it. You know something . . . sometimes it seems as if you are doing more than just endure it . . . that you refuse to admit it's there.

DIMETOS. When the wind turns . . .

SOPHIA [*hysterically*]. There's a rotten carcass on that rock, Dimetos!

DIMETOS. Sophia!

SOPHIA. Then tell me what's in your mind!

[*Dimetos is too exhausted, too desperate, to put up any further defence.*]

DIMETOS. A dream . . .

SOPHIA. When?

DIMETOS. The night before last.

SOPHIA. The day Danilo was here?

DIMETOS. Yes.

SOPHIA. What happened?

DIMETOS. I can't remember.

SOPHIA. Try.

DIMETOS. I have. I woke up with my hands . . . desperate . . . they had to do something . . . but it eludes me. There are moments when I seem on the point of remembering . . .

SOPHIA. I'll help you.

DIMETOS [*frightened*]. No.

[*Pause . . . Sophia and Dimetos look at each other in their separate and private desperations.*]

SOPHIA. It's . . . Lydia . . . isn't it?

DIMETOS. She's still hanging there. I can't get her down. Time is passing, Sophia. . .

SOPHIA. That's what is really stinking in this room. She messed herself when she reached the end of that rope. I had to clean her. [*She goes to the window.*] Lydia. [*Pause.*] There is a woman somewhere, sitting . . . immobile but not frozen . . . she will move again. Warm and beautiful, but one eye . . . her head is turned in profile . . . is fixed on something evil, ugly . . . like a hawk's eye. I found her . . . at the end of a long walk . . . which I had taken to put a lot of distance between myself and something I was afraid of. . . something inevitable.

It wasn't easy.

As I walked, the day changed . . . the sun bleached all colour out of the world . . . places and things which I passed, and knew, were strange and ugly. But I kept on . . . because I had an appointment. My sense of it was so strong I started to run. The road got stonier and stonier.

I reached the pool. The water was dark, and turgid. The day was night. That is where I found her . . . sitting, waiting for me . . . her knees drawn up under her chin. Her feet are misshapen . . . her hair, long and soft, lies gently around her face. But it's all a lie. There is something wrong with her. She keeps company with a donkey, an owl, a griffin, a bat and an old, million-year-old turtle.

There is a terrible familiarity between herself and the entrance to hell, which is just behind her.* She goes in and out. She was waiting for me. If I could tell you . . . If you could help me . . . I loved Dimetos.

[*She leaves the window and goes to him. He no longer registers her presence. She puts out a hand and touches him gently and then laughs for the second time. At the end of it she leaves him. Dimetos is alone.*]

DIMETOS. Time is passing . . . nowhere to nowhere . . . Time is at work . . . [*Pause.*] Work . . . Work!

The effect produced in any mass by a force acting against iner-tia or resistance . . . an effect that may merely result in strain or produce motion of the mass . . . the rate of work is Power . . . because power takes account of Time . . . Force, work, power! Apply them . . . [*Using his beach debris he goes to work.*] . . . make a tool, a Machine That Will Stop Time . . .
Machine, a primary machine.
The lever! First order. Fulcrum between force and weight . . . crowbar, pumphandle . . .

[*It doesn't stop time.*]

No. Second order. Weight between fulcrum and force . . . wheel-barrow, nutcracker . . .

[*It also doesn't stop time.*]

No. Third order. Force between weight and fulcrum . . . treadle

of a lathe, sugar tongs, forearm . . . No. Still passing . . . moving
. . . Motion!
Every body will maintain its state of rest or of uniform motion
in a straight line unless compelled by some external force to
change that state and this rate of change is directly proportional
to the force and takes place in the direction of that force.
. . . to every action there is an equal and opposite reaction . . .
. . . because every particle of matter in the universe attracts
every other particle with a force whose direction is that of the
line joining the two and whose magnitude is directly as the
product of the masses and inversely as the square of the distance from each other . . . Time stinks. Time stinks! [*He is totally
defeated.*] What must I do?

LYDIA'S VOICE. Keep calm. Don't be frightened. Can you hear
me clearly?

DIMETOS. Yes.

VOICE. Your hands. Find your hands. Look at them. They are
useless. The only tool a man can make that will help him hold
time, is a Story. The theory is very simple: adapting the principle
of a lever of the first order we will place in exact opposition, on
a common pivot, the clean edges of a beginning, and an end.
The beginning, Dimetos. Make a beginning . . .

DIMETOS. Beginning . . . 'The point at which anything starts or
commences . . .' Once upon a time . . .

VOICE. Now the end.

DIMETOS. For ever after.

VOICE. And now the pivot.

DIMETOS. Pivot . . . 'That on which anything turns or depends . . .
the cardinal, central or vital point . . .' There was.

VOICE. Now put them together.

DIMETOS. Once upon a time . . . there was . . . for ever after. Once
upon a time . . . there was . . . for ever after.

[*He begins to play with the words . . . repetition of them all in sequence
and individual elements. From a clumsy, awkward start we see a facility*

*develop. He tries every conceivable variation. At the end he is handling them with the facility of a consummate story-teller.*]

VOICE. You've made your tool, Dimetos. Now comes the hard part. Use it.

DIMETOS. Once upon a time, there was . . . a man . . . who dreamt he was a horse. He had fallen out of the world into a place where it was cold and dark and he was frightened. And because he was an animal, that fear lasted for ever. There was no hoping or waiting for help, just successive eternities of cold mud, the darkness in his very open eyes, and nowhere to go. He tried, but there was nowhere else to go.

And so, it was from nowhere that she came. And from her first sound and touch, to the last heavy loss of her weight when she went back to nowhere, he trusted her. He wasn't alone.

They pulled him up. He galloped away. And the place where he had been, the thing that had happened to him, also went back to nowhere. But that night under a tree, with the world around him once again the way it was when he first found it, he remembered her and wanted her. And because of this, his desire to possess her was so great that that night he dreamt his hooves turned into hands. Because of this, he had to stand very still, hold on to the grass very tight, because he couldn't walk. The danger of falling again was very real. Another eternity of fear followed until she came a second time, from nowhere, and was on his back again. She was laughing and he understood from that, that she wanted him to gallop away with her into the world. But he couldn't move. His hooves were hands. He was frightened of falling. So she left him.

And because of this, his torment was so great that that night, he dreamt he was a man. He could walk. His hands were free. He could work. And because he was a man, he could hope now and wait. And while he was hoping and waiting he put his hands to work making a world for her so that he could hear her laugh again the way she had when he was a horse. Eternities of making and working passed while he waited and hoped. He mastered the four elements of the universe. He disciplined water in pipes, air in bellows, fire in furnaces and the earth he shaped with the extravagance of a profligate. But she never came.

And because of this, his despair was so great, that that night he dreamt his hands without himself. A voice was talking to them: 'All you ever wanted to do was possess. All you've ever made were tools and machines to help you do that. It is now time for the skills you scorned. Find something and hold it. Close that powerful hand on a thing. Yours. Hold it! The act of defiance man has made his creed. The mortal human hold! Now give it away. Don't be frightened. Only to your other hand. It will still be yours. That's right. Hold it. Tight. That was a terrible second when they were both empty. One still is. Find something. Quickly! Now comes the hard part . . . so listen carefully. Each must give what it has got to the other, at the same time. You must give and take with the same action.

Again . . . and again . . .

[*Dimetos's hands juggle. He starts to laugh . . . and laughs and laughs.*]

And now, because your gaiety is so great, the last skill of all. Hold them out, and wait . . .

CURTAIN

# THE GUEST

*devised by*

Athol Fugard and Ross Devenish

*The Guest at Steenkampskraal* had its world première on BBC2 on 5 March 1977. It was released in South African cinemas as THE GUEST on 13 September 1977. Director: Ross Devenish. Cast:

| | |
|---|---|
| MARAIS | Athol Fugard |
| VISSER | Marius Weyers |
| OOM DOORS | Gordon Vorster |
| TANT CORRIE | Wilma Stockenström |
| DOORSIE | James Borthwick |
| LOUIS | Emile Aucamp |
| LITTLE CORRIE | Susan Maclennan |
| BRENDA | Trix Pienaar |
| STUURIE | Thomas Masicane |
| LILLY | Grace Ndlovu |

This script is based on an episode in Leon Rousseau's *Die Groot Verlange* (Cape Town: Human & Rousseau, 1974). The authors wish to thank the following for permission to quote: Human & Rousseau (*The Soul of the Ape*; *The Soul of the White Ant*; *My Friends the Baboons*) and J. L. van Schaik, Pretoria ('Die Spinnerak-rokkie', 'Diep Rivier', and 'Die Lied van Suid-Afrika', in Eugène N. Marais, *Versamelde Gedigte*; 'Lotos-land' in *Gedigte van A. G. Visser*).

We would also like to thank the many people who helped in the making of the film, especially Leon Rousseau, Eugène Charles Marais, and Bill Morton.

# NOTES ON CHARACTERS

A. G. VISSER. Forty-eight years old. Marais' doctor and very close friend. In South African literature Visser occupies a place in every sense as big as that of Marais. Like the latter, a complex and sophisticated man of the world. Studied for his medical degree in Edinburgh. It is doubtful whether at any point in Marais' life he had as total a friendship with any other man. A marvelous sense of humor and rapier-quick wit.

OOM DOORS. In his late sixties. The typical patriarch, strong and resolute in his own world. The encounter with Marais, however, becomes an excursion into an area of human behavior about which he knows nothing and with which he cannot cope—a transition from easy optimism at the beginning of the film to defeat at the end.

TANT CORRIE. Oom Doors' wife, a few years younger. A firm but compassionate woman, marked by a hard life and bitter experience. Like the rest of her family, this simple Afrikaner woman understands nothing of Marais' dilemma. In the final analysis, however, she forgives him for everything because of the pain she witnesses. Marais' incredible charisma and charm is not without its effect on her, especially during the period of his recovery.

DOORSIE. Shy and introspective. A physically big man but also gentle, with a sly sense of humor when relaxed. Like his father, Oom Doors, and for that matter the rest of the family, he has an absolute faith that a righteous life needs no other wisdom than that contained in the Bible. In this the family is archetypally Calvinist. Shares with his mother a compassionate response to the hell that Marais lives through at Steenkampskraal.

LOUIS. The polar opposite of Doorsie his brother—extrovert and brash. Shares his father's naïve conviction that fresh air and farm food will cure all Marais' troubles. When this in fact doesn't happen, he loses all patience with the latter's condition. There is finally a substantial measure of ill feeling between him and

Marais, to the extent that Louis virtually waits for the relapse that overwhelms Marais at the end of the film.

LITTLE CORRIE. Nine years old. The youngest of Oom Doors' children. A plain, almost unattractive little girl—particularly during the first half of the film when she treats Marais with suspicion and fear. Once Marais' recovery has started and he succeeds in winning her friendship, this changes. The trust he wins and the pleasure he gives leads to a strong change in our image of her. The natural innocence of a child surfaces and we end up liking her.

BRENDA. Thirty-six years old. A widow.

STUURIE. An African employee. Entrusted with the task of collecting Marais' weekly supply of drugs from Dr. Visser.

LILLY. An African domestic employee.

Road. Exterior. Day.

*Highveld winter landscape. Wide and empty. A farm road in the Heidelberg district of the Transvaal. Moving slowly along it is a herd of cattle, followed by an African shepherd in an old overcoat. A car drives up and is forced by the animals to slow down. The shepherd breaks into a jog beside it, waving his kierie and shouting to clear a path. Framed by one of the windows of the car is the pale and gaunt face of a man. He is staring vacantly into space. No reaction to what is happening around him. The car clears the herd of cattle. The African watches it disappear in a cloud of dust. The car carefully negotiates a drift in the Suikerbosrivier.*

Car. Interior. Day.

*The driver. A handsome, well-groomed man in his late forties, his apparent ease belied by the occasional and furtive glance at his passenger.*

Car. Interior. Day.

*The passenger sitting impassively. His devastated condition now fully apparent.*

Road. Exterior. Day.

*The car passes a signboard displaying the words 'Steenkampskraal Doors Meyer.'*

Car. Interior. Day.

*The two men.*

DRIVER. Simple decent people. You'll like them. Please, boetie, don't waste any energy or time being embarrassed. They've been told just as much as they need to know.

*The passenger looks at the driver.*

PASSENGER. How much was that, Andries? How much does anyone need to know about Eugène Marais?

*The two men are Andries Visser and Eugène Marais. The year is 1926.*

Farmhouse. Exterior. Day.

*Oom Doors, Tant Corrie, Doorsie and Little Corrie on the stoep watching the approach of the car. It drives past a smiling Louis into the farmyard. Oom Doors leaves the group on the stoep to meet the guests. With the exception of*

*Visser's occasional visits, these five people will be Marais' only civilized company over the next few months.*

Car. Interior. Day.
*Visser and Marais. Visser opens his door. Marais doesn't move.*

VISSER. Eugène?

*No response from Marais who is watching Oom Doors approach.*

Eugène, please!

Car. Interior. Day.
*Oom Doors' face and voice startlingly large at the window on Marais' side.*

OOM DOORS. Welcome to Steenkampskraal, Advocate Marais.*

*Marais doesn't respond.*

Car. Exterior. Day.
*Marais, Visser with a suitcase and his doctor's bag, and Oom Doors. Marais is wearing a pair of white tackies without laces, white trousers held up by a tie around his waist, shirt with a crumpled collar and open at the neck, and a black blazer beneath an overcoat. A sense of total physical neglect. He shakes hands with Oom Doors indifferently.*

VISSER. Good afternoon, Oom Doors.

OOM DOORS. Hello, Doctor! Come meet the family.

*Oom Doors takes the suitcase from the back of the car.*

VISSER. How's the leg, Oom Doors?

OOM DOORS. Ag, much better thank you, Doctor. Much better. You know, I had to kick Stuurie's backside the other day and it didn't hurt a bit.

*He laughs at his own joke.*

VISSER. Good afternoon, Tant Corrie, Doorsie.

TANT CORRIE. Afternoon, Dr. Visser.

Farmhouse. Exterior. Day.
*The stoep. Oom Doors and his family, Visser and Marais.*

OOM DOORS. Advocate Marais, this is my wife, Corrie.

TANT CORRIE. Pleased to meet you.

OOM DOORS. And my son, Doorsie, and this is our little laat

lammetjie . . . this is Little Corrie . . . and it was Louis who opened the gate for you.

*Hands are shaken.*

TANT CORRIE.  I've just taken some rusks out of the oven.

*Marais looks desperately at Visser.*

VISSER.  I think Advocate Marais would like to rest first, Tant Corrie. He's . . .

TANT CORRIE.  Of course.

OOM DOORS.  Yes, follow me.

*Oom Doors leads Marais and Visser through the house.*

Bedroom. Interior. Day.

*Oom Doors ushering Marais and Visser into the bedroom which Marais will occupy during his stay at Steenkampskraal.*

OOM DOORS.  Well . . . it's not as grand as you're used to I'm sure, but we'll do our best to make you comfortable.

VISSER.  We know you will, Oom Doors. I'll just help Advocate Marais to unpack, then I'll be with you . . .

OOM DOORS.  So . . . just call if you need anything.

*Oom Doors leaves the room, closing the door carefully behind him. Visser looks anxiously at Marais, then helps him take off his overcoat.*

VISSER.  Sit down, Eugène.

*Marais sits on the bed. After closing his eyes for a few seconds he looks around the room. Visser opens the suitcase and starts to unpack. One of the items in the suitcase is a small leather pouch which we will come to know well. Visser places this on a little table beside Marais' bed.*

I also brought your papers on the baboon.* They'll move a table in here as soon as you're ready to start working again.

MARAIS.  Where will they put it, Andries? Three beds?

*The two men look at each other.*

VISSER.  Louis and Doorsie have agreed to sleep in here with you until you feel better. [*Sits beside Marais on the bed.*] Listen, Eugène . . . boetie . . . I know it won't be easy, but you've done it before and you can do it again.

MARAIS.  Easy? No, Andries. You don't know. [*His condition has*

*deteriorated still further: he is sweating and trembling slightly.*] When will
I see you again?

VISSER. Oh, don't think like that, boetie. Steenkampskraal isn't
all that far from Heidelberg. I'll come out whenever I've got a
spare moment.

*Visser stands up.*

MARAIS. Not yet! We . . . haven't discussed everything properly.

VISSER. Yes we have.

MARAIS. You can't just leave me like this . . .

VISSER. I have to, Eugène.

*Visser takes a small glass phial out of his pocket.*

MARAIS. It's not going to work, Andries.

VISSER. Yes it will. Here. Better take these now.

*Visser hands the phial over to Marais. This has the effect of silencing him. He
then leaves the room immediately. It is with a sense of relief that he closes the
door behind him.*

Voorkamer. Interior. Day.

*Oom Doors and Visser. A large and comfortable room very typical of the
period. Family portraits are amongst those of the presidents of the former
republics. Visser hands over to Oom Doors the box of pills.*

VISSER. I've brought you a week's supply, Oom Doors. You know
how many to give.

OOM DOORS. Ja, ten in the morning and ten in the evening until
you tell me otherwise.

*The subject has obviously already been discussed with Oom Doors who has
memorized instructions.*

VISSER. Under no condition more or less until you hear from me.
We must give him time to settle in first. Now, when I think we
are ready to start reducing the dosage, I will either come out
myself or send you a letter with Stuurie when he comes to fetch
a week's supply.

OOM DOORS. That's on Mondays.

VISSER. Right. Now warn Stuurie that he must not take any mes-
sages from Advocate Marais to anyone in town.

OOM DOORS. Yes, Doctor.

VISSER. Remember what I said, Oom Doors . . . he's a . . . he's very sick so it won't be easy, but Advocate Marais could become Chief Justice if we can get him back to good health. Who else will know where they are?

OOM DOORS. Nobody, Doctor.

Farmyard. Exterior. Day.
*Louis and Doorsie are examining Visser's car. Oom Doors and Visser stand to one side exchanging a last word.*

VISSER. Oom Doors, try to get the others to understand. You're all still strangers to him. He will feel lonely and . . . embarrassed . . . because of his condition . . . to start with. But most important of all, under no circumstances more or less than I told you.

OOM DOORS. Yes, of course.

VISSER. He's a very sick man but also a very clever one. And when a clever man gets desperate . . .

OOM DOORS. I understand, Doctor. But Steenkampskraal will get him right.

VISSER. I hope so, Oom Doors, because he is also a very dear friend of mine.

OOM DOORS. Doctor, we will treat him like one of the family.

VISSER. Thank you.

OOM DOORS. Goodbye.

TANT CORRIE. Doctor! Doctor!

*Oom Doors halts the Doctor's progress to the car.*

A karmenaadjie. We slaughtered yesterday.

*Tant Corrie gives Dr. Visser a small basket, neatly covered with a cloth.*

VISSER. Tant Corrie, you're a dear. Thank you.

Car. Interior. Day.
*Visser driving back to Heidelberg. No 'appearances' now that he is alone.*

Farmyard. Exterior. Day.
*Oom Doors, Tant Corrie, Louis and Doorsie watching Visser's car driving away. They stroll back to the house.*

DOORSIE. He looks sick, hey, Pa?

OOM DOORS. Ja, well that's why he's here. Fresh air and your mother's cooking . . . that's what he needs. [*Afterthought*] . . . And his medicine, of course.

LOUIS. How must we call him, Pa? 'Advocate' Marais or 'Mister' Marais?

OOM DOORS. Hell, Louis, I don't know. Maybe he's even a bloody professor!

*Father and sons, particularly Louis, enjoy the implied importance of their guest.*

Bedroom. Interior. Day.

*The leather pouch which Visser unpacked. It is open and has produced a hypodermic syringe, candle stub and teaspoon. Marais is preparing an injection. He is suffering acutely. Over these images we hear Marais' voice, calm and detached.*

MARAIS [*voice-over*]. It is to those temperaments in which pain is a predominant element of consciousness, and in which some quality of suffering is inseparable from thought, that all joy-creating poisons constitute the greatest threat. All of them have one property in common . . . the first, and chief, physiological effect is a temporary feeling of happiness which wears off as the poison is eliminated by the system.

Kitchen. Interior. Night.

*Oom Doors, Doorsie, Louis and Little Corrie seated at a large table, ready to start supper. Two vacant places. Tant Corrie knocks on Marais' bedroom door, and when there is no answer she tries the handle.*

TANT CORRIE. Mr. Marais? Mr. Marais? The door is still locked.

OOM DOORS. Come over here. The doctor said the pills would make him sleepy.

TANT CORRIE. But he must also eat, Doors.

OOM DOORS. Ja . . . ag, Louis, won't you go outside by the window and see if he's all right.

Bedroom. Interior. Night.

*The room in darkness. Marais lying on his bed, staring vacantly at the window. He hears something tapping at it. He lights a candle and goes to the window. In its light we see Marais' face reflected in the glass.*

LOUIS. It's only me—Louis! [*Pause.*] Supper's ready . . . something wrong, Mr. Marais?

*Marais stares around him, almost as if he were seeing the room for the first time, unaware now of Louis's voice.*

Kitchen. Interior. Night.

*Oom Doors, Tant Corrie, Louis, Doorsie and Little Corrie eating. Relaxed and easy conversation. The subject is Marais. Louis shows how impressed he is by the fact that Steenkampskraal has been honored by such an important guest.*

LOUIS. How many books do you think he's written, Pa?

OOM DOORS. How many? [*Snort of admiration.*] More than I could ever read in what's left of my time . . . that's for sure.

LOUIS. Maybe we'll be in one of them one day. With a picture. How's that? Louis Meyer and Eugène Marais!

*All laugh.*

TANT CORRIE. Leave the poor man alone now.

LOUIS. We're not saying anything bad, Ma.

TANT CORRIE. I didn't say you were. But I think all this sort of talk is just going to make things harder for him. Let's treat him like . . . one of the family . . . like any other ordinary person.

LOUIS. But he's not, Ma. Dr. Visser said so himself.

DOORSIE. What is now actually wrong with him, Pa?

OOM DOORS [*in all innocence*]. Man, as I understand it from the Doctor, it's a sort of fever.

DOORSIE. Fever?

OOM DOORS. Mm. You know, hot and cold with shivers and so on. One thing I do know, his medicine is bliksem strong.

Kitchen. Interior. Night.

*Oom Doors, with spectacles, reading from the Bible. Listening respectfully, the rest of the family.*

OOM DOORS. '. . . de amandelboom zal bloeijen, en dat de sprinkhaan zich zelven een last zal wezen, en dat de lust zal vergaan: want de mensch gaat naar zijn eeuwig huis, en de rouwklagers zullen in de straat omgaan.'*

*Closes the Bible, takes off spectacles; all kneel.*

Almighty and merciful Father, we thank thee for this day, for food, clothing and shelter . . . and please God, extend thy mercy to the sick man who has taken shelter under our roof. Hallowed be thy name. Amen.

Dream. Rock ledge. Exterior. Night.

*Marais and baboons. Sounds of an African night. Baboons huddled together on the rock ledge. Marais, naked, is huddled among them.*

Bedroom. Interior. Night.

*Marais stumbling about, totally disorientated.*

MARAIS.  Don't throw! Don't throw stones!

*Doorsie and Louis wake up. A moment of complete confusion until the candle is lit. Louis jumps out of bed.*

LOUIS.  Mr. Marais!

MARAIS.  Leave them alone . . .

*Louis grabs Marais and shakes him.*

LOUIS.  Mr. Marais!! Wake up!

*Marais slowly establishes himself in the reality of the room. He looks at the window. There is nothing there. Doorsie attempts, unsuccessfully, to get Marais back to his bed. Doorsie returns to his own bed. The two brothers look at Marais, Marais looks at them. Embarrassed smiles from Doorsie and Louis.*

LOUIS.  Are you O.K., Mr. Marais?

*Doorsie stretches out of his bed to blow out the candle.*

MARAIS.  No!

*Doorsie leaves the candle burning.*

What's the time?

*The two brothers exchange looks.*

LOUIS.  Time? We don't worry too much about the time here, Ad . . . Mr. Marais . . . uh . . . Pa's got the clock.

*Marais is staring at the window.*

MARAIS.  What's the date?

LOUIS.  Date?

DOORSIE.  Monday.

MARAIS.  The date!

LOUIS. June 1926.

*Another exchange of looks passes between the brothers.*

Bedroom. Interior. Dawn.

*The first light of dawn. The door opens and Oom Doors enters silently. He goes to Louis's bed and shakes him.*

OOM DOORS. Hey, Louis . . . sh-sh-sh . . . Wake up! Be quiet.

*Goes over to Doorsie and he too is wakened.*

Kom, Doorsie . . . wake up . . . don't disturb the Advocate.

*Oom Doors goes over to Marais' bed and carefully places ten little pills and a glass of water beside it.*

Kitchen. Interior. Dawn.

*Oom Doors is seated near the stove pulling on his boots. Doorsie and Louis rush in and dress in front of the fire. The warmth it provides is not enough to stop them feeling the chill of a highveld winter's morning.*

OOM DOORS. Everything all right?

LOUIS. Ag, ja. He had a bad dream, that's all, Pa.

*Oom Doors pours coffee and produces rusks.*

OOM DOORS. Well, there's a lot of work to be done. Here's some nice coffee. Come.

Bedroom. Interior. Day.

*Marais' first day at Steenkampskraal. The room is like a prison cell. Most of the time he stares vacantly about him, or at objects in the room. Slowly the light in the room fades . . . outside the sun sets. It is almost time for Oom Doors to bring the pills.*

Bedroom. Interior. Night.

*Marais waiting tensely. Knock on the door. Oom Doors' voice from the other side.*

OOM DOORS' VOICE. Mr. Marais! Are you awake?

MARAIS. Come in.

*Door opens and Oom Doors comes into the room carrying a glass of water. He obviously feels awkward and uncomfortable.*

OOM DOORS. Mr. Marais . . . your medicine . . .

*The ten little pills are very small and white in his large farmer's hands. Marais takes them. A strained pause as Oom Doors stands, uncertain.*

Is there anything else I must do, Mr. Marais?

MARAIS. No, that is all.

*Oom Doors is still not certain whether he must go or stay.*

That is all, thank you!

OOM DOORS. Sorry, Mr. Marais.

*He withdraws, still carrying the glass of water.*

Kitchen. Interior. Night.

*Oom Doors outside the bedroom door. He hears the key turn in the lock.*

Bedroom. Interior. Night.

*Marais. He is preparing an injection. Sleeve of his left arm rolled up. We see the arm for the first time. It is in a dreadful condition as a result of years of injections. Throughout this ritual his face is taut and desperate. Once again we hear Marais' voice . . . cold and detached.*

MARAIS [*voice-over*]. The supreme danger which lies in the use of intoxicants as a cure for mental suffering and which often renders the remedies worse than the disease is of course the morbid organic changes resulting from habitual use. Cessation of use causes what are known as symptoms of abstinence, of a severity and painfulness proportionate to the usual dose and the duration of the habit. These symptoms are always painful and a dose of the poison invariably affords relief from their immediate effects. Long-continued usage therefore sets up in time the so-called 'double pull'—the craving for the characteristic euphoria and a dread of the painful symptoms of abstinence. There is a continual alternation between the deepest gloom of abstinence and a mental state . . . which through continuous use of the drug resembles sluggish mental anaesthesia rather than positive happiness. But for the individual concerned this temporary respite is preferable to the normal condition of suffering.

Kitchen. Interior. Night.

*Oom Doors, Tant Corrie, Little Corrie, Louis and Doorsie. Marais' place at the table is again empty.*

TANT CORRIE. Corrie, you go knock on the door and tell Mr. Marais supper is ready.

*Little Corrie shakes her head vigorously.*

178

What's the matter with you, child?

LITTLE CORRIE. He's strange.

OOM DOORS. It's all right. Louis.

*Oom Doors gestures that his son should go instead. Louis gets up with obvious irritation. He goes to Marais' bedroom and rattles the knob of an obviously very locked door.*

LOUIS. Mr. Marais! Mr. Marais!

*The family at the table listens in silence; Louis comes back and sits down.*

Pa, I'm hungry.

*Oom Doors clears his throat and starts to say grace.*

OOM DOORS. Zegen Heer hetgeen wij eten, laten wij Uw Naam nimmer vergeten. Amen.\*

Bedroom. Interior. Day.

*Another day in the prison cell for Marais, a day without prospects or interest. Suddenly Marais hears something that attracts his attention. He goes over to the window and sees Stuurie on horseback, setting off for Heidelberg. Marais knows that Stuurie will be bringing the new week's supply from Dr. Visser.*

*As the day continues, the effect of the morning's injection begins to wear off. Marais begins to experience the painful symptoms of withdrawal to which we have heard him refer. He paces up and down endlessly . . . smokes continuously.*

*At last Stuurie returns. Marais has thought of something. Anxiously he begins to look around the room. He finds a book in one of the drawers. He sits down pretending to read, waiting for the knock that he knows must eventually come.*

Bedroom. Interior. Day.

*Marais reading. Knock on the door.*

MARAIS. Come in.

*Oom Doors enters.*

OOM DOORS. There's a letter for you, Mr. Marais.

*Marais tries to smile.*

MARAIS. Oh. Spilhaus. Thank you. Sit down, Oom Doors.

OOM DOORS. How are you feeling today?

MARAIS. Not too well. I had another bad night.

OOM DOORS. Ja. My sons tell me you are not sleeping too well. Is there nothing else we can do for you?

MARAIS. Thank you, Oom Doors, but Dr. Visser and I have tried everything. Only the pills really help. That's the trouble with malaria . . .

OOM DOORS. Malaria?

MARAIS. Yes. Once it's in the bloodstream it's virtually impossible to get it out. I picked it up in East Africa.

*His performance is very good; he offers Oom Doors a cigarette; for the moment Oom Doors is fooled.*

There were fourteen of us. I had organized an expedition to get ammunition and medical supplies through to our people.

*Oom Doors nods. He also has memories.*

OOM DOORS. The war?

MARAIS. Yes.

OOM DOORS. Ja, in the end, you know, we ended up counting our bullets more carefully than I've ever counted the money in my pocket. It almost hurt to take aim at a rooinek and pull the trigger. [*Laughs.*] What happened to the expedition?

MARAIS. They died. One by one. It's a terrible region for malaria.

OOM DOORS. Terrible.

MARAIS. In the end it was just a Dr. Schultz and myself. But even we had caught it. An Indian doctor kept us alive . . . with the pills. That's how it all started.* It varies of course. Sometimes, for years, I can do with virtually nothing. Other times, when it gets out of hand, I've got to increase the dosage.

OOM DOORS. Yes, of course.

MARAIS. In fact, I think it has come to that again.

*Oom Doors, nodding his head, is listening innocently.*

OOM DOORS. What do you mean, Mr. Marais?

MARAIS. I think I should increase the dosage for the next few days. Fourteen or even sixteen pills instead of ten.

*Pause. Without giving anything away, Oom Doors is suddenly on his guard.*

OOM DOORS. Mr. Marais, Dr. Visser won't like that at all you know. He's trying to reduce the number of pills, not increase them.

MARAIS. He doesn't know how badly I've been sleeping.

OOM DOORS. But I told him in my last letter, and he said I mustn't change anything unless he tells me to.

MARAIS. I'm not asking for the lot!

OOM DOORS. Please, Mr. Marais. With these pills and things, I don't know what is a lot and what isn't.

*Marais is aghast with the knowledge that he has failed.*

You must excuse me now. This brandsiekte is beginning to get out of hand, you know. Castor oil for cows . . . that's what I know about.

*Oom Doors doesn't give Marais a chance to say anything more. He leaves the room.*

Farmyard. Exterior. Day.

*Marais and Little Corrie. Little Corrie is swinging, singing softly to herself. Marais is sitting on a bench in the sun. His rejection of Steenkampskraal and its people is summed up in the indifference with which he watches the child. Suddenly Little Corrie realizes that Marais is watching her. Immediately her humming stops and she stares back at Marais. Intimidated by her look he gets up and goes back inside.*

Kitchen. Interior. Night.

*Oom Doors and family, and this time also Marais. The evening meal . . . Calvinism and healthy appetites. Oom Doors says grace.*

OOM DOORS. Zegen Heer hergeen wij eten, laten wij Uw Naam nimmer vergeten. Amen.

*Everyone sits with bowed head except Marais. He becomes aware of someone watching him. It is Little Corrie. Another moment between the two of them.*

We're going up into the randjies tomorrow, Mr. Marais. Would you like to come with?

MARAIS. I'll see how I feel.

OOM DOORS. Fresh air will do you good. You know all this lying in bed can make a man feel worse than he really is.

LOUIS. We must take guns, Pa!

OOM DOORS. Mm.

LOUIS. It's getting to time for the guinea-fowl.

*Marais pecks away apathetically at his food.*

OOM DOORS. Yes, there's guinea-fowl and quail and partridge.

LOUIS. Do you hunt Mr. Marais?

MARAIS. I have.

LOUIS. Doorsie is the marksman in our family.

DOORSIE. You're too impatient, that's all.

OOM DOORS. He's right you know.

*Louis shakes his head and smiles at Marais. Tant Corrie has been watching Marais with quiet concern.*

TANT CORRIE. Mr. Marais, please try to eat something.

MARAIS. I'm . . . sorry, I'm not hungry. Please excuse me.

*Marais gets up and leaves the room. The family eats in silence for a few seconds. Oom Doors shakes his head.*

LITTLE CORRIE. When's he going?

TANT CORRIE. Corrie!

*Oom Doors puts down his knife and fork and looks at his daughter sternly.*

OOM DOORS. Advocate Marais is a guest in this house. Don't let me ever hear you ask that question again.

Bedroom. Interior. Night.

*Doorsie and Louis in their nightclothes, watching Marais. The latter's condition has deteriorated still further. Although asleep, he is tossing restlessly in his bed and sweating.*

LOUIS. Look. And that's what Pa calls getting better.

*Marais has not put the hypodermic syringe back in its box. The two brothers see it for the first time.*

DOORSIE. He's sicker than we think.

LOUIS. Fancy yourself as a doctor, hey?

DOORSIE. Don't joke about it, Louis. The man is suffering.

*Louis goes over to Marais' bedside intending to blow out the candle beside him.*

What're you doing?

LOUIS. Ag no, man! I can't sleep with that damned light . . .

*Doorsie forces Louis to give up the attempt and sullenly Louis gets into bed.*

DOORSIE. He's in for another bad night.

LOUIS. And so are we.

*Marais, who is dreaming, opens his mouth in a silent scream; over this image we hear Marais' voice and we dissolve through to Marais sitting on his bed talking.*

Bedroom. Interior. Night.

MARAIS. . . . we were standing in the dark . . . watching it . . . when the baby cried for the first time. Hansie! Do you know what you are looking at? Something that millions of people never saw because they died . . . too soon.

*Louis, who is trying to sleep, opens his eyes and glares at Marais; unaware of the discomfiture that he is causing, Marais continues.*

King Harold felt it was an omen of misfortune. Tamaria could never remember its name. She called it 'Eugène's star.' It has an orbit of the most extreme ellipticity. At aphelion, Halley's Comet is thirty-five times more distant from the sun than the earth is at its mean distance.

*Louis's anger can scarcely be contained, but Marais still continues.*

When it comes back, Hansie, we'll all be . . .

LOUIS [*shouting*]. Marais! Shut up! I want to sleep!

*Slowly Marais blows out the candle and then lies down.*

Dream. Exterior. Night.

*The pale square of a window. The silhouette of a dark form appears slowly. As if watching a print in a developing tray, the head of a baboon floats into focus out of the darkness.*

Pantry. Interior. Day.

*Tant Corrie at work trying to ignore an argument between Oom Doors and Marais.*

MARAIS[*off-screen*]. The difference between ten and twelve is absolutely negligible. If you know nothing about the quantities involved then let me assure you, I do.

OOM DOORS [*off-screen*]. Mr. Marais. Please be reasonable . . .

Voorkamer. Interior. Day.

*Marais, pale and trembling with anger. He hasn't shaved for a few days. A harassed and distressed Oom Doors.*

MARAIS. It's outrageous. You're treating me as if I were . . . a ten-year-old child.

OOM DOORS. Mr. Marais!

MARAIS. I've lived with my illness for thirty years now. Do you think I've learnt nothing about it?

OOM DOORS. Be reasonable, Mr. Marais. Dr. Visser gave me specific instructions . . . ten in the morning and ten at night . . . and not to change anything unless he told me to. Now please try to understand. I'm a farmer. I know nothing about these things.

MARAIS. Well, I do. So I suggest you let me look after the pills. Where are they?

OOM DOORS. Mr. Marais.

MARAIS. Oom Doors . . . !

OOM DOORS. I can't. I promised.

*Marais' face hardens.*

MARAIS. Right! Then I'm warning you . . . you take full responsibility for whatever happens to me.

Bedroom. Interior. Day.

*Marais comes in from his argument with Oom Doors and slams the door behind him. He leans against it and closes his eyes. He then pulls himself together and scratches around in a drawer for paper and pen. With a trembling hand he starts to write.*

MARAIS [*voice-over*]. Andries, in the name of God, I must have more.

Kitchen. Interior. Night.

*Oom Doors, Louis, Doorsie and Tant Corrie. Doorsie is checking the mechanism of a rifle. Tant Corrie, with sewing box, is doing some mending. Louis and Oom Doors are at the table, with paper, pen and ink for a letter which Oom Doors is going to dictate.*

LOUIS. Wragtie, Pa, you don't know what it's like in there.

OOM DOORS.  We also hear him.

LOUIS.  You've got walls between you and him. We're in the same room. And that medicine of his is beginning to stink now. I get naar when I go in there.

*Doorsie interrupts quietly.*

DOORSIE.  I can stick it out.

*Louis looks at his brother in amazement.*

LOUIS.  That's not what you said last night.

DOORSIE.  Ja well, you know what it's like when you want to sleep. But hell, Louis . . . so does he. If it's hard for us . . . ! I don't want to be in his shoes.

LOUIS.  He hasn't got any.

TANT CORRIE.  Louis!

OOM DOORS.  You're forgetting your place and your manners, my son. Now come on . . . let's get on with the letter.

*Louis withdraws into a taciturn silence after this reprimand; Oom Doors starts dictating and Louis writes.*

'Dear Dr. Visser' . . . have you got . . . ? 'I take my pen in hand to write to you and tell how things are here at Steenkampskraal . . . here at Steenkampskraal' . . . big letter 'S' and full-stop . . . 'Mr. Marais . . .' No. No. Make that 'Advocate Marais is fine . . .'

*Louis stops writing and looks up at his father, dumbfounded; Oom Doors is embarrassed.*

It's true. It's happening just like the Doctor said it would. Write.

*With a shake of his head Louis returns to the letter; Oom Doors continues.*

'. . . Advocate Marais is fine . . . but he is being a bit difficult about the pills. A little bit difficult about the pills . . .' Fullstop. 'However . . . I have not given in to him.'

Farmyard. Exterior. Day.

*Oom Doors talking to Stuurie who is ready for his weekly ride into Heidelberg.*

OOM DOORS.  Now, Stuurie, this goes to the Doctor, hey.

*Stuurie nods and rides off.*

Bedroom. Interior. Day.

*Marais alone, asleep. Knock on the door. Tant Corrie comes in with a tray. Her calling of his name wakes him. Food is the last thing Marais needs.*

TANT CORRIE. Mr. Marais . . . Mr. Marais.

MARAIS. Please, Tant Corrie!

*She has obviously resolved to be firm.*

TANT CORRIE. No . . . you listen to me. You've hardly eaten anything since you've been with us. I've watched you get weaker, not stronger. If that is all Steenkampskraal can do for you . . . [*Changes her tone.*] Just a bowl of soup?

*Marais yields, Tant Corrie watching him eat.*

What is it with those pills, Mr. Marais?

MARAIS. Didn't Dr. Visser tell you as well? I'm a sick man.

TANT CORRIE. Ja, but they're like a devil in this house . . . putting you and Doors against each other . . . angry voices! No, it's not right.

*Marais stops eating.*

MARAIS. I'm sorry, Tant Corrie . . . but I . . . I can't help myself.

*Tant Corrie and Marais look at each other. There is an honesty in the encounter and on the woman's side some premonition of what lies ahead.*

Stoep. Exterior. Day.

*Marais is waiting desperately for Stuurie's return. The road remains agonizingly empty. He paces up and down frantically, constantly watching the road.*

Farmhouse. Exterior. Day.

*Marais and Stuurie. Stuurie arrives on horseback. He hands Marais a letter.*

MARAIS. Is that all?

STUURIE. Ja, Baas.

*Marais opens the letter and starts to read. From his reaction we can surmise what Visser's reply was to his desperate plea. There is no escape from what lies ahead. He crumples the letter and throws it away as he walks back to the house.*

Kitchen. Interior. Day.

*Tant Corrie, Little Corrie, Doorsie and Louis. From the voorkamer come the sounds of another scene between Oom Doors and Marais. Tant Corrie is trying to get rid of Little Corrie.*

TANT CORRIE.  Go play outside.

LITTLE CORRIE.  I don't want to.

TANT CORRIE.  Do as I say!

*Little Corrie leaves the kitchen. Louis can't take it any longer. He gets up and moves to the front door.*

Keep out of it, Louis.

Voorkamer. Interior. Day.

*Oom Doors and Marais. Oom Doors is seated, his head between his hands, trying to block out the sound of Marais' voice. Marais—one hand on the table, the other clutching his stomach—is in a terrible condition. Severe chronic spasms make it almost impossible for him to stand.*

MARAIS.  Oom Doors, I promise you, if you help me . . . I won't ask you again.

OOM DOORS.  *Mr. Marais! I am only following Dr. Visser's instructions . . . read the bloody letter yourself if you don't believe me, man!*

MARAIS.  Then drive me into Heidelberg . . . a few moments with Dr. Visser . . . just let him see the state I'm in.

OOM DOORS.  Mr. Marais, *you are not listening to what I am saying!!!* Dr. Visser won't be back in Heidelberg . . .

MARAIS [*violently*].  You're lying! You're all lying to me!

*This is too much for Oom Doors and he walks towards the door.*

No! Don't go! I didn't mean it. Listen . . . [*Grabs hold of Oom Doors to prevent him leaving the room.*] I'll do anything Oom Doors . . . anything you say. Only, please help me. It's worse than hell, man . . . I can't stand it any longer . . .

OOM DOORS.  But if I give to you today, there won't be enough left for the rest of the week, man.

MARAIS.  We'll send to Dr. Visser for more. I'll explain it was all my fault.

OOM DOORS.  He won't. He warned me.

MARAIS.  I . . . I . . . I'll go with less tomorrow.

*Louis, followed by Tant Corrie and Doorsie, enters the room from the kitchen.*

LOUIS.  Give it to him, Pa!

TANT CORRIE.  No, Doors.

MARAIS. For God's sake have pity . . . !

OOM DOORS. Take him to his room.

*Doorsie has to literally tear Marais away from his father.*

MARAIS. Oom Doors . . .

DOORSIE. Please come, Mr. Marais . . .

MARAIS. Oom Doors . . .

OOM DOORS. All right, Mr. Marais. All right. Just go to your room.

*Doorsie manages to get Marais out of the room.*

TANT CORRIE. Do you know what you are doing?

OOM DOORS. No.

Bedroom. Interior. Night.

*Marais alone. Barely able to control his hands, he prepares the pills and injects himself with the double dose. For a few desperate seconds he waits for it to take effect. Relief is almost immediate. He closes his eyes, his face relaxes, his breathing slows down. Euphoria.*

MARAIS [*voice-over*]. In such cases life becomes a continual struggle to render permanent by excessive use the very fleeting happiness these poisons bring . . . the bonds of civilized life are
eagerly snapped, where the strongest springs of human
conduct—love of friends and relatives, position, honor—are
restraints more powerless than plumed reeds to stop the whirl-
wind in its course. Everything held priceless in normal life is
carelessly cast into the maelstrom. The sufferer drifts into a
vicious circle and, like the scorched fly, spins in vain upon the
axis of his pain.

Pantry. Interior. Day.

*Doorsie and Marais. An old-fashioned galvanized iron bath of very hot water. Steam fills the small room. Marais is seated in it. Doorsie pours pot after pot of hot water into the bath. Now holding a pot of scalding water, he hesitates.*

MARAIS. Pour it.

DOORSIE. But I can't put my hand in it, Mr. Marais.

*Marais can hardly speak.*

MARAIS. Not hot enough.

DOORSIE. But you'll burn yourself, Mr. Marais.

MARAIS.  For God's sake do as I tell you . . . it's not hot enough.

*Doorsie pours.*

More!

Kitchen. Interior. Day.

*Doorsie and Tant Corrie. Tant Corrie is at the stove. Every plate has a kettle or pot of steaming water on it. Doorsie hands over an empty kettle.*

DOORSIE.  More.

*He leaves with a full kettle from the stove.*

Pantry. Interior. Day.

*Marais and Doorsie. Marais is immersed up to his neck in the scalding water. A frightened Doorsie is emptying yet another kettle.*

MARAIS.  Stuurie?

DOORSIE.  Any minute now, Mr. Marais.

*As Marais splashes the scalding water over himself, we hear his voice; the observer in his mind is still alert.*

MARAIS [*voice-over*].  There remains the question . . . what is it about the euphoric poisons that make them so irresistible to man and the baboon? In the psyche of an animal such as man, dominated by the new 'causal' mind, the pain of the survival struggle has a single focus . . . the consciousness. Both man and the baboon experience consciousness as something based on pain and suffering.

Pantry. Interior. Day.

*Doorsie and Marais. Doorsie, under Marais' instructions, is preparing an injection. The syringe is very small in Doorsie's huge hands as he hands it to Marais. Marais holds out his left arm. Doorsie grasps it tightly above the elbow.*

MARAIS.  Tight. Tighter. Give me the syringe. (*Injects himself and closes his eyes; the hand with the syringe hangs limply outside the bath*) Get out. Get out!

*Doorsie leaves. Through the dense haze of steam we see Marais' face relax as the drug takes effect.*

Dream. Interior. Night.

*Marais, fifteen years younger than the man at Steenkampskraal, and his tame*

*baboon, Piet. The rondavel Marais lived in at Bobbejaankloof during his years
in the Waterberg. He becomes aware of a shadow at the window. He watches
it with detached curiosity for a moment, then taking up an oil lamp he moves to
the door. He opens it and steps outside.*

## Dream. Exterior. Night.

*Marais and baboons. He steps out of the rondavel. Dimly he sees round him a
number of baboons. He stares at them and they stare back at him, as if
expecting something. Eventually they move off into the darkness and he follows.
It is very dark and the light from his lamp is all but useless. Dark forms
converge on him—the baboons are frightened of the dark. A sense of this
communicates itself to Marais who becomes aware of the importance of his
light. He tries to protect it from the wind but it is too late. The flame is blown
out. Whatever terror the night holds now seems very near. The man is rapidly
losing his self-assurance and is identifying more and more with the animals. He
finds it very difficult to keep up with them, stumbling and falling over rocks and
the roots of trees as they move into Bobbejaankloof. Eventually he finds it
impossible to keep up with the animals, who are now in full flight. When he
realizes his position as the fatal straggler, he makes a renewed effort to catch up
with the troop. This final effort fails and he abandons himself to total animal
terror. At this point we start to see images of a prowling leopard ... the
baboons' arch-foe. Marais' anxiety and desperation turn into terror. He looks
up and sees the leopard on the branch above him.*

## Veld. Exterior. Day.

*Marais fleeing. For a moment a sense of continuity between this and the
preceding dream sequence. We then realize he is in fact running away from
Steenkampskraal.*

## Pantry. Interior. Day.

*Tant Corrie and Lilly. Lilly is sweeping. Tant Corrie enters with some veget-
ables that she has just collected. She goes over to the table to put them down. She
pauses for a moment and listens. The house is silent. She quickly leaves the
pantry.*

## Kitchen. Interior. Day.

*Tant Corrie knocks on Marais' bedroom door. There is no answer. She opens
the door quietly and looks inside. Marais' bed is empty.*

## Farmhouse. Exterior. Day.

*Tant Corrie comes running out of the house.*

TANT CORRIE. Doors! Doors!

Veld. Exterior. Day.
*Marais fleeing from Steenkampskraal. Louis and Stuurie on horseback, moving at a steady canter along a footpath.*

Road. Exterior. Day.
*Oom Doors and Doorsie rattling along the road to Heidelberg as fast as their old Ford will take them.*

Veld. Exterior. Day.
*Marais running. The horsemen.*

Road. Exterior. Day.
*The old Ford.*

Veld. Exterior. Day.
*Marais running. He is becoming exhausted.*

Veld. Exterior. Day.
*The horsemen.*

Veld. Exterior. Day.
*Marais climbing up a grassy slope. In the valley below, horsemen approach.*

Ford. Interior. Day.
*Marais, unconscious, lies in the back of the Ford.*

Farmhouse. Exterior. Day.
*Little Corrie playing outside sees the Ford drive up. Marais is unloaded and carried by Doorsie towards the house. Oom Doors and Louis follow.*

Stoep. Exterior. Day.
*Marais, Oom Doors, Doorsie and Tant Corrie. Marais is carried past an appalled Tant Corrie into the house. Tant Corrie sees Little Corrie playing and realizes that she too has seen Marais' return to Steenkampskraal.*

Bedroom. Interior. Day.
*Louis, Doorsie and Marais. Doorsie dumps Marais on his bed. He is unconscious. Doorsie takes the door key from the inside of the lock and puts it on the outside. He leaves the room with Louis, locking the door behind them.*

Stoep. Interior. Day.
*Louis is nailing the window closed from the outside.*

Kitchen. Interior. Day.
*Louis, Doorsie, Oom Doors and Tant Corrie. The men are slumped in chairs,*

*exhausted. Tant Corrie looks at them. She picks up the key that is lying on the table in front of Oom Doors.*

TANT CORRIE.  He's a human being, Doors, not an animal. [*Hands the key to Doorsie.*] Unlock the door.

*Doorsie hesitatingly gets up and opens the door for Tant Corrie. She goes in, carrying a saucepan of hot water.*

Bedroom. Interior. Day.

*Tant Corrie, Doorsie and a still-unconscious Marais. Tant Corrie is loosening Marais' clothing so that she can wash off some of the dirt from his flight from Steenkampskraal.*

TANT CORRIE.  Take off his jacket.

*The two of them lift Marais and slowly remove his jacket.*

I never expected it of you, Doorsie.

Kitchen. Interior. Day.

*Oom Doors, Louis, Doorsie and Tant Corrie. A furious argument between Oom Doors and his sons. In the bitterness of accusations and counter-accusations we see the corrosive effect Marais has had on this nexus of family relationships.*

LOUIS.  Are we supposed to be his bloody nursemaids?

OOM DOORS.  Who do you think you are talking to?

LOUIS.  Be reasonable, Pa. Who told us he was going to behave like a . . . a . . . I don't even have a word for it.

TANT CORRIE.  Dr. Visser. He warned us, Louis, when he asked us the first time.

LOUIS.  He said he was a sick man, Ma, not a mad man . . . and even that's not the truth.

OOM DOORS.  Louis, I'm beginning to lose my temper with you . . .

LOUIS.  Then you must maar lose it, Pa, because wragtie I've had enough. I'm not sleeping in that room anymore.

DOORSIE.  Then move out. I'll stay in there with him.

LOUIS.  So it's Doorsie the Samaritan now!

DOORSIE.  He is sick, boet!

LOUIS [*very angry now*].  Doorsie! If you tell me that once more . . .! Sick! You know what he really is, don't you? Why're we bluffing ourselves? Malaria! Those bloody pills aren't medicine. It's drugs he's taking. He's worse than a dronklap. . . . It's the end as far as I'm concerned . . . and if Pa doesn't like it, I'll leave Steenkampskraal. We're wasting our time. He'll never get better.

Bedroom. Interior. Day or night.

*A sequence of images which reflect the start of the cycle of Marais' recovery: Doorsie lighting the candle beside Marais' bed; Marais sitting lifelessly in a chair while his bed is being made; Tant Corrie bringing Marais' food; Marais propped up in bed, being shaved by a nervous Doorsie; Doorsie preparing an injection for Marais.*

DOORSIE. Only four tomorrow.

*We see the number of pills being reduced and the improvement in Marais' condition. Marais' voice, calm and detached, is heard over these images.*

MARAIS [*voice-over*]. Man is born an instinctive animal. The baby clings to the mother, cries for food, and instinctively knows what to do when offered a breast. There is no memory, no conception of cause and effect, no consciousness. Then, as it grows, the new mind slowly emerges and as this happens, the instinctive soul becomes just as slowly submerged. It is this new mind which has helped man to conquer the driest deserts, the highest mountains, the deepest valleys and the frozen poles, and still to survive. But nature demands payment for all she gives. The baboon and man pay an enormous price for their psyche, a price which is bound surely but slowly to bring about their natural extermination.

Bedroom. Interior. Day.

*Marais alone in a chair at the window: a serene image of a man who is starting to live again. The window has been opened . . . the curtains billow out gently in the breeze.*

Bedroom. Interior. Day.

*Doorsie, Marais and Visser. Close-up of a trembling hand and cut-throat razor. It is Doorsie's. He is shaving a still very weak Marais. Visser, sitting in a chair, is watching the operation with gentle amusement.*

DOORSIE. Look.

VISSER. I think you're doing very well. A little more practice,

Doorsie, and you could set yourself up in business. I'll tell you this much . . . I'd rather take out his tonsils than attempt what you're doing.

*Doorsie wipes away sweat with the back of his hand.*

DOORSIE. Don't say that, Doctor. You make me more nervous. [*Turns back to Marais and his partly lathered face.*] Make like so, Mr. Marais.

*He pulls a face . . . there is an inaccessible tuft of hair on Marais' upper lip. A few more agonizing strokes with the razor and the job is finished.*

MARAIS. I'll try tomorrow, Doorsie.

DOORSIE. Thanks, Mr. Marais.

*Doorsie leaves the room.*

VISSER. Any work yet?

MARAIS. You must be joking, Andries.

VISSER. Ah . . . that will come next. You're over the worst now.

*Marais looks at him.*

Don't you think so?

*Marais smiles strangely; Visser speaks with confidence.*

We're going to get you off it this time, Eugène. Some mail for you. Do you want me to read it for you?

*Marais shakes his head.*

MARAIS. No. Later.

VISSER. Your friend in Cape Town.

MARAIS. Uh. Wilhelm Spilhaus.

*Visser takes out his stethoscope and begins his examination.*

VISSER. Eugène . . . you've got your hands on your life again. Don't let go, boetie.

MARAIS. Of course not. You said it yourself, Andries . . . I'm over the worst. It was just a question of time. Why do you think I agreed to come here?

*As Visser completes his examination.*

Diagnosis?

VISSER. Hm . . . interesting . . . very . . . interesting . . . a coronary . . .

*Looks round to see the surprised look on Marais' face.*

. . . pentameter.

*Marais smiles.*

MARAIS.  Rhyming?

VISSER.  No.

MARAIS.  Let's hear it.

VISSER.  It's something like . . . 'Thou hast nor youth, nor age, but as it were, an after dinner sleep dreaming on both.'*

*They both smile.*

Farmhouse. Exterior. Day.

*Little Corrie playing with a doll.*

LITTLE CORRIE.  . . . brought her a new doll, the other fairy brought her new shoes . . .

*Marais appears round a corner. Little Corrie stops as soon as she sees him.*

MARAIS.  Go on with your story.

*Little Corrie stares at him.*

What's her name?

*Little Corrie doesn't respond.*

Do you know where the fairies live? In there.

*He points to the door leading to a cellar under the house.*

LITTLE CORRIE.  No.

MARAIS.  I've seen them, Koekie.

LITTLE CORRIE.  My name is not 'Koekie.'

MARAIS.  I'm going to call you 'Koekie.'

LITTLE CORRIE.  My name is 'Corrie.' And there are no fairies in there.

MARAIS.  How do you know?

LITTLE CORRIE.  Because!

*She picks up her doll and runs away. Marais watches her go . . . registering no response to her rude rejection. Then, slowly, he starts to smile. There is a twinkle in his eye.*

Farm. Exterior. Day.

*Marais strolling around the farm. He looks around with interest, pausing from time to time to examine things.*

Farmhouse. Exterior. Day.

*Tant Corrie baking bread in the bakoond outside the kitchen door. Marais is sitting nearby, carving a piece of wood with a pocket knife and listening to her.*

MARAIS. Veld is looking good, Tant Corrie.

TANT CORRIE. Ja, but it needs rain.

*Smiles to herself and shakes her head; looks up to see Marais staring at her inquiringly.*

Just remembering what it looked like when we first came. Nineteen hundred and five: homestead burnt down. Bare veld. We outspanned and put up our tents there where the kraal is now. Bitter hearts. The two boys still small; myself out of the concentration camp;* Doors as long a prisoner of war. We had nothing when we started . . . except that bitterness.

MARAIS. Which camp, Tant Corrie?

TANT CORRIE. Turffontein. The race course. Ja. Two years. The longest two of my life. Not even the drought in nineteen ten and nineteen eleven seemed to last as long. It wasn't the Almighty's mercy we were waiting for, but an end to man's stupidity. Don't talk to me about the English! Those first few years, Doors and the two boys worked like kaffirs on this land, Mr. Marais. [*Pause; looks at Marais.*] Don't judge us harshly. Life hasn't been easy for us . . . droughts, locusts, the English. I know my men aren't gentle . . .

MARAIS. I haven't judged anyone, Tant Corrie. I hope no one has judged me.

*Marais presses into the sand at his feet the end of the stick he has been carving. It leaves a perfect, miniature footprint.*

Farmhouse. Exterior. Day.

*Marais and Little Corrie. A large number of the miniature footprints lead into the darkness of the cellar. Marais and the little girl are squatting side by side. She is very impressed.*

MARAIS. What do you say now, Koekie?

LITTLE CORRIE. How many do you think there are?

MARAIS. I'm not sure.

LITTLE CORRIE. What do they look like?

MARAIS. I'll tell you. Come with me.

Farmyard. Exterior. Day.
*Marais and Little Corrie sitting on the roots of the alhambra tree. She listens very attentively to his story.*

MARAIS.
'n Feetjie her vir haar
Uit spinnerak 'n doek vergaar;
'n Rokkie wit soos heuningwas
Het sy toe aanmekaar gelas.

Maar nouliks was dit om haar lyf,
Toe kom 'n windjie, vlug en styf,
En met die uiting van sy sug
Daar trek ons Feetjie deur die lug!

Haar maatjies staar haar treurig aan,
Hoe sy hoog oor die bome gaan,
Tot sy met heel haar rokkie fyn
Daar in the verte glad verdwyn!

As jy 'n rokkie ooit besit
Van spinnerak of jets soos dit,
Pas op hoe jy jou dan verroer,
'n Windjie mag jou glad vervoer!*

Waenhuis. Interior. Day.
*Oom Doors and Marais hauling out of a corner the parts of an old liquor still. Marais examines them.*

OOM DOORS. My father was the last one to use it. When he died, my mother made us take it down. [*Laughs at the memory.*] It was the only thing they ever argued about . . . his mampoer. He liked his dop.

MARAIS. Is the condenser here? On the top.

*Another laugh from Oom Doors.*

OOM DOORS. Condenser? I don't know about these things. But there's something here . . . [*Rummages around in another corner.*] Here.

MARAIS. That's it. I could get this to work again.

OOM DOORS. Well, go ahead. To tell you the truth I don't mind a drop myself.

*Oom Doors stops laughing abruptly. His manner changes. Marais understands.*

MARAIS. I've never been a heavy drinker. I don't mean to start now.

*Oom Doors gives a weak, apologetic smile.*

OOM DOORS. I'm sorry . . . please, Mr. Marais . . . I'm sorry. Ah, to hell with this 'Mr.' and 'Advocate' business. . . . Listen, I've said it before and I'll say it again, because it's the truth. I'm only a farmer, and maybe not such a good one at that . . . there are some things I don't understand, and . . . wragtig Oedjeen . . . you're one of them. Make allowances, man.

*Marais hesitates for a second, then turns back to the dismantled still.*

MARAIS. We'll need something to put the mampoer in.

Waenhuis. Interior. Day.
*Marais putting the still together. He is being watched by a very interested Stuurie.*

MARAIS. Do you know what this is for, Stuurie?

*Stuurie smiles.*

Waenhuis. Interior. Day.
*Marais and Stuurie. The still is now in operation.*

Waenhuis. Interior. Day.
*Business operations: Stuurie is serving mampoer to a queue of Africans through a window. Visser and Marais sample the contents of one of the bottles. Stuurie is seen in the background, busy selling.*

VISSER. Unmistakable . . . the bouquet, the body . . . Steenkamp-skraal '26.

*Marais smiles, Visser raises his glass.*

To a good year. You have hidden talents, Eugène.

MARAIS. Just a good memory, and a little elementary science. There were quite a few stills around in the Waterberg during my time there . . . and one or two very potent recipes. Dr. Visser doesn't approve?

VISSER. Nor for that matter disapprove, Advocate Marais. It's just that being a doctor I find myself, of necessity, advocating the cause of moderation.

MARAIS. Then by all means plead it . . . but as one advocate to another, let me just say that I don't think you stand a chance. The judge . . . is biased. Name me a civilization, Andries—or for that matter a race or tribe of men—that has not had its euphoric drug, not made. . . . You'll forgive me quoting myself . . . 'Habitual recourse to the use of a poison to induce a feeling of happiness as a remedy for the pain of consciousness . . .'

*Stuurie approaches.*

Ah! Stuurie. Finished?

*Stuurie gives Marais a small tin in which he has placed the day's takings. In return Marais gives him a bottle of mampoer. As Stuurie leaves, Marais rattles the tin triumphantly. Visser and Marais laugh.*

Orchard. Exterior. Day.

*Marais and Visser walking near the sheep kraal.*

MARAIS. '. . . that with thy potent rhetoric stealest away the purposes of wrath, pleadest effectually for relenting pity, and through one night's heavenly sleep callest back to the guilty man the visions of his infancy, and hands washed pure from blood . . .'

VISSER. Beautiful . . .

MARAIS. But?

VISSER. Dangerous rhapsodies.

MARAIS. I know. I'm not justifying anything, Andries . . . merely stating a fact. That's all Stuurie wants. How did you yourself describe it in 'Lotos-land?' . . . ' 'n salige niksdoen en droom.'*

VISSER. That's cheating, Eugène. There's more to the poem than just that line. It pleads the cause of moderation. Not excess.

*Marais smiles.*

MARAIS. Do me the honor.

*Visser climbs onto the kraal wall. The sheep become part of his audience.*

VISSER. All right. From when Naudé speaks up. Naudé addresses the nation:

''n Vyand bedreig ons, O Broeders,
En 'n vyand op wie ons moet let;
Te glad sit jul tawwerts, O Moeders,
Trekkerswee is per slot trekkersvet!

Veel beter om eind'loos te swerwe,
Teen gevare ons moet weer te staan,
As hier in gemak te verderwe
En in smorende vet te vergaan!

Veel voorspoed word later 'n ketting
En 'n dwing'land die luie gemak;
Te gronde gaan ons deur vervetting:
Môre trek ons van hier sak en pak!' . . .

. . . Die aand nog het Koos van der Merwe
En Naudé die ou vet-span verlaat;
Hul bene na swoege en swerwe
Is al weer van normale formaat.

Maar hoe die met die ander gesteld is,
Dit weet Nugter. 'n Rondloper-Ier
Beweer dat hul almal gesmelt is
En derhalwe die naam Vet-rivier!*

*Visser's delivery is brilliantly comic. Marais enjoys the performance.*
Bedroom. Interior. Day.
*Marais and Visser. The skull of a chacma baboon.*
MARAIS. *Papio ursinus ursinus.*
VISSER. A lovely little old lady.
MARAIS. First citizen of the world . . . and the reason? A soul that
had escaped the shackles of instinct and was able to memorize
the relationship between cause and effect. Prime attribute of the
new mind.
*The room reflects Marais' recovery and renewal: there is now only one bed and
a table has been moved in; it is already cluttered with specimens from the veld,
papers, pen and ink.*
VISSER. *Cogito ergo sum?*
MARAIS. I think, therefore I am? Come on, Andries. You're a
surgeon. Put eyes in those sockets.

VISSER. So?

MARAIS. *Suffero ergo sum.* It hurts, therefore I am.

VISSER. Oh, no, boetie. [*Kisses the skull.*] *Amo ergo sum.*

*They laugh.*

Farmyard. Exterior. Day.
*Marais and Visser at the latter's car.*

MARAIS. How's your writing going, Andries?

VISSER. You tell me.

*He takes a sheet of paper out of his jacket and hands it to Marais.*

MARAIS. Another poem?

VISSER. After you've corrected it.

*Marais accepts the piece of paper. Visser hesitates before driving off. Something is obviously on his mind. Visser takes a letter out of his pocket and offers it to Marais who recognizes the handwriting.*

MARAIS. Brenda.

*He makes no move to take the offered letter.*

VISSER. She's passing through Heidelberg in a week or so.

MARAIS. And?

VISSER. She wants to know if there's a chance of seeing you.

MARAIS. What did you say?

VISSER. I haven't replied yet.

MARAIS. What does 'our doctor' advise?

VISSER. To avoid emotional complications . . . both of you.

*Marais smiles cynically.*

MARAIS. That won't happen, Andries. It's all over. But I never did say goodbye to her properly, or thank you for helping us.

VISSER. Your doctor doesn't remember a thing, and he hopes for his sake that you will do the same. I'll arrange with my driver to bring her out.

*A pause, then Visser drives off.*

Kitchen. Interior. Night.
*Tant Corrie and Marais. A quiet moment between the two of them. The*

*evening meal is obviously over. Tant Corrie is sewing, Marais staring intro-spectively at the coals in the grate.*

TANT CORRIE. Dr. Visser seemed very pleased with your progress.

MARAIS. Yes.

TANT CORRIE. Then why aren't you?

MARAIS. Who said I wasn't?

TANT CORRIE. You don't look it.

MARAIS. Pleased? My name is Eugène Marais, Tant Corrie. I'm fifty-four years old.

TANT CORRIE. What does that mean?

MARAIS. I don't know.

*A helpless shrug of the shoulders completes the sentence. Tant Corrie reacts with characteristic determination to Marais' mood of somber pessimism.*

TANT CORRIE. I'll tell you what *I* know. You are getting better. Dr. Visser has every reason to be pleased. You already look years younger. Your . . . your friends will hardly recognize you when you go back.

MARAIS. Steenkampskraal must take all the credit for that, Tant Corrie. You've all been very . . . patient.

*Pause.*

TANT CORRIE. Only friends, Mr. Marais? No family?

MARAIS. Family? Of course. We Marais are like the baboon . . . you'll find us wherever it's possible to survive. There's a troop of us down in the Cape, another in the Free State . . . Pretoria . . . [*His voice trails off into silence; he knows he hasn't answered her question.*] I've got a son. My wife died . . . a long time ago. [*Moves to go to his bedroom.*] Goodnight, Tant Corrie.

TANT CORRIE. Goodnight, Mr. Marais.

Bedroom. Interior. Night.

*Marais at his table reading a manuscript. He starts writing. We hear his voice.*

Waterberg. Exterior. Day.

*We see the Marais of the Waterberg years. He is a younger, more agile Marais than the one we have come to know. The countryside is as Marais describes it . . . verdant and rich.*

MARAIS [*voice-over*]. My first acquaintance with the baboons of Doornhoek took place under the most favorable of circumstances. There had been a succession of very good rainy years in the Waterberg before my arrival there. As the prophet aforetime declared, 'The wilderness was like Eden and the desert like the garden of the Lord: joy and gladness were found therein.'* [*Through his binoculars, he sees the troop of baboons in the distance.*] It goes without saying that our troop of baboons enjoyed this state of affairs to the full. They were fat and frolicsome and more beautifully bearded than we ever saw them afterwards. We little knew when we first settled in, that happiness was only on the surface and that the shadow of perpetual tragedy always darkened the lives of these baboons.

Bobbejaankloof. Exterior. Day.
*Marais approaches the troop to feed them. A warning bark. A fight breaks out among some adults.*

MARAIS [*voice-over*]. The older individuals were at first very chary of approaching me. I was able in time to approach within a few yards of them and it was then apparent that it was I, rather than the chacmas, who needed to be distrustful and continually on guard. I was never attacked, although dangerous threats were a daily occurrence and of such a nature that in the beginning I had always to be armed. But a better understanding was gradually established as we got to know each other.

Bobbejaankloof. Exterior. Day.
*Marais has been feeding the troop for some months now. The baboons eagerly come forward as he approaches them.*

MARAIS [*voice-over*]. The circumstances which rendered these clever and extremely nervous animals indifferent to the presence of their arch-foe, man, were due to a long succession of events. . . . The South African War had left the area in unpeopled solitude for a number of years and, when eventually the families returned, they were for several more years without rifles and ammunition. The baboons were very quick to realize the helplessness and took full advantage of it.

Bobbejaankloof. Exterior. Day.

*Marais near the baboon sleeping-place in the late afternoon. He looks up at the cliff face to which the baboons retire during the hours of darkness.*

MARAIS [*voice-over*]. The baboons generally reached their sleeping-place some time before sunset. Among the younger members of the troop this was the favorite time for frequent romping games. It was especially the hour of the little ones. With the setting of the sun, however, and the first deepening of the shadows, a singular transformation came over the entire scene. Silence fell upon them. In few phases of their behavior did the troop of baboons appear to me more human-like than in the unquestionable expression of this evening melancholy. The older ones assumed attitudes of profound dejection. It is hardly possible to avoid the conclusion that the chacma suffers from the same attribute of pain which is such an important ingredient of human mentality, and that the condition is due to the same cause, namely, the suffering inseparable from the new mind which like man the chacma has acquired in the course of its evolution.

Stoep. Exterior. Day.

*Tant Corrie, Marais, Little Corrie and Brenda. Tant Corrie, Marais—in a suit—and Little Corrie are posing for a photograph which Brenda is taking: Tant Corrie—erect and severe; Marais—smiling; Little Corrie—glowering suspiciously at the camera. The click of a shutter. We see Brenda for the first time, winding forward the spool of a box Brownie. Parked behind her in the farmyard is Dr. Visser's car.*

BRENDA. There . . . that should make Albertus happy . . . if it comes out. [*To Tant Corrie.*] . . . my son and Mr. Marais' most dedicated pupil.

TANT CORRIE. Would you like tea in the voorkamer?

BRENDA. It's quite pleasant out here on the stoep.

TANT CORRIE. Then make yourselves comfortable. I've got everything ready.

*Tant Corrie disappears through the front doorway. Brenda and Marais sit. So does Little Corrie, but at a distance. Brenda smiles at her, but gets no response. The little girl watches the woman with smoldering dislike. Brenda takes in the view from the stoep.*

BRENDA. So this is it.

MARAIS. Steenkampskraal.

BRENDA. Andries' few letters said nothing. It's gentler than I had imagined.

MARAIS. Spring, Brenda. It was a bleak landscape when I arrived. There's still time for a few late frosts.

BRENDA. How are you?

MARAIS. Fine. And you?

*She smiles at him, ignoring the question. He stares back calmly. Tant Corrie returns to the stoep with an obviously special tray of tea and cake. She realizes that Brenda and Marais would like to be alone.*

TANT CORRIE. There—if you want anything I'll be in the kitchen. [*To Little Corrie.*] And you? Holiday? Come. Your mother's only got two hands; she needs four.

*A final uncompromising exchange between Brenda and Little Corrie before the latter follows her mother into the house.*

BRENDA. Your little friend doesn't like me. You're going to break another heart, Eugène.

MARAIS. Koekie? Strange child. She does believe in fairies though. Will you pour?

*Brenda doesn't move, but stares frankly at Marais.*

BRENDA. You're looking much better than I had imagined. Relaxed . . . alive . . . and you're writing again, Andries tells me.

MARAIS. I've had the time. They live a quiet life here.

BRENDA. Poetry?

MARAIS. Not much. I'm putting all my energy into my *magnum opus* . . . The Soul of the Ape.*

BRENDA. Back to your baboons again.

MARAIS. Back? [*Shakes his head, smiling.*] I never left them.

*Brenda is still staring at him; he pours the tea.*

Tell me about Albertus.

BRENDA. I've got him in a good school now . . . and he misses you . . . your walks in the veld . . .

MARAIS. I was hoping the microscope would keep him busy.

*Brenda laughs.*

BRENDA. Too busy. It's becoming impossible to get him away from it to do his homework. He gets his best marks in nature study though.

MARAIS. Excellent.

Farm. Exterior. Day.

*Marais and Brenda sitting beside a small stream.*

BRENDA. How much longer do you think you're going to stay here?

MARAIS. Not much. I've had all the rest I need now.

BRENDA. Andries says you might be moving to Pretoria . . . you've applied for a post at the zoo.

MARAIS. I'm only thinking about it. Gustav Preller is talking to Malan, Minister of the Interior,* on my behalf. But I'm in two minds . . . if it's a purely administrative post, there won't be time for any research . . . that is what I need. I'm tired of writing vacuous newspaper articles for people who are too lazy to think for themselves. If I work seriously now, there might just be enough time left for me to apply myself to what I really have to do. So don't attach any significance . . .

BRENDA. Eugène . . . stop! You're not talking to me. Stop running away. I know it's over. I simply came to see you . . . because . . . well it does help to know you're alive and well.

*Pause.*

MARAIS. It wouldn't have worked, Brenda. You know me well enough to know that.

BRENDA. Please . . . anything, but don't say you're sorry. I'm not.

MARAIS. I wasn't going to.

Farmyard. Exterior. Day.

*Visser's car. The driver is waiting to leave. Marais and Brenda. Marais opens the door for Brenda.*

MARAIS. Give this to Albertus. Tell him it's the lower jawbone of the black-backed jackal. I found it in the veld.

BRENDA.  Thank you Eugène, live . . . and work. You've got so
much to give. I hope some day you'll find somebody who
can . . .

MARAIS.  Goodbye, Brenda.

BRENDA.  Goodbye, Eugène.

*The car drives away and Marais watches it for a long time.*

Bedroom. Interior. Night.

*Marais is preparing an injection. There are only two pills.*

Suikerbosrand. Exterior. Day.

*Marais and Doorsie. Marais has a snake firmly grasped in his hand, its mouth
squeezed open. He scrapes a small stick along the upper jaw to reveal the
needle-sharp fangs . . .*

MARAIS.  . . . see . . . the hole through which the poison comes . . .
not at the end. . . . If it was, the fang would be plugged by the
flesh of the animal it bites, and the poison wouldn't come
through. The hole is just above the point . . . the point makes an
open path through the flesh for the poison. The first hypodermic, Doorsie. Mine is just a copy of this.

Termitary. Exterior. Day.

*Marais and Doorsie. Marais is cutting into an anthill.*

DOORSIE.  They'll be flying soon. Not long till the first rains.

MARAIS.  That's right. The nuptial flight. That's how it all starts,
Doorsie. In the dry districts they sometimes have to wait for
years before they get the chance to fly. Imagine it. Years under-
ground in darkness waiting for that one moment, and when it
comes . . . might only last for three seconds. For a distance of
only three yards, they will enjoy the exquisite thrill of flight. . . .
To really understand this antheap, Doorsie, try to think of it as a
single animal . . . some of the termites forming the mouth and
stomach, others the weapons of defense, and still others the
sexual organs . . . and to call the queen the brain of that animal
is almost to do her a disservice. She's the soul.*

*Doorsie is watching Marais' assault on the termitary.*

DOORSIE.  If that's true, Mr. Marais, then what you're doing now
is mos a sin isn't it?

*Marais looks down at the broken termitary.*

MARAIS. And those?

*He indicates the two dead guinea-fowl.*

DOORSIE. We'll eat them tomorrow.

MARAIS. My curiosity is also an appetite, Doorsie.

DOORSIE. Maybe . . . but I didn't hear you say grace.

*Marais smiles.*

Man can ask too many questions, Mr. Marais. You know what
the Preacher said in the Bible: 'For in much wisdom is much
grief: and he that increaseth knowledge increaseth sorrow.'*

MARAIS. I wish I had your faith, Doorsie. My mother died in my
arms. Just before the end there was an expression . . . a look in
her eyes. I asked her what it was she saw. She said . . . 'Nothing.
There is nothing.'

*The two men sit in silence in the fading light.*

Bedroom. Interior. Day.

*Marais and Visser. Marais' suitcase, half-packed, is open on the bed.*

VISSER. Be reasonable, Eugène . . . you're down to half a grain a
day . . . in a few more weeks you'll be off it completely. You're
writing again . . .

*Marais is very irritable and angry.*

MARAIS. I am not.

VISSER. What's that?

*He gestures to the table and its manuscripts.*

MARAIS. I've gone as far as I can here on Steenkampskraal. Can't
you understand, Andries?! If I'm lucky, I see you once a week
for an hour . . . for the rest . . . the Meyers are decent people
and I have come to like and respect them . . . but for God's sake,
man, there's no intellectual stimulus or provocation. I'm living
on old ideas.

VISSER. Eugène! I'm not asking you to stay here indefinitely.

MARAIS. It feels like that. The cure has become a prison sentence.
No, Andries. I've had enough.

*He resumes packing. Visser watches him.*

VISSER.  I'm not just talking to you as a doctor or as a friend. There's more involved in the life and work of Eugène Marais than just a patient's recovery or a friendship . . .

MARAIS.  Stop that nonsense, Andries! My life is my own. [*Abandons packing and sits down on the bed.*] It won't ever be a national monument . . . too much has happened already. I've tried before, you know. I've been on it for thirty years now. The most I can hope for is to keep it under control.

VISSER.  No. As a doctor I refuse to accept that. Eugène, have you forgotten what you were taking before you came here? In one week you pumped enough into yourself to kill sixty men!

MARAIS.  For God's sake, Andries. Sixty men—one man . . . ten grains—half a grain . . . eight pills—two pills. Listen, boetie, it's got nothing to do with either arithmetic or chemistry. What do you want? No . . . don't tell me. I can hear your inimitable phalanx of bedside platitudes lining themselves up. Me . . . sober? . . . sensible? . . . normal? . . . happily married for ever after? Stop wasting your time, Andries. It's as much a part of me now as the spelling of my name. If you want me for a friend, accept me for what I am.

*Visser listens quietly. Marais, all his energy spent on the foregoing outburst, sits down on his bed, exhausted. A moment's silence between the two men. Visser fills it by apparently examining some specimen from Marais' table. When he eventually speaks it is without looking at his friend.*

VISSER.  How long has it been now . . . the two of us?

*Marais, unable even to consider the question, shrugs his shoulders.*

You're right. Two years, three years . . . what does that measure? Nothing. Arithmetic. I could take out your appendix, boetie, through a hole so small you wouldn't be able to slip a cufflink through it . . . if you ever have one again. But . . .

*Marais looks at his friend and smiles wryly.*

MARAIS.  I know. It would be so simple wouldn't it if you could apply your scalpel with the same precision and efficacy in other directions as well?

VISSER. Yes. I would have liked to have believed there was something I could do to . . .

MARAIS. Remedy life.

VISSER. I see. That is the name of the ailment now?

MARAIS. Yes. Diagnosed as such a few thousand years before Christ by the nameless author of an Egyptian papyrus. Title: Dialogue between the writer and his soul. In it the writer came to the conclusion that the very existence of life was founded on sorrow and pain, and that there was ultimately only one perfect remedy . . . to put an end to one's existence. The Sotho have a nice turn of phrase for that . . . *peli n'daba* . . . 'end of dialogue.'

VISSER. There's a morbid streak of self-indulgence in your nature, Eugène. You haven't got a monopoly on pain and sorrow, you know. I too had a wife. Her name was also Lettie. But I also try to . . . sing . . . Eugène.

MARAIS. Try to? Come on, Andries . . . 'Die Sanger van die Suikerbosrand'* will have his special place in our language for as long as it is spoken. But . . . don't try to teach me your song, boetie, because, if you succeeded . . . [*Pause.*] There is one mystery above all others that awed the Bushman: how a string of badger sinew, pulled taut over an empty pumpkin gourd . . . could make a sound that in turn could make men laugh or cry, dance or wait for rain. It so impressed them as one of the ultimate mysteries that they decided that men thought, dreamt and imagined with strings . . . that every man in fact had one song all of his own.* Sounds like their word for 'soul' doesn't it? All right. How much longer did you want, Andries?

VISSER. No. No more arithmetic.

MARAIS. How much longer, Andries?

VISSER. You're a bastard, you know that?

MARAIS. Then why do you persist?

VISSER. Medical ethics.

MARAIS. All right, Doctor . . . how much longer?

VISSER. Two weeks.

MARAIS. Let's get on with it then. Tell Oom Doors to reduce the dosage to one every second day.

Stoep. Exterior. Day.

*Marais watching Visser's car as it drives away from the farmyard. When it is out of sight he walks back to the steps leading up to the stoep. Little Corrie is sitting there watching him. Marais smiles at her, she frowns back. Despite this we sense that the relationship between the two of them is very intact. He sits beside her.*

MARAIS. Yes, Koekie.

LITTLE CORRIE. Why were you cross with the doctor?

MARAIS. Who says I was cross?

LITTLE CORRIE. I heard you.

MARAIS. I wasn't cross with the doctor.

LITTLE CORRIE. Who then?

MARAIS. Myself, I suppose.

LITTLE CORRIE. Why?

*Marais looks at the little girl in silence for a few seconds. The innocence of her question brings into sharp focus his sense of himself and his dilemma.*

MARAIS. For always being a guest, in someone else's home.

LITTLE CORRIE. Haven't you got a home?

*Marais smiles.*

MARAIS. Come to think of it, I have, Koekie. Let's go for a walk in it.

Veld. Exterior. Day.

*Marais and Little Corrie.*

MARAIS. It's beautiful, isn't it, Koekie?

LITTLE CORRIE. But it's not green.

MARAIS. You must learn to see and love it for what it is. Don't ask it to be something else. It's dry, but not dead. There's a lot of life down there.

Veld. Exterior. Day.

*Marais and Little Corrie out in the open veld. He parts a tuft of grass, exposing a nest of the yellow-breasted pipit . . . three eggs, speckled and blotched with various shades of brown.*

MARAIS. There, I've spent hours trying to find one of these nests . . . even when it was only a few yards away from me as this one was.

*Little Corrie looks at the nest.*

LITTLE CORRIE. Three babies.

MARAIS. Not yet . . . but they'll try. They've got a lot of enemies. Sometimes they fly so high you can't see them.

LITTLE CORRIE. Do you think they can hear the angels singing up there?

Veld. Exterior. Day.

*Marais walking, deep in thought.*

MARAIS [*voice-over*]. You will look in vain in nature for love, sympathy, pity, justice . . . protection of the weak and innocent. From the very beginnings of life we hear a chorus of anguish. Pain is a condition of existence. Escape from pain is the purpose in all striving.

Road. Exterior. Day.

*Stuurie, on horseback, returning to Steenkampskraal from Heidelberg. Marais is suddenly in front of him. Stuurie starts to smile. Marais doesn't return the greeting.*

MARAIS. Give!

*Stuurie, still smiling, hands over to Marais the box of pills. Marais takes them and walks down to the stream where he fills the syringe.*

Kitchen. Interior. Night.

*Oom Doors is trying to read from the Bible. The family in attitudes of complete defeat. They cannot avoid listening to Marais' near-hysterical euphoria from the bedroom . . . laughter, and for the most part, incoherent babbling. The noise virtually drowns Oom Doors' voice. We cut between Marais addressing his reflection in the window of his room and the family seated round the kitchen table. Oom Doors shows his agitation as he has to raise his voice to be heard above Marais. Each of the family's faces, seen for the last time, communicates the personal experience that the encounter with Marais has meant to the individual concerned. It is their home. He was their guest. Oom Doors—total bewilderment; Tant Corrie—compassion and defeat; Louis—resentment; Doorsie—acceptance; Little Corrie—fear.*

MARAIS. Blus uit, O Diep Rivier, die vlam van haat;—Die groot verlange wat my nooir verlaat.*

OOM DOORS. '. . . de priester en de profeet dwalen van den sterken drank; zij zijn verslonden van den wijn; zij dolen van sterken drank; zij dwalen in het gezigt, zij waggelen in het gerigt.'*

MARAIS [*off-screen*].

> Ek sien van ver die glans van staal en goud,
> Ek hoor die sag gedruis van waters diep en koud;
> Ek hoor jou stem as fluistering in 'n droom,
> Kom snel* . . .

[*On-screen.*] Happiness can be bought for a penny and carried in the waistcoat pocket . . . [*Laughs.*] The chancery of dreams. The seven heavens above the seventh heaven.

OOM DOORS [*off-screen*]. 'Want alle tafels zijn vol van uitspuwsel en van drek, zoodat er geene plaats schoon is . . .' [*On-screen.*] 'Zoodat er geene plaats schoon is. Wien zou Hij dan de kennis leeren?'*

*Marais is heard off-screen, laughing.*

MARAIS. All the candles are alight. Desdemona lives again, black man!

OOM DOORS [*off-screen*]. '. . . en wien zou Hij het gehoorde te verstaan geven? den gespeenden van de melk?' [*On-screen.*] ' . . . den afgetrokkenen van de borsten? Want bet is gebod op gebod, gebod op gebod, regel op regel, regel op regel, hier een weinig, daar een weinig. Daarom sal Hij door belagchelijke lippen . . .'*

MARAIS [*off-screen*]. The evil is undone. With hands washed pure from blood, you can enjoy her most subtle perfection. She lives! Iago has not distilled his poison. Start again. Take up your candle, Othello. [*On-screen.*] If I quench thee, thou flaming minister, I can thy former light restore.*

OOM DOORS [*off-screen*]. '. . . regel op regel, hier een weinig, daar een weinig.' [*on-screen*.] 'Daarom zal Hij door belagchelijke lippen, en door eene andere tong . . .'

MARAIS [*off-screen*]. Put out the light and then again put out the light. If I quench thee, thou flaming minister, I can thy former light restore if I repent me. But once put out thy light.\* Poor Othello. Doubt, darkness and death.

OOM DOORS [*defeated*]. Louis . . . go tell Dr. Visser to fetch him.

Car. Interior. Day.
*Visser and Marais driving back to Heidelberg.*

MARAIS. Stop the car.

VISSER. Why?

MARAIS. I want to say grace.

Veld. Exterior. Day.
*Marais and the veld. We hear his poem, 'Die Lied van SuidAfrika.'*

MARAIS [*voice-over*].

> Sy sê: 'Ek vorder as 'n heil'ge reg
> Die vrug van eindelose pyn;
> Ek smyt hulle oor die berge weg,
> En smoor hulle in die sandwoestyn.'
>
> Sy sê: 'Nooit her ek iets gegee;
> Ek laat hulle honger, dors en bloei;
> Hulle worstel deur en sterf gedwee,
> En min my as 'n vlam war skroei.
>
> Tien male moes bulle veg vir my,
> Tien male moes hulle kerm en stoei,
> Tien male in die stof gebrei,
> Tien male opstaan weer en bloei.
>
> My liefde duld geen ewenaar—
> Vergeefs die weeklag van die vrou,
> Van kleintjies al die stom gebaar:
> My liefde verg 'n enkel trou.

Hulle diepste hoop is lang verteer,
Vergaan in rook en as en bloed,
Hulle sak aanbiddend om my neer,
Ek voel hulle trane op my voet.

Ek adem nooit hulle name meer,
Nooit kon ek hulle kinders noem;
In vreemde tale hoor ek weer
Die dowwe fluistering van hulle roem.

En vlymend as 'n swaard, geheg
Bly van my liefde slegs die pyn;
Ek smyt hulle oor die berge weg,
En smoor hulle in die sandwoestyn.'*

*Andries Visser gets out of the car and watches his friend. His face expresses for us in these final moments our sense of the enigma of Eugène Marais.*

*Text on screen:* Ten years later, on the farm 'Pelindaba' in the Pretoria District of the Transvaal, Eugène Marais, suffering acutely again from withdrawal symptoms, shot himself.

# A LESSON FROM ALOES

In celebration of
Elizabeth Magdalena Potgieter*

# CHARACTERS

PIET BEZUIDENHOUT, *an Afrikaner, in his mid-forties*
GLADYS BEZUIDENHOUT, *his wife, at the same age*
STEVE DANIELS, *his friend, a Coloured man, the same age*

A LESSON FROM ALOES was first performed at the Market Theatre, Johannesburg, on 30 November 1978, directed by the author with the following cast:

| | |
|---|---|
| PIET BEZUIDENHOUT | Marius Weyers |
| GLADYS BEZUIDENHOUT | Shelagh Holliday |
| STEVE DANIELS | Athol Fugard |

After replacing himself with Bill Curry, Fugard transferred the play to the Baxter Theatre, Cape Town, on 3 January 1979, and from 3–27 January 1980, Fugard directed a Canadian cast in the Montreal production at the Centaur Theatre.

A LESSON FROM ALOES was performed at the Yale Repertory Theatre on 28 March 1980, directed by the author, with the following cast:

| | |
|---|---|
| PIET BEZUIDENHOUT | Harris Yulin |
| GLADYS BEZUIDENHOUT | Maria Tucci |
| STEVE DANIELS | James Earl Jones |

This production moved to the Playhouse Theatre, Broadway, 17 November 1980–8 February 1981. Meanwhile, the first London production, with the original cast (including Bill Curry as Steve), opened at the Cottesloe Theatre on 10 July 1980, directed by Ross Devenish.

*The action of the play moves between two areas representing the backyard and the bedroom of a small house in Algoa Park,* * *Port Elizabeth.*

# ACT ONE

## Scene 1

*The backyard. It is cluttered with a collection of aloes\* in a variety of tins of all shapes and sizes.*

*There is a gate with a nameboard: Xanadu.*

Piet, *seated at a garden table with an aloe in front of him, is studying a small field book on the plants.\* He is wearing spectacles, short trousers, no shirt and sandals without socks.* Gladys, *behind sunglasses, sits very still on a garden bench.*

*Time: late afternoon.*

PIET [*reading from the book*]. '. . . small, glaucous leaves, erect or incurved . . .' [*Studies the specimen in front of him, then turns back to the book.*] 'Tuberculate-based . . .' [*Turns to the glossary at the back of the book.*] Tuberculate . . . 'Having knobby or warty excrescences.' [*Back to the entry he was reading.*] 'Tuberculate-based soft prickles on both surfaces.' [*He holds the book at arm's length for a comparison between the illustration and his plant. He shakes his head.*] No. That's not it.

[*He closes the book, and takes off the spectacles. He gets up quietly, the aloe in his hands, and looks at Gladys.*]

GLADYS [*without moving*]. I'm awake.

PIET. Well, my dear, we have a stranger in our midst. Aloe Anonymous! Because that is what it is until I know its name. I've been through my book twice, page by page, but there is nothing that looks quite like it. I don't think I can allow myself to believe I've discovered a new species. That would be something! I'd name it after you, my dear. Hail aloe Gladysiensis! Sounds rather good, doesn't it? [*He reads the other aloes.*] Hail ferox! And you aristata . . . arborescens . . . ciliaris . . . and now Gladysiensis! Welcome to the most noble order of Eastern Cape aloes. An impressive array of names, isn't it? And knowing them is important. It makes me feel that little bit more at home in my world. And yet, as little Juliet once said: 'What's in a name? That which we call a rose | By any other name would smell as

221

sweet.'* [*These lines, and all his other quotations, although delivered with a heavy Afrikaans accent, are said with a sincere appreciation of the words involved. He thinks about those he has just quoted.*] Alas, it's not as simple as that, is it?

GLADYS. Are you talking to me?

PIET. Who else, my dear?

GLADYS. The aloes . . . or yourself. I'm never sure these days.

PIET. Names are more than just labels. [*He sits beside her on the bench.*] Petrus Jacobus Bezuidenhout. [*He gives a little smile.*] 'So, would Petrus, were he not Petrus called, | Retain that dear perfection which he owns without that title?'

GLADYS. What are you talking about?

PIET. The balcony scene. Where the little lady laments Romeo's name. I was just thinking about mine, trying to hear it as others do.

GLADYS. And?

PIET. Nothing . . . except that when other men say Piet Bezuidenhout it is me they are talking about. Yes! That is what's in a name. My face, my story in mine, as much as theirs, is in Romeo and Juliet. 'Then deny thy father and refuse thy name.' Hell! I don't know about those Italians, but that's a hard one for an Afrikaner. No. For better or for worse, I will remain positively identified as Petrus Jacobus Bezuidenhout; Species, Afrikaner; Habitat, Algoa Park, Port Elizabeth, in this year of our Lord, 1963 . . . and accept the consequences.

[*He looks at his wrist watch.*]

GLADYS. What is the time now?

PIET. Just on four o'clock.

GLADYS. It's passing very slowly, isn't it?

PIET. Yes, it is. The sun is as lazy as we are this afternoon.

GLADYS [*shaking her head*]. It's because we're waiting.

PIET. Let me get you something to read.

GLADYS. I'm all right.

PIET. I've got today's paper inside.

GLADYS. Stop fussing, Peter. I've learned how to sit and wait. When should we expect them?

PIET. I didn't fix a definite time. I just said, 'Supper.' So what do you think? Half-past six? Seven? They won't be too late because of the children. If we start to get ready at five, we should be all right. Everything under control in the kitchen?

GLADYS. Yes.

PIET. Then relax, my dear. Enjoy the sunshine.

GLADYS. I'm perfectly relaxed.

PIET. Good.

GLADYS. You're the one who can't keep still.

PIET [*he moves back to the garden table where we first saw him*]. Just tidying up my mess.

GLADYS. I hope I'm not getting too much sun.

PIET. No danger of that on an autumn afternoon. This is the start of our gentle time, Gladys . . . our season of mists and mellow fruitfulness, close bosom friend of the maturing sun.* On the farm there was almost a sense of the veld sighing with relief when autumn finally set in. We certainly did. Man and animal. Months of grace while we waited for the first rains.

GLADYS. My skin can't take it. I learned that lesson when I was a little girl.

PIET. Sunburn.

GLADYS. Yes. A holiday somewhere with my mother and father. On the very first day I picked up too much sun on the beach and that was the end of it. My mother dabbed me all over with calamine lotion to soothe the pain. I can remember looking at myself in the mirror . . . a frightened little white ghost. Mommy was terrified that I was going to end up with a brown skin. But she needn't have worried. It all peeled away and there I was, the same as before.

PIET. The voortrekker women had the same problem. That's where the old white bonnet comes from. Protection.

GLADYS. I think it was Cape Town. Not that it made any

difference where I was. All I remember of the outside world was standing at a window and watching the dogs in the street go berserk when the dirt-boys came to empty the bins. Heavens! What a terrible commotion that was. A big gray lorry with its mountain of rubbish, the black men banging on its side shouting, the dogs going for them savagely ... [*Breaking out of her reverie.*] I think I need my sun hat.

PIET. Don't move. [*He walks to the back door.*] Where is it?

GLADYS. In the bedroom.

[*Piet goes into the house—the bedroom—and returns a few seconds later with the sun hat.*]

PIET. Here you are, my dear. [*Gladys doesn't take the sun hat.*] Anything wrong?

GLADYS. Did I put away my diary?

PIET. I didn't notice.

[*After a moment's hesitation, Gladys walks awkwardly into the house.*]

GLADYS. I'll ... I'll just ... [*She enters the bedroom and unlocks a dressing-table drawer and takes out her personal diary. She looks around the room and then hides it under the mattress on the bed. She steadies herself and returns to Piet.*] Safe and sound.

PIET. I'll never interfere with it, my dear.

GLADYS. I know that!

PIET. So, where were we? Yes, our nameless friend. [*He holds up the unidentified aloe.*] I'll have to wait for it to flower. That makes identification much easier. And it will! It's got no choice. I've put it in a tin, so it needs me now. A little neglect on my side and it will be into a drought as fearsome as anything out there in the veld. If plants have feelings, this is as bad as keeping animals in cages. It's the roots that upset me. Even with all my care and attention they are still going to crawl around inside this little tin and tie themselves into knots looking for the space creation intended for them.

GLADYS [*obviously not listening to him*]. And you are quite certain they're bringing the children?

PIET. Yes. I very definitely made it an invitation to the whole family. It's high time we saw our godson again. Children grow fast at his age. And little Lucille should be quite the young lady by now.

GLADYS. How many of them are there again?

PIET. Steve and Mavis, the three girls, little Pietertjie and then the two of us. Eight all told. It will be quite a party. Have we got enough to feed the hungry hordes?

GLADYS [*betraying her nervousness*]. More than enough. That's not going to be the problem.

PIET. Then what is? [*Gladys doesn't answer.*] They're not strangers, Gladys. It's Steve and his family.

GLADYS. It's a big family.

PIET. We've had them all here before and you coped splendidly.

GLADYS. That was some time ago. I'm out of practice, remember. I know what's going to happen. You and Steven will end up in a corner talking politics all night and I'll be left with the rest of them, trying to make polite conversation. I can't even remember their names, Peter!

PIET. Mavis, Lucille, Charmaine . . .

GLADYS. And then that little boy . . . !

PIET. Yes, I know. Little Pietertjie can get a bit boisterous at times, but don't worry, my dear. Steven knows how to handle him. You must admit the girls are well behaved. You always admired their manners, remember? Please and thank you and speak when you're spoken to. Please relax, my dear. You won't have any trouble.

GLADYS. Well . . . you can't deny we are going to be crowded.

PIET. Yes, I do. Observe. [*Placing two tables in front of the garden bench.*] The festive board! [*Positioning chairs. He works hard at trying to allay Gladys's anxieties.*] The Lord and Lady of the Manor . . . our two honored guests . . . and then in descending order of age . . . Lucille, Charmaine, Beryl and little Pietertjie. [*Gladys studies the seating arrangement in silence.*] Does that look crowded?

GLADYS. No.

PIET. Then what's the matter?

GLADYS. You've got the little boy next to me.

PIET. Because Steve is sitting there and I thought . . . All right, all right! We'll change it around. In ascending order of age: Pietertjie here and then Beryl, Charmaine and Lucille next to you. How's that?

GLADYS. Thank you. It's not that I don't like children . . .

PIET. Say no more, my dear. I understand. [*He surveys the table.*] We mustn't forget your brass candlesticks. That was an inspired thought. Alfresco and candlelight. It's going to look very good. Continental!

GLADYS. Don't expect too much from me. I can only manage cold meats and salads.

PIET. Have we got a little pudding?

GLADYS. Yes. Jelly and custard. I've tried my best, Peter!

PIET. I know that, my dear. I was just thinking of the children.

GLADYS. If you want the menu, it's assorted cold meats . . . ham, brawn and polony . . . three salads . . potato mayonnaise . . .

PIET. What could be better? A cold buffet! It's going to be a warm evening. I must remember to chill the wine.

[*Looks at his wrist watch.*]

GLADYS [*anxiously*]. Is it time?

PIET. No, not yet.

GLADYS. How much longer?

PIET. Let's try to forget it, my dear, and enjoy what's left of the afternoon. That's why it's passing slowly. We're flattering time with too much attention.

GLADYS. You can't exactly blame us. They'll be our first visitors since I've been back. [*If she waits for Piet to respond. He doesn't.*] You do realize that, don't you?

PIET. Yes, now that you mention it. All the more reason for a celebration.

GLADYS. I won't have any trouble finding something to write in my diary tonight. 'At last! Other people! Just when it was beginning to feel as if Peter and I were the last two left in the world. Steven and his family came to supper.'

PIET [*back with his unidentified aloe*]. So . . . What I'll do is make some notes and go to the library and sit down with Gilbert Westacott Reynolds—*The Aloes of South Africa*. A formidable prospect! Five hundred and sixteen big pages of small print . . . and that is not counting General Smuts's foreword. A life-time's work so that ignoramuses like myself can point to an aloe and say its name. And make no mistake about it . . . I want to. So . . . let us attempt a sketch. What is it that makes knowing them so important?

GLADYS. Aloes?

PIET. No, their names. Just names in general. Yours, mine . . . anything! There's a lot of mystery in them, isn't there?

GLADYS. Peter and Gladys Bezuidenhout, Xanadu, 27 Kraaibos Street, Algoa Park. It sounds very ordinary to me.

PIET. Because it's your own. Familiarity has bred contempt. I can remember very clearly how, when we first met, 'Gladys Adams' was a name to conjure with.

GLADYS. Oh come, Peter!

PIET. It's the truth, my dear. How did you feel about mine?

GLADYS. I liked it. Very much. It was certainly much longer than anything I'd hoped for. I thought it had a strong earthy sound . . .

PIET. Yes, it has that. Bezuidenhout! Origin: Dutch. The first one arrived in 1695.

GLADYS. But to be quite frank, I wasn't sure that Gladys went with it.

PIET. Really? Gladys Bezuidenhout. Sounds all right to me.

GLADYS. Familiarity has bred contempt, Peter.

PIET. Touché! But it goes even deeper than that. What's the first thing we give a child when it's born? A name. Or when strangers meet, what is the first thing they do? Exchange names. According to the Bible, that was the very first thing Adam did in Eden. He named his world. 'And whatsoever Adam called every living creature, that was the name thereof.' No. There is no rest for me until I've identified this.

GLADYS. Can I see it?

[*He passes her the aloe.*]

PIET [*looking in his field book*]. This is the nearest I could get to it. Aloe humilis. But it's not right, is it?

GLADYS. They all look alike to me. Thorns and fat, fleshy leaves.

PIET. Of course. The distinguishing characteristics of the genus, the family being *Liliaceae*. Protection against grazing animals and the storage of moisture during periods of drought. But what species?! Ay, there's the rub.*

GLADYS. Do any of them have any scent?

PIET. No. That they don't have. But the old people used to make a purgative from the bitter juice of the leaves. And they are mentioned in the Bible.

GLADYS. Really, Peter! That doesn't help them. Purgatives and the Bible! It only makes it worse.

PIET. How do you mean?

GLADYS. Well, they're not very pretty plants, you know. Is there a good word for something you can't and don't want to touch? That would describe them.

PIET. A rose has also got its thorns.

GLADYS. There's no comparison! They've got a lovely scent, they're pretty to look at and so many beautiful colors. But these . . . [*She pushes the aloe away.*] No, thank you.

PIET [*looking around at his collection*]. This is not fair to them. An aloe isn't seen to its best advantage in a jam tin in a little backyard. They need space. The open veld with purple mountains in the distance. This one . . . arborescens . . . I think it is possibly my favorite . . . we had one on the farm growing around a goat kraal. Eight-, ten-foot high and so thick a chicken couldn't push its way through. You should have seen that when it was flowering. A veritable forest of scarlet spikes with the little suikerbekkies . . . honey birds . . . sucking up the nectar. Or even old ferox, with all its thorns! A hillside covered with them in bloom! 'Damp clods with corn may thank the showers | But when the desert boulder flowers | No common buds unfold.' Roy Campbell. He understood them. 'A glory such as from scant seed | The thirsty rocks suffice, to breed | Out of the rainless glare.'* And remember, it's a defiant glory, Gladys. That veld is a hard world. They and the thorn trees were just about the only things still alive in it when I finally packed up the old truck and left the farm. Four years of drought, but they were flowering once again. I'm ashamed to say it, but I resented them for that. It's a small soul that resents a flower, but I suppose mine was when I drove away and saw them there in the veld, surviving where I had failed.

GLADYS. Is that the price of survival in this country? Thorns and bitterness.

PIET. For the aloe it is. Maybe there's some sort of lesson for us there.

GLADYS. What do you mean?

PIET. We need survival mechanisms as well.

GLADYS. Speak for yourself, Peter. I'm a human being not a . . . prickly pear. [*Piet stares at her, appalled.*] What's the matter?

PIET. The prickly pear isn't an aloe, Gladys.

GLADYS. Please Peter . . . !

PIET. It's not even indigenous, my dear. The jointed cactus is a declared weed.

GLADYS. This conversation is upsetting me, Peter.

PIET. Sorry, my dear. What . . .

[*Gladys moves abruptly into the house. She returns a few seconds later with a tablecloth, which she tries, without too much success because of her agitation, to spread over the 'festive board'.*]

PIET. Sorry, my dear. What have I said?

GLADYS. We've already had droughts, prickly pears and despair. I suppose we'll be into politics next and the black man's misery. I'm not exaggerating, Peter. That is what a conversation with you has become—a catalogue of South African disasters. And you never stop! You seem to have a perverse need to dwell on what is cruel and ugly about this country. Is there nothing gentle in your world?

PIET. Is it really as bad as that?

GLADYS. Yes, it is. And don't make me feel guilty for saying it. [*She gestures at the aloes.*] Look at them! Is that what you hope for? To be like one of them? That's not the only possibility in life, you know. If that's what your expectations have shrunk to, it's your business, but God has not planted me in a jam tin. He might have cursed you Afrikaners, but not the whole human race. I want to live my life, not just survive it. I know I'm in this back-yard with them, but that is not going to happen to me.

PIET. I . . . [*He makes a helpless gesture.*] . . . What can I say? I'm sorry you don't like them.

GLADYS. Don't like them! It's worse than that, Peter. [*He looks at her.*] I'm going to be very honest with you. They frighten me. Yes, thorns and bitterness? I'm afraid there's more than that to them. They're turgid with violence, like everything else in this country. And they're trying to pass it on to me.

PIET [*carefully*]. What do you mean, my dear?

GLADYS. Don't worry. I won't let it happen. I won't!

[*She pauses.*]

PIET [*trying to break the mood*]. Well . . . [*Looks at his wrist watch.*] Time to get ready. They'll be here soon.

GLADYS [*looking fearful*]. Who?

PIET. Steve and Mavis.

[*They pause, looking at each other.*]

GLADYS. Yes, of course.

PIET. I'll look after the table.

GLADYS [*moving her hands to her face*]. I think I have picked up too much sun, you know. I feel quite flushed. I wonder if we've got any calamine lotion in the house?

[*She goes into the house. Piet adjusts the tablecloth and follows her.*]

## Scene 2

*The bedroom. Gladys is at her dressing table. There is a knock on the door. She tenses.*

PIET. Can I come in? [*Pause.*] Gladys!

GLADYS. Yes?

PIET. Can I come in?

GLADYS. One moment. [*She looks back abruptly at her bed, where her diary is hidden. She retrieves it, and after a few desperate seconds of trying to find another hiding place, sits down with it at her dressing table.*] All right!

[*Piet enters. He has a towel around his waist, having just bathed.*]

PIET. I thought you might be changing.

GLADYS. I will in a minute.

PIET. Well, I'll make a start. I won't be long. [*In the course of this scene he changes into a safari suit, with short trousers, long socks and brown shoes.*] Shorts won't be out of place, will they? It's not really a formal occasion, and it is outdoors. I am sure you ladies will look after the finery.

[*He becomes conscious of her sitting very still at the dressing table.*]

PIET. Were you busy with your diary?

GLADYS. What do you mean?

PIET. Making your entry for the day.

GLADYS. It's too early for that. Nothing has happened yet.

PIET. True. But, as you said, my dear, you will certainly have subject matter tonight.

GLADYS. I was just paging through it.

PIET. Reading the old ones.

GLADYS. That's right. Reminding myself of the exciting life I've been living. [*She opens her diary, but in such a way that he can't see it.*] This hasn't been such a good week. Let's see . . . an old woman looking for work, the meter reader . . . who else? Oh yes! Those little black boys selling brooms and baskets. But they're always around. Last week I had a gentleman from the Watchtower Society* at the front door. That was a long talk. I was a bit nervous at first because he asked if he could come in, but he turned out to be very nice. Do you know they've got a date worked out for the end of the world? It's not far off, either. I almost told him there are times when I think it has already happened. [*Piet smiles.*] I'm not joking. It can be very quiet here in the house when you're at work. If I haven't got the radio on or a car isn't passing in the street, it's hard sometimes to believe there is a world out there full of other people. Just you and me. That's all that's left. The streets are empty and I imagine you wandering around looking for another survivor. If you ever find one, Peter, you must bring him home.

PIET. Well, I've got news for you. I found six of them and they'll be arriving in a short while. I know it's been a quiet time, but under the circumstances, don't you think that's been for the best?

GLADYS [*with a little laugh*]. Quiet time! You're an unpredictable mixture of understatement and exaggeration. I never know which to expect. How long have I been back? Six months? Seven?

PIET. Nearly seven.

GLADYS. And you don't find it strange that in all that time not one of our friends has been around to see us, or invited us to see them? Solly, or Mervyn, or Betty . . . there was never any short-age of comrades in the old days. Is it because of me?

PIET. No. You mustn't think that.

GLADYS. Then say something! Every time I mention it you either ignore me, or change the subject.

PIET [*trying to placate her*]. All right, my dear! Relax.

GLADYS. God I wish you would stop saying that!

PIET. There's no mystery, Gladys. A lesson in human nature maybe, but that's all. It's a dangerous time and people are frightened.

GLADYS. Of what?

PIET. Isn't that obvious?

GLADYS. I don't know. You tell me.

PIET. The police raids, then Steve going to jail, the banning of the congress . . . everyone has crawled away into his own little shell.* It's as simple as that. Why do you shake your head?

GLADYS. It's too simple.

PIET. Most explanations of human behavior usually are.

[*He makes a move to leave the bedroom.*]

GLADYS. Peter . . .

PIET. Yes, my dear?

GLADYS. Is there something I don't know?

PIET [*evenly*]. If there is, I know nothing about it as well.

GLADYS. Then I am even more surprised at how easily you accept the situation.

PIET. I don't accept it easily, but there is nothing else to do. I can't change human nature.

GLADYS. Not even a complaint about its lack of courage and faith. After all it has meant the end of 'The Cause.'

PIET. No. I don't want to sit in judgment on others.

GLADYS. And what about you, Peter?

PIET. Why should I be any different? Anyone is justified in feeling nervous and uneasy these days.

GLADYS. The word was frightened. [*She pauses.*] Well?

PIET. Yes, I am.

GLADYS. That's very hard to believe. Watching you with your aloes, quoting your poetry . . . in spite of all that has happened, you've still got a whole world intact. You seem very safe to me.

PIET. The aloes give me pleasure, Gladys, not a purpose. [*She smiles.*] What's the matter?

GLADYS [*closing her eyes*]. Don't say anything! I am going to try to remember. And no prompting. [*She quotes from memory*.] 'There is a purpose to life, and we will be measured by the extent to which we harness ourselves to it.' And the author . . . Thoreau.*

PIET.  Correct.

GLADYS.  Word perfect?

PIET.  Yes.

GLADYS [*delighted with herself*]. So I get full marks! That's encouraging. After all, it was quite a few years ago. Can you remember when?

PIET.  No.

GLADYS.  Oh, Peter! How sad. Our very first meeting . . . the concert . . . when you walked me home afterward.

PIET.  Yes, yes, of course. I had forgotten.

GLADYS.  But I'm cheating a little. I only remember it that clearly because I wrote it down that night and read it to myself many times afterward. That's how my diaries started, you know. The very first entry. I was so impressed with the words and your faith in them. [*Closing her eyes again as she tries to remember*.] You said good night to me on the verandah and I let myself into the house. My mother was still awake, and angry. I tried to apologize to her for being late, but she wouldn't accept it. Just sat there in bed, propped up against her pillows, ignoring me. I made her a cup of Ovaltine, went to my room, sat down at the dressing table and wrote: 'There is a purpose to life . . .' [*Very proud of herself*.] How's that?

PIET.  Very good.

GLADYS.  Do you still believe it?

PIET.  Yes. It's not as easy as it used to be, but I still do.

GLADYS.  I envy you, as I did then. Nothing seemed more without purpose than the Gladys Adams I looked at in the mirror, in that stale room, with my mother sick and sulking on the other side of the wall. She had a purpose. A terrible determination not to die. I'm not exaggerating. Dr. Finnemore said her last six years were a miracle. I was convinced she was going to live longer than me. At times I still find it hard to believe that she is dead and I'm the one who's alive. It's very unfair. That was another entry in the first diary. 'My mother died today. I haven't cried yet, and I don't think I'm going to.'

PIET. Don't brood about bygones, my dear. It's all over and done with. [*Trying to change the subject.*] That one must be nearly full now.

GLADYS. How do you know?

PIET. Page a day. It's nearly a year since I gave it to you.

GLADYS [*sharply*]. I see. It's going to be like a birthday, is it, or our anniversary? A date that mustn't be forgotten. 'Give Gladys another diary.'

PIET. Right. I'll forget it if you want me to.

GLADYS. Just like that? That's more than I could do.

PIET. I'll try.

GLADYS. No, don't do that. It was a very touching gesture, even though I wasn't in a state to appreciate it at the time. [*Opening the diary.*] I've kept the card. I use it as a marker. [*Reading.*] 'Take this sweet soul! We'll start again. | They've come and gone and all in vain | For we live on.' It was so appropriate. Where does it come from?

PIET. Henry Wadsworth Longfellow.*

GLADYS [*holding her diary*]. I'd be lost without this. It's where I keep all my little secrets. A woman needs them, and as you know, I did lose all of those I once had. You were given a receipt for them, remember? A little piece of paper torn from a grubby notebook.

PIET. Yes, I do. But that is something we must try to forget, Gladys, not remember.

GLADYS. Yes I realize that. But I can't help myself sometimes. There's so much that keeps reminding me. After all, it was in this very room. He sat down here, opened the first one, and started to read . . .

PIET [*his desperation growing*]. I remember it very clearly, my love! I was here! With you! [*He pauses.*] Maybe if we changed the room around . . . rearranged the furniture! That might help. What do you think?

GLADYS.  You could try.

PIET.  I know what it really needs, though. More light! This is a dark little room. I know what that means. I've had my occasions to sit brooding in them as well. That's the answer, Gladys! As soon as we've got a little something together in the bank again I'm going to put another window in that wall. Light! That's what we need. And we'll change the furniture as well. It will be a different room. I should have thought of it before.

GLADYS [*she hasn't been listening to him*].  Yes . . . you led them in and then stood there next to the doorway. I can't remember much about you after that. I was still trying to get into my dressing gown. Then the one in charge saw them on the table, asked you what they were . . . you told him . . . he apologized to me nicely and started to read them . . . page by page. I couldn't believe it was happening. Did I ever get my dressing gown on?

PIET.  Please . . .

GLADYS [*violently*].  That's an important question, Peter! Did I ever get my dressing gown on?

PIET.  No.

GLADYS.  So I just stood there. . .! What did I look like?

PIET.  For God's sake, Gladys! What do you want?

GLADYS.  An answer to a simple question! What did I look like?

PIET.  You had just woken up, you were sleepy, you didn't know what was going on . . .

GLADYS [*she gazes into the dressing-table mirror*].  Me.

[*Pause.*]

PIET.  They won't visit us again, Gladys.

GLADYS.  What makes you so sure of that?

PIET.  Because there is nothing to be found here, and they know it. They're not fools. *Please* believe me. Where's my Bible?

[*He finds it on a bedside table.*]

GLADYS. What are you going to do with that?

PIET. Listen to me now. On this book ... on my mother's grave ...

GLADYS. Oh shut up! Just say what you want to.

PIET. The search that night had nothing to do with you person-ally. They were looking for ... God knows what! ... banned literature, political secrets that didn't exist.

GLADYS. And instead they found my diaries, and they did take them away and they haven't given them back!

PIET. I'm still trying. That's why I've kept the receipt.

GLADYS [outraged]. You what?

PIET. Kept the receipt.

GLADYS. Get it. [He hesitates.] Where's that receipt, Peter? [He produces it from inside the Bible. She can barely articulate.] What's written on it?

PIET [reading the scrap of paper]. 'Gladys Bezuidenhout's diaries ...' then Strydom's signature, the date and our address.

GLADYS. Tear it up. [He hesitates.] Tear it up! Small pieces. [He does so. She holds out her hand, takes the pieces and puts them down carefully on the dressing table. For a few seconds she lapses into an almost bland normality.] There. I've cancelled those years. I'm going to forget I ever lived them. They weren't just laundry lists, you know. There were very intimate and personal things in those diaries, things a woman only talks about to herself. Even then it took me a lot of trust and courage to do that. I know I never had much of either, but I was learning. [Her hysteria begins to surface again.] You were such a persuasive teacher, Peter! 'Trust, Gladys. Trust yourself. Trust life.' There's nothing left of that. [She brandishes her diary.] Must I tell you what I've been trying to do with this all day? Hide it. It's been behind the dressing table ... under the mattress ... Can you think of somewhere really safe? Where nobody would find it, including yourself? There isn't, is there? Do you know what I would really like to do with this? Make you eat it and turn it into shit ... then maybe everybody would leave it alone. Yes, you heard me correctly. Shit! I've learned

237

how to use my dirty words. And just as well, because there's no other adequate vocabulary for this country. Maybe I should do that in case they come again. A page full of filthy language. Because that is what they were really hoping for when they sat down with my diaries. Filth!

PIET. I don't know what to say.

GLADYS. Thank God! Because if you were to tell me once more that they won't come again . . .! To start with, I don't believe you, but even if I did, that once was enough. You seem to have a lot of difficulty understanding that, Peter. It only needs to happen to a woman once, for her to lose all trust she ever had in anything or anybody. They violated me, Peter. I might just as well have stayed in that bed, lifted up my nightdress and given them each a turn. I've shocked you. Good! Then maybe now you understand. Yes, I can see it. You are frightened.

PIET. That's right.

GLADYS. Of me?

PIET. For you. Please be careful.

GLADYS. You're too late with that advice. You should have given it to the Gladys Adams you conjured with, instead of persuading her that life was to be trusted. Not that she needed it. She'd been warned. She knew the dogs are mad.

PIET. What do you mean?

GLADYS. Exactly what I've said. Our dogs are mad. They're guarding our dirtbins, not us. I discovered that as a little girl. Forgetting it was the biggest mistake I ever made . . . and it was you who made me do it. Are you feeling guilty?

PIET. Yes. I know that nothing of what you've been through would have happened if you hadn't married me.

GLADYS. That's perfectly true. Which makes you as responsible for my condition as them. [*Stopping herself.*] No . . . No . . .! Why don't you stop me?

PIET [*nearly frantic*]. I can't! I've tried.

GLADYS [*appalled*]. I didn't mean that. I'm sorry. [*She pauses . . . then quietly . . .*] What are we going to do, Peter?

PIET. About tonight?

GLADYS. And tomorrow . . . and the next day . . .

PIET [*trying his utmost to calm her down*]. I know. First thing . . . I want you to lie down and relax in a nice hot bath. I'll run it for you. Just lie down and relax. And while you're doing that, I'll take a bus into Gelvandale and put off Steve and Mavis . . .

GLADYS. No.

PIET. Just listen! I'll take the wine I bought and have a drink with them at their place. It won't be obvious. I'll say . . . something has come up at work . . . overtime . . .

GLADYS. No. Don't you think we're coping with enough lies already? Let them come. I'll be all right. [*Piet is not convinced. Gladys puts her diary down on the dressing table.*] There. No more hiding it away . . . or anything. Don't you trust me?

PIET. Of course I do. But are you quite sure you want them to come?

GLADYS. Yes. And to prove it, I'd like to change now, please.

PIET. Sorry, my dear. I'll . . . I'll start to get things ready.

GLADYS [*as he is leaving the room*]. I am trying, Peter.

PIET. I know that. [*Piet goes out, leaving Gladys alone at the dressing table.*]

## Scene 3

*The backyard. Piet is laying the table. Gladys comes out of the house. She has changed and has a shawl over her shoulders. Her manner—quiet and composed—is in direct contrast to the violence and hysteria in the bedroom. Piet watches her expectantly. She goes to the table.*

GLADYS. Is this where Mavis sits?

PIET. Yes. [*Gladys places a little parcel on the table.*] What is it, my dear?

GLADYS. A small gesture, that's all. A little embroidered hand-kerchief. It's not very much, but the needlework is very fine. My mother would never let a visitor leave the house without some little souvenir of the occasion.

PIET. That's a lovely thought, Gladys. And you look splendid!

GLADYS. Thank you. [*She looks at the table.*] Well, you're quite right, Peter. It is going to look very good.

PIET. Everyman's altar to the civilized virtues . . . a well-laid table with food waiting and friends coming. The candlesticks create a sense of occasion, don't they? You wouldn't like to do your fancy thing with the serviettes, would you?

GLADYS. If it will make you happy. [*She sits down at the table and starts to fold them.*] You look nervous, Peter. Please don't worry about me. I promise everything will be all right.

PIET. I can see that! I'm just over-anxious for us all to have a good time tonight.

[*He takes a little book out of his pocket.*]

GLADYS. What are you reading?

PIET. My little book of quotations. I'm looking for a few strong lines for a toast when we sit down to eat.

GLADYS. What have you found?

PIET [*opening the book and reading*]. Where is it? . . . Where is it? . . . Yes! 'Sweet is the scene where genial friendship plays | The pleasing game of interchanging praise.' Oliver Wendell Holmes. There's that. Then this: 'What is the odds so long as the fire of soul is kindled at the taper of conviviality, and the wing of friendship never moults a feather.' Charles Dickens. Or this: 'Thy friendship oft has made my heart to ache: | Do be my enemy—for friendship's sake.' William Blake.*

GLADYS. Let me hear the second one again.

PIET. 'What is the odds so long as the fire of soul is kindled at the taper of conviviality . . .'

GLADYS. Yes, that's the one. Tapers . . . candles! It fits in.

PIET. I never thought of that! Settled. I shall now commit it to memory.

[*Gladys watches him as he paces up and down, memorizing the lines.*]

GLADYS. Steven means a lot to you, doesn't he?

PIET. Yes, he does. After you, I owe him more than anybody else in this world. If it wasn't for Steve, I suppose I'd still be sitting in a little room somewhere hating rain . . . because it had come too late. That's how I ended up when I left the farm. A little room in Havelock Street. I used to pull the curtains and put cotton wool in my ears so that I wouldn't hear it.

GLADYS. That doesn't sound like you.

PIET. It was me all right. [*He goes into the house and returns with a few more items for the table.*] Doesn't seem right, does it, that something so important in your life should depend on chance? Because that is all it was. It could just as easily not have happened. But one of the other bus drivers was sick one morning and they took me off the Humewood run and put me onto No. 11 . . . Market Square to Cadles. I was even fed up about it. Instead of that nice drive next to the sea, it was into that ugly Coloured area with all the factories. But it also happened to be the morning the bus boycott started.* I'd heard talk about it in the sheds, but so what! It had nothing to do with me. Politics! . . . [*He smiles.*] until I drove my empty bus through that crowd walking to work. Hell, Gladys, it was a sight! Men, women, even school children, walking and laughing and full of defiance. Bitter and hard as I was inside, I felt emotions. At first I tried to ignore them. I said to myself the people were being stupid. Why make an issue of a penny? That's all the fares had been increased by. But they didn't think that. They carried on walking and waving at me and my empty bus. Steve had a position on the corner of Standford and Kempston roads. I'd see this man standing there handing out pamphlets or addressing a little crowd. Then one morning the police moved in and arrested him. I was parked at a bus stop across the road when it happened. Into the van he went and I thought that was the end of it. Not a damn. Next day he was back again. The comrades had bailed him out. That's when I thought: To hell with it. I want to hear what this little bugger is saying. And anyway my bus was empty as usual. So I stopped and got out. I got a little nervous with all of them watching me as I walked over. I was the only white there. When

I got to them I said I just wanted to listen. The next thing I knew is they were cheering and laughing and slapping me on the back and making a place for me in the front row. [*He pauses.*] I don't know how to describe it, Gladys . . . the effect that had on me. It was like rain after a long drought. Being welcomed by those people was the most moving thing that has ever happened to me. Feelings about life and people, which I thought had withered away like everything else on the farm, were alive again. I was so emotional I didn't even hear what Steve said when he carried on talking. Something about a penny and the price of bread. I fell in beside him when they started walking and when he turned off to go to the building site, where he was working, I carried on alone. Into town and straight to the head office where I handed in my notice. They docked off a week when they paid me out. Deserting my bus while on duty. The next day I was back on that same corner, and a week later I was handing out pamphlets with Steve. The bus company won in the end. They got that penny from the people. I thought we had failed, but not Steve. He said he'd expected it. The really important thing was that those two weeks of boycott had raised the political consciousness of the people. They had acted politically, some of them maybe for the first time in their lives. My first lesson from Steve, and the most important one. An evil system isn't a natural disaster. There's nothing you can do to stop a drought, but bad laws and social injustice are man-made and can be unmade by men. It's as simple as that.* We can make this a better world to live in. [*Gladys has been listening and watching very attentively.*] You've been very patient with me.

GLADYS. It wasn't difficult. I saw the man I first met very clearly again. It's been a hard time for you, hasn't it?

PIET. No more so than for everybody else, and certainly less than for Steve.

GLADYS. Well at least the two of you will be able to salvage our friendship tonight. [*A pause. Piet doesn't respond.*] That's at least some consolation, isn't it? [*Piet hesitates.*] What's the matter?

PIET. He's leaving, Gladys.

GLADYS. What do you mean?

PIET Steve and Mavis and the children are leaving the country. They're going to settle in England.

GLADYS. How do you know?

PIET. He told me.

GLADYS. For good?

PIET. Yes.

GLADYS. When?

PIET. Next week. [*They pause, then Piet goes into the house and returns with something else for the table.*]

GLADYS. You're joking.

PIET. I'm not.

GLADYS. Well ... that's a surprise ... to say the least. Steven leaving. I always thought of him as being like you, hanging on to the bitter end. [*Shaking her head in disbelief.*] I don't know what to say.

PIET. Neither do I.

GLADYS [*her tone hardening*]. No. I'm wrong. I do. Good for Steven! And England! From all I've heard, it's a very different world to this one. They are very lucky.

PIET. He's leaving on an exit permit, Gladys.

GLADYS. So?

PIET. He can't come back.

GLADYS. So!

PIET. I don't think it's all that easy for him. This is his home as much as it is ours.

GLADYS. No. I know I was born here, but I will never call it that. Why didn't you tell me earlier?

PIET. I don't know. Maybe because I also find it so hard to believe.

GLADYS. Believe what? That he doesn't love 'home' as much as you? It's almost a joke, you know, coming after all you've just been telling me.

PIET. You're being very hard on him, my dear.

GLADYS. Of course. Because I'm jealous. I'd never persuade you to go, would I?

PIET. I haven't had to survive a banning order for three years and then six months in jail.

GLADYS. That's not such a high price to pay for coming to your senses. I still think he's lucky and I still envy him for getting out.

PIET. Anyway, he's certainly doing that. At first I thought he meant Middelburg or Graaff Reinet, or something like that. He's got family up there. That's where Mavis and the children went when he was inside. I think I said as much. But he just stood there on the pavement smiling at me in a funny sort of way. [*Shaking his head.*] I think I'd rather forget that moment with him.

GLADYS. Why?

PIET. It was as if we were embarrassed by each other.

GLADYS. You didn't tell me that either. I'd imagined a warm reunion of old friends.

PIET. No, it wasn't quite that. But maybe it's not surprising. We were caught on the wrong foot. I certainly was. I didn't even know he had been released from jail and suddenly there he was walking toward me on Main Street.

GLADYS. Go on.

PIET. I never thought I'd feel like that with him . . . you know, forcing myself to make polite conversation as if he was some-body whose name I had forgotten. I asked him about Mavis and the children and that's when he said: 'We're leaving, Piet.' When I finally understood what he meant, I didn't know what to say. I still don't. All I could think of was to ask him and the family to come around for a farewell meal. He said, 'Yes.' That's all.

GLADYS. So if you hadn't bumped into him, you might not have seen him again.

PIET [*hurriedly*]. No. He said he intended coming out to see us and say good-bye before leaving.

GLADYS. He left it very late.

PIET. I'm sure he's been busy . . . packing up and . . . it's a big move.

GLADYS. So there goes Steven! You're not left with much now are you? . . . Me! . . . And I don't think I qualify as a comrade. I don't want to rub salt into your wounds, Peter, but I can't help being just a little cynical at this moment about the 'struggle' all of you were so passionately committed to. I used to think there was something wrong with me when I heard everyone carrying on about 'the cause,' 'freedom,' 'the people.' You see, I never thought things were as bad as you made out. Some of the talk even made me a little nervous. Yes! You never realized that, did you? You were too busy believing that life had a purpose and I was too ashamed to say it made me nervous. But I can remember very clearly how frightened some of the talk made me. 'Over-throwing the regime' sounded very violent to me. [*With a little laugh.*] Not much chance of that now, is there, with everybody . . . how did you put it? . . . crawled away into his own little shell. Snails aren't the most revolutionary of God's creatures.

PIET. They weren't empty slogans, Gladys. To misquote the Bard: The weakness lay not in our ideals, but in ourselves.*

GLADYS. Yes, of course. But not all of you surely? Just the one.

PIET. What do you mean, my dear?

GLADYS. Don't do that, Peter. You know very well what I mean. The informer. [*Piet doesn't respond.*] I'm not imagining things, am I? Just before I went away wasn't everybody whispering about there being an informer in the group? And that is how the police . . .

PIET. Yes, yes. You're right.

GLADYS [*finishing the sentence with quiet deliberation*]. . . . and that is how the police knew that Steven was going to break his Banning Order and be at the party.

PIET. I said you were right, my dear.

GLADYS. Have you never worked out who it was?

PIET. No.

GLADYS. Did you try?

PIET. Oh yes. I spent a lot of time doing that while you were away.

GLADYS. And?

PIET. I stopped myself.

GLADYS. Why?

PIET. I discovered that if I tried hard enough I could find a good reason for suspecting everyone. I wouldn't have had any friends left if I carried on.

GLADYS. But on the face of it you haven't, Peter.

PIET. Steve and five other friends are on their way to us at this very moment. Let me see if I can remember my toast. [*He studies his book of quotations.*] 'What is the odds so long as the fire of soul . . . is kindled at the taper of conviviality . . .'

GLADYS. It's just as well, I suppose, that I decided not to go to that party. I would have been a very likely suspect.

PIET. I don't think so, my dear.

GLADYS. Not to you, obviously. But I'm sure the others would have had their doubts. After all, it was no secret that I didn't share everyone else's enthusiasm for 'the cause.' [*Piet remains absorbed in his book of quotations.*] It's no use, Peter.

PIET. What?

GLADYS. I'm sorry, but I've got to ask it. Do the others think it's you?

PIET [*trying very hard to avoid her question*]. I told you, my dear, on my side I could find a good reason . . .

GLADYS. Peter. Do all the others think it's you?

PIET. I don't know.

GLADYS. Are you lying to me, or yourself?

[*She waits.*]

PIET. Yes. It looks as if . . . they all think . . . I'm the one.

GLADYS. What about Steven?

PIET. No! He wouldn't be coming here if he thought that.

GLADYS. He's not here yet.

PIET. He didn't cross to the other side of the street when he saw me coming.

GLADYS [*outraged*]. Who did that?

PIET. It doesn't matter.

GLADYS [*quietly*]. My God! I want to scream. Maybe swearing would be better. How long have you known?

PIET. It isn't something I 'know' in that way. There's no one day on which a drought starts. But there were meetings to which I wasn't invited and then, as I said, I realized people were avoiding me. There is only one conclusion.

GLADYS. And you didn't tell me because you thought it would aggravate my condition. Didn't you know I'd realize it sooner or later? I haven't been made that insensitive.

PIET. It's not as simple as that, Gladys. Obviously I wanted to avoid upsetting you. But even without that, could we have talked about it? [*He speaks with deep emotion.*] Sat down and discussed over supper the fact that I was considered a traitor? That's the correct word. Could you have made a simple entry to that effect in your diary? God! It's the ugliest thing that has ever happened to me. It makes me feel more ashamed of . . . myself, my fellow men . . . of everything! . . . in a way I never thought possible. [*Gladys has been watching him very carefully.*] What's the matter?

GLADYS. I'm trying to see you as others do.

PIET. And?

GLADYS. It's not true, is it?

[*Piet stares back at her for a long time before turning away.*]

PIET [*vacantly . . . looking at his wrist watch*]. They should be here any minute now. I'll . . . I'll light the candles.

GLADYS [*getting up, she goes to the table*]. Yes, it looks very good. I'm going inside. Call me . . . if they come.

[*She walks into the house, leaving Piet alone in the backyard.*]

CURTAIN

# ACT TWO

*The backyard about two hours later. Piet is still waiting. He looks at his watch and after a moment's hesitation, he goes into the house and puts on the outside light. He returns to the backyard, blows out the candles and starts to clear the table.*

*After a few seconds he hears the 'Marseillaise' being played on a harmonica in the darkness beyond the backyard gate. Piet hurriedly resets the table. Steve appears out of the darkness.*

STEVE [*respectfully, but with an exaggerated degree of authority*]. Excuse me, sir! [*He flashes some sort of identity card.*] Security Branch. I wonder if you could help me?

PIET [*playing along*]. Yes, my good man. What can I do for you?

STEVE. I'm looking for a mad Afrikaner, who recites English poetry. He stays around here somewhere.

PIET [*pretending outrage*]. A what?

STEVE. His name is Piet Bezuidenhout.

PIET. Did I hear you right? An Afrikaner, reciting English poetry! And a Bezuidenhout at that!

STEVE. I told you he was mad, sir.

PIET. It's worse than that, my good man. There's a name for his sort. Why do you think we lost the Boer War? And what do you think is making your people so cheeky these days?

STEVE [*whips off his hat; is suddenly servile*]. Sorry, sir.

PIET. Subversive elements like him. English poetry! If I was you I would choose my company more carefully in future.

STEVE. Is it all right if I visit you instead, then?

PIET. Have you got a bottle? [*Steve produces a bottle of wine from the side pocket of his jacket and holds it.*] Come inside.

STEVE. Thank you, sir. [*He lets himself into the backyard.*]

PIET [*moving to the house*]. They've arrived, Gladys!

STEVE [*obviously very embarrassed*]. Hold on, Piet! Hold on, man! I'm alone. Mavis couldn't make it. Charmaine has come down

248

with something. Looks like the flu. With the trip coming up so soon, Mavis thought it best to stay at home with the children.

PIET. Don't give it a thought. I'm sorry to hear about Charmaine, but if my memory doesn't fail me, the two of us were enough for a good time in the past.

STEVE [*with forced exuberance*]. Right! Where do we start? [*Before Piet can answer.*] Ja, of course! You ready? [*Steve puts down his hat, buttons up his jacket, adopts a very formal stance and then launches into a recital of Longfellow's 'The Slaves' Dream'.*]

> Beside the ungathered rice he lay,
>     His sickle in his hand;
> His breast was bare, his matted hair
>     Was buried in the sand.
> Again, in the mist and shadow of sleep,
>     He saw his Native Land.
>
> Wide through the landscape of his dreams
>     The lordly Niger flowed;
> Beneath the palm-trees on the plain
>     Once more a king he strode;
> And heard the tinkling caravans
>     Descend the mountain road.
>
> He saw once more his dark-eyed queen
>     Among her children stand;
> They clasped his neck, they kissed his cheeks,
>     They held him by the hand!—
> A tear burst from the sleeper's lids
>     And fell into the sand.
>
> And then at furious speed he rode
>     Along the Niger's bank;
> His bridle-reins were golden chains,
>     And, with a martial clank,
> At each leap he could feel his scabbard of steel
>     Smiting his stallion's flank.

Before him, like a blood-red flag,
   The bright flamingoes flew;
From morn till night he followed their flight,
   O'er plains where the tamarind grew,
Till he saw the roofs of Caffre huts,
   And the ocean rose to view.

At night he heard the lion roar,
   And the hyena scream,
And the river-horse, as he crushed the reeds
   Beside some hidden stream;
And it passed, like a glorious roll of drums,
   Through the triumph of his dream.

The forests, with their myriad tongues,
   Shouted of liberty;
And the Blast of the Desert cried aloud,
   With a voice so wild and free,
That he started in his sleep and smiled
   At their tempestuous glee.

He did not feel the driver's whip,
   Nor the burning heat of day;
For Death had illumined the Land of Sleep,
   And his lifeless body lay
A worn-out fetter, that the soul
   Had broken and thrown away!

[*Steves's delivery is awkward and amateurish and before long he starts floundering for the words. Piet prompts him to start with, but eventually takes over. Steve, one beat behind, struggles to keep up as Piet gets into his stride and then gallops splendidly to the end of the poem. We are obviously watching a little scene that has taken place many times in the past. The effect is both comic and moving. When it is finished, there is a pause as the two men look at each other.*]

PIET [*quietly*]. Welcome, Steve.

STEVE. Hello, you mad Afrikaner.

PIET [*embarrassed by the emotion he feels*]. I'll get the wine.

STEVE [*handing over his bottle*]. Let's open mine!

PIET. This puts my humble offering to shame. We'll save it for the feast. Have you eaten?

STEVE. Later.

PIET. Make yourself at home, man! Take off your coat. The night is still young.

STEVE. Okay. Bring on the dancing girls!

[*Piet goes into the house . . . the bedroom. Gladys is sitting at her dressing table.*]

PIET. Steve's arrived.

GLADYS. I heard his voice. And the others?

PIET. No. Charmaine is sick. That's why he's late. Mavis stayed behind to look after her. Come and join us, my dear, even if it's only for a few minutes. Let's end the day on a happy note. It's the Steve we knew. He wouldn't have come if everything wasn't all right.

GLADYS. I will. Just leave me for a little while.

[*Piet rejoins Steve in the backyard.*]

PIET [*holding up a bottle of wine*]. 'A draught of vintage that hath been cooled a long age in the deep delved refrigerator!' I told you to take off your coat, man! You look like a bloody bank manager. [*His happiness knows no bounds.*] Hell, Steve, this calls for a toast.

STEVE. Just as long as I don't have to make a speech.

PIET [*laughing at a memory*]. I can remember an occasion when that did not present a problem.

STEVE. When was that?

PIET. Your very first visit to us here. No? [*He raises his glass.*] 'To the birth of a man!' Come on, Steve! What's the matter with you? My godson.

STEVE. Hey, by the way! Little Pietertjie's birth.

PIET. That's right. We were still busy unpacking and sorting things out in there when you arrived from the hospital.

STEVE. Of course. Hell, Piet, that goes back a few years now, hey? He turns seven next birthday. I couldn't believe it when they woke me up in the waiting room and said: 'It's a boy, at last, Mr. Daniels.' What the hell was it you wanted me to call him again?

PIET.  Gorki . . . and I still think you should have done it.

STEVE.  Haaikona Piet! *You* go to school with a name like that and see what the other kids do to you.

PIET.  To hell with them! Gorki Daniels! It's got a ring to it, man.

STEVE.  That was quite a night, hey?

PIET.  Memorable, my friend. Memorable. Obviously, there had to be a toast to your son, and a speech from you.

STEVE.  Then one to the house, and a speech from you!

PIET.  What came next? The future!

STEVE.  That was a speech from both of us, wasn't it?

PIET.  Correct. I proposed, you replied. But the trouble really started when we decided that a general toast to the comrades was not good enough, that all of them merited individual recognition. And if you remember, our membership was quite healthy in those days.

STEVE.  Ja, no chance of getting drunk on that now, hey? So there's our toast. To the good old days! If nothing else, they produced a few revolutionary hangovers.

PIET  [*restraining him from emptying his glass, and raising his own*]. 'What is the odds . . .' [*Piet has forgotten the toast. His spectacles and little book of quotations come out hurriedly.*] 'What is the odds so long . . .' [*He finds the correct page.*] 'What is the odds so long as the fire of soul is kindled at the taper of conviviality and the wing of friendship never moults a feather.'

STEVE.  Jesus, Bezuidenhout! How the hell do you do it?

PIET.  What?

STEVE.  All your quotations and poetry. You should have been a schoolteacher, man.

PIET.  I tried to be a farmer, Steve, and the poetry starts where that ends . . . with a few seconds of silence out in the veld under a very hot sun.

STEVE.  You've never told me that one.

PIET. I know, but only because I've tried very hard to forget it. And I thought I had . . . but it's been a lot in my thoughts lately.

STEVE. What happened?

PIET. Nothing. That's the whole point to the story . . . nothing. One of the last little chores of Baas Bezuidenhout on the farm was to put on his black suit and join an African family that had worked for him—and his father before him—around a little grave out in the veld. A baby had died. Gastroenteritis. There hadn't been a drop of clean water on Alwynlaagte . . . the farm . . . for God alone knows how many months. They hadn't 'dug' that hole, Steve. They'd used a pick and crowbars to break into the ground, it was so dry.

Anyway . . . when it came to my turn to say a few words . . . [Piet shakes his head.] That hole with the little homemade coffin at the bottom defeated me. I had dug plenty of them as deep as that, but to plant trees or fence posts, or to lay in a dipping tank.

A sense of deep, personal failure overwhelmed me. They waited—I don't know how long—until I just shook my head and walked away.

I lasted out another three months on the farm, and that is how I passed the time. There was this little book of poetry and stories in the house. I read through it many times, looking for something I could have said out there in the veld.

STEVE. Did Baas Bezuidenhout ever find it?

PIET. No. But I learned a few poems while trying. Seen any of the old crowd since you've been out?

STEVE. Only Solly. He's been damned good, helping us with our boat tickets, you know, and everything. Got his lawyer to sort out the Exit Permit and to have my Banning Order relaxed for these last few weeks. But he's the only one.

PIET. Yes, things have been very quiet lately.

STEVE. So he was saying. But even if they weren't, I don't want to know or talk about it.

PIET. I was just wondering . . .

STEVE. No, sure, sure. It's just that I've had enough, Piet.

PIET. I understand.

[*An awkward silence between the two men is broken by Gladys's appearance.*]

GLADYS. Hello, Steven!

STEVE. Gladys! Long time no see, hey!

[*They shake hands. Steve and Gladys treat each other with a stilted politeness and formality.*]

PIET. Good to see him here again, isn't it?

GLADYS. Yes, it is. I'm sorry Mavis couldn't come. Peter told me about . . . which one is it that's sick?

STEVE. Charmaine.

GLADYS. What a lovely name.

STEVE. Mavis is also sorry she couldn't make it. She really was looking forward to seeing you again.

PIET [*pulling out her chair*]. Here, my dear. A glass of sherry?

GLADYS. Yes, please. [*Piet walks into the house.*]

GLADYS. And bring out the plate of snacks! I put them in the fridge. [*Turning to Steve.*] We'd given up hope of seeing you.

STEVE. Ja, sorry about everything. [*Trying to break the ice.*] So, how things been with you, Gladys?

GLADYS. Oh, just the same old humdrum existence. I putter about the house and Peter goes for long walks in the veld looking for aloes.

STEVE. Ja, so I see. [*Gesturing at the aloes.*] This is all new.

GLADYS. Peter's new hobby, now that there's no politics left. Aloes. He takes it very seriously. He's got a little book and he knows all their names.

STEVE. I prefer flowers myself.

GLADYS. That makes two of us. We tried to lay out a little flower bed here once . . . Roses! . . . But the soil is very poor. Come, let's sit down. So, Steven, you're on your way to England. I couldn't believe my ears when Peter told me.

STEVE. Next week.

GLADYS. So I gather. You're very fortunate, you know.

STEVE. You reckon so, Gladys?

GLADYS. To be leaving this country! You don't have any doubts, surely? You of all people.

STEVE [*with an embarrassed little laugh*]. Well, the children are excited, that I can say for sure.

GLADYS. And so they should be. It will be a marvelous experience. Travel broadens the mind.

STEVE. Ja, I'm glad for their sakes. It's just that I don't know how much broadening mine can take. I'm forty-two, Gladys, and I've spent most of those years here in Port Elizabeth. It's going to be a big change.

GLADYS. But for the better. You must think positively.

STEVE. You're right. It's hard to imagine anything worse than the past years. [*Trying to move the conversation along.*] One thing I can say is that I'm not looking forward to the boat trip too much.

GLADYS. One of the mail ships?

STEVE. *Windsor Castle*. I know I'm going to be seasick all the way! And I can't swim, you know.

GLADYS. You're joking.

STEVE. Truly. I love my fishing, but when it comes to getting into that water . . . ! No, thank you!

GLADYS. Well, don't worry about it. They've got life-belts and all sorts of things that will keep you floating in case something happens . . . which is most unlikely.

STEVE. What's it going to be like, Gladys?

GLADYS. What?

STEVE. England. All I know about it is what I've seen on the bioscope and pictures in books. They always make it look very pretty. [*She is staring at him.*] Is it really like that?

GLADYS. Why do you ask me?

STEVE. You're from England, aren't you?

GLADYS. What makes you say that?

STEVE. Oh, your manners and the way you speak. Not rough and ready like Piet and myself. Sorry . . . I always thought.

GLADYS. That's all right. In a way I suppose I am from England . . . now. [*She gives a little smile.*] I've been there many times.

STEVE. Tell me about it.

GLADYS. What do you want to know, Steven?

STEVE. Anything. Very cold in winter, hey? Solly warned me about that. He's been over a couple of times. That's all little Beryl talks about . . . making a snowman. Did you ever do that?

GLADYS. No. There are no snowmen in my memories.

STEVE. But it's summer there now.

GLADYS [*another smile*]. Of course. It will never be anything else. [*Before she can say anything more the backyard light goes out.*] Oh dear! What's happened now?

STEVE. The light's gone, Piet!

PIET [*calls from offstage*]. Oh no, it hasn't. [*Piet comes out of the house carrying the two brass candlesticks—the candles alight—a plate of snacks and a glass of sherry.*] 'Put out the light, and then put out the light. | If I quench thee thou flaming minister | I can thy former light store should I repent me. | But once put out thy light . . .'*

STEVE. Fancy stuff, hey!

PIET. How's your glass?

STEVE [*emptying it*]. Empty.

PIET. And now, ladies and gentlemen, to keep the tradition alive, another toast. To your new pastures!

[*They all raise their glasses.*]

GLADYS. New pastures.

STEVE. Ja, Gladys was telling me about them.

GLADYS. Later.

PIET. All packed and ready for the big move?

STEVE. Ag no man, Piet!

PIET. What's the matter?

STEVE. You promised me a good time.

PIET. And you're going to get it.

STEVE. Then don't ask questions like that. Packed up and ready?

You must be joking. If you really want to know what that is all about, Piet, you just go sit in your lounge with some empty suitcases and boxes and let Gladys start to empty the drawers and the cupboards and the wardrobe and pile it all around you. And then you must choose, hey! What you want to take with you, what you'll give to your old Auntie Bettie in Salisbury Park or what you'll just maar throw away. [*Shaking his head ruefully.*] I don't know where we kept it all, Gladys. Mavis just keeps coming with more and more . . . and then the children! Please pack this, Daddy, please pack that, Daddy. You ought to see the place. It looks as if burglars have been in the house ransacking it. And you know me, Piet! I'm one for having things nice and tidy. I've packed and unpacked those bloody suitcases I don't know how many times already, trying to fit in all the damned things. Excuse the language, Gladys, but that is how I feel about it. When I left the house to come here tonight I put my foot in my own face—our wedding photo! . . . so that started Mavis crying . . . you know, bad luck!—and then I stood on that table lamp covered with sea-shells. You know the one, Piet, with all the mother-of-pearl. My dad made it. It was going to be my special souvenir of this place in our home over there.

GLADYS. I'm sure you'll be able to fix it, Steven.

STEVE. Maybe. I didn't even look to see how broken it was, I was so the hell-in, Gladys. Just slammed the door on the lot . . . wife, children, suitcases, broken glass . . . [*Piet laughs.*] It's no joke, man. It's a life lying around on that lounge floor like a pile of rubbish. That's what I'm trying to squeeze into a few old suitcases. And the worst part is that you start to hate it. Sometimes I think we should just chuck the whole lot away. Get onto that boat with a pair of pajamas each and a toothbrush. Start over there with nothing. But there's no winning. Because just when you're feeling like that, out of a box or a cupboard drawer comes something you'd forgotten about . . . and before you know it, you're sitting there on the floor smiling at a memory. [*He goes through his coat pockets and finds an old snapshot.*] Get your glasses.

PIET [*he puts on his spectacles and takes the snapshot*]. What do I see?

STEVE. Me and my dad.

PIET. And this?

STEVE. Hell, you are blind. Can't you see? It's a fish. Look again.

PIET. Hell, Steve, it's big!

STEVE [*proudly*]. Of course, that's just it. Why do you think we found somebody with a camera and a spool? And in Fairview. [*Studies it himself.*] How can I throw this away? Want to see, Gladys? Me and my dad.

GLADYS. You look just like him.

STEVE. It was the biggest moment in the old man's life. And I was there when he caught it. Maitland surf! Friday afternoons after work we used to trek out from Fairview on his bike. Winter, it was dark before we were halfway there. Hell, that last stretch across the sand was a slog! He made me push the bike, and I was still only a pikkie.

We had one hole we always fished. And he caught, hey! The white boys used to come past with their fancy rods and reels empty-handed, while we had Steenbras tails flapping around us on the sand. The old man had patience. That was his secret. I can still see him . . . sitting next to the fire, his rod in front of him . . . waiting, for the big one. [*He laughs.*] And that night it came. Piet . . .! With its first run it walked him down the beach and into the darkness. He managed to turn its head and get it back to our spot, and then it was off again. Three times! With me next to him shouting: 'Don't lose it, Daddy! Don't lose it!' The reel seized up. Solid! But by then the fish had had it as well. He pulled it in hand over hand. A thirty pound bloody mussel-cracker! It lay there on the sand like a sack of potatoes while we cried with happiness.

But the real fun came the next morning trying to get it onto the bicycle. He wouldn't gut and scale it. Not a damn! Fairview had to see it the way it was when he caught it. We ended up tying it to the crossbar and walking home, him pushing and me behind holding up the tail. Haai! That old man!

PIET [*filling glasses*]. What was his full name?

STEVE. Willem Gerhardus Daniels. But everybody just called him Uncle Willie.

PIET. I like the Willem Gerhardus. That name belongs to this world as surely as any one of those aloes. I'd like to raise my glass to Willem Gerhardus Daniels.

[*Gladys does the same. There is a pause . . . Steve shakes his head.*]

STEVE. No don't let's get sentimental about him, Piet.

PIET. I meant it, Steve.

STEVE. I'm sure you did. It's just that if you'd seen him at the end you wouldn't want to do that. All he wanted from life was to work, feed his family and wait for another big one. That's not asking for a lot, hey? But it was still too much for a Coloured man.

They kicked us out, Gladys. Separate Group Areas.* Fairview was declared white and that was the end of us.

Every penny he had saved was taken by the lawyers. He tried to fight it, you see. Petitions and court cases that went on and on. When we finally piled our furniture onto the back of the lorry he was broke. That was quite a day! The old man took out his Bible and cursed that little bit of ground before we drove away. It's still empty, you know. No whitey has built on it yet.

Strange the things you remember! We had an auntie staying with us. She was a bit simple. I worked it out the other day . . . my father's brother-in-law's sister-in-law . . . Ja! Anyway, it was she and me on the back of the lorry on top of the furniture, me with the chickens and the old auntie with a big pumpkin in her lap!

But that finished Willem Gerhardus. He hadn't just lost his house and his savings, they also took away the sea. I mean . . . how the hell do you get from Salt Lake to Maitland on a bicycle?! He tried the river a few times, but that wasn't for him.

I'll never forget one day in the backyard there at Salt Lake. I had started to get a bit conscious about things, and I was going on about our rights and what have you. He just listened. When I

was finished he shook his head and said: 'Ons geslag is verkeerd.' Hell, that made me angry! And I told him we have only
ourselves to blame if we let them walk over us. He just shook his
head and repeated himself: 'Ons geslag is verkeerd'

Sorry, Gladys. That means . . . how would you say it nice in
English, Piet?

PIET. Our generation . . . our race is a mistake.

STEVE. Ja, something like that. And maybe he was right after all.
[*He pauses.*] I like the sound of my own voice tonight, hey,
Gladys?

GLADYS. Don't apologize for that. So do I! I'm just sorry your
memories are so-so.

STEVE. You're very polite. I hope they're all like you in England.

GLADYS. I'm not being polite, Steven. I meant it. We haven't had
a visitor for a long time. Isn't that so, Peter?

PIET. Yes, that's true.

GLADYS. And with Steven leaving, heaven alone knows when we'll
get another. That's a disturbing thought, isn't it? You could find
yourself talking to your aloes for quite a long time yet, you
know.

PIET [*he is uneasy about the direction the conversation is taking. He turns to
his aloes.*] What do you think of them, Steve? So far I've got
nine of the indigenous Eastern Cape species. There's twenty all
told. Not bad for six months, is it?

GLADYS [*to Steve*]. You see, there is no chance of persuading him
to leave. I must confess I don't really understand why. It's all got
to do with him being an Afrikaner and this being 'home' . . .
because like you, Steven, I'm more than prepared to call some
other place that. But not Peter. If those aloes can survive
droughts, so can he!

PIET. Come. Let me show you the collection. [*He puts on the outside
light.*] Right. Where do we begin? These two. Both saponarias.
You wouldn't think so, would you? The range of variation within
a species is quite remarkable. 'Nature refusing to be shackled by
the fetters of a man-made system.' Here we have ferox . . .

arborescens . . . ciliaris . . . it's a sort of climbing aloe. Pushes its way through dense undergrowth to reach the sun. [*To Gladys.*] All right, my dear? [*Back to Steve.*] What I would really like to do, Steve, is get in a few nice rocks and a load of good red soil and build a little natural habitat in this corner . . . for the dwarf species.

STEVE. You were surprised when I told you I was pulling out, weren't you?

GLADYS. Surprised? That's putting it mildly, Steven. It left him speechless. He only managed to tell me tonight. It might not have been so bad if it was one of the others . . . but you, of all people!

PIET [*quietly to Gladys*]. Let me speak for myself.

GLADYS. Haven't I told the truth?

PIET [*turning to Steve*]. Yes, I was . . . but is that so strange, Steve?

STEVE. No, of course not. I was just saying . . . But then, what did you expect, Piet? That I would come out of jail, go home quietly and sit out the rest of my Banning Order? And when that was up and they slap on another five years, just go on sitting there waiting for charity from the comrades to feed my family? That's a hell of a contribution to the struggle! Or does the cause need a few martyrs now to get it going again? I'm not going to be one, Piet.

PIET. You're also doing it, Steve. Don't put words in my mouth. I think I understand.

STEVE. What?

PIET. Your reasons for leaving.

STEVE. What are they?

PIET. Hell, Steve . . . !

STEVE. I'm being serious, man! I want to know how much you understand.

PIET. Let's talk about something else, Steve.

STEVE. Ag, come on, Piet! There's no time left for polite conversation. And certainly not between the two of us. Here, look at that. [*He produces a card from his back pocket and throws it down on the table.*] My membership card of the Amalgamated Building Workers Union of South Africa. It certifies that Steven Daniels is a qualified bricklayer and mason. Four years apprenticeship and twenty years experience. You know what that means, Piet? [*Holding out his hands.*] These are useful. They can do a job, and they can do it bloody well. The G.M. plant at the bottom of Kempston Road . . . I laid two thousand four hundred bricks there one day, Piet. Using these is the only way I can feed and clothe my family. I've got nothing else! They haven't worked for four years now. Look at them. They're softer than Mavis's. They might as well fall off for all they mean in my life now. And I must feel guilty about leaving?

PIET. Steve . . .

STEVE. No, let me finish. I've paid my debts in full, Piet. I don't owe this damned country a thing anymore. And let me tell you something, if they ever get their hands on you, you'll feel the same. You'll also get out.

PIET. You're arguing with yourself, Steve. I haven't accused you of anything.

STEVE. Thanks, Piet. That's big of you. But if ever you want to, just remember it's easier for you.

PIET. I know that.

STEVE. If I had a white skin, I'd also find lots of reasons for not leaving this country. [*He pauses, then sits down in a chair.*] Hell, that's crude! Doesn't sound like the Steve Daniels you used to know, hey? Sorry people . . . sorry, sorry. Jesus, I spend a lot of time apologizing for myself nowadays. If it's any excuse, I'm just as bad at home. Mavis says I left my manners behind in jail.

GLADYS. Oh dear, is the party over?

[*Neither man responds. She gets up and quietly starts to stack plates and cutlery.*]

PIET [*the unidentified aloe in his hands*]. I found this one this morning, but I'm buggered if I can identify it.

STEVE. I've lost more than just my manners, Piet. There was

262

nothing to do inside, when they weren't questioning me, except think. So I did a lot of that. Too much, I suppose, but what the hell! You can't stop yourself.

It all came down to one question, Piet. Why was I really there, inside? Don't tell me about the party at Betty's and the Special Branch catching me having a drink, singing freedom songs on the sly, with the comrades. That's not what I mean. My life had been in a mess long before they walked in that night. Why? And for what?

You understand what I'm asking?

Tell me one thing we've achieved that makes it worthwhile staying here and messing up my children's lives the way I have mine. Because that's what will happen. We've only seen it get worse. And it's going to go on getting worse. But I know why now.

We were like a bunch of boy scouts playing at politics. Those boer-boys play the game rough. It's going to need men who don't care about the rules to sort them out. That was never us.

GLADYS. I'll leave the wine.

STEVE. My turn for a toast! Your glass all right, Gladys? [*He fills up his own.*] I always had a feeling you never cared much for our politics. Here's your chance. [*He raises his glass.*] What do they call it, Piet? A lost cause!

[*Gladys exits into the house with the dinnerware.*]

PIET. My turn to say no. I won't raise my glass to that.

STEVE [*studying him carefully before speaking*]. You confuse the issue for me. I got no problems with old Solly in his nice house out at Humewood.* He gives me boat tickets, I give him an easy conscience. And anyway, he's got a factory full of my people making him richer. I'm not saying his heart isn't in the right place. Hell man, he's proved it! Same for the others. They all got their hearts in the right place . . . [*A sudden bitterness comes into his voice.*] . . . so I got no problems in saying good-bye to them next week. Because I know I'll see them all over there if it ever gets rough for them as well! [*Gladys returns.*] But you? No, Gladys is right. I can't see you doing that. Piet Bezuidenhout will be here at the end even if it means being the last one left. You're fooling yourself, Piet, if you think there's any hope. Do what I'm doing, man. Get out. Join me in England. We can sit back and talk as much and as loud as we like . . . because that's all we ever did here. Somebody was telling me there's a place over there where you can stand up on a box and say anything you like.

GLADYS. Poor Peter! It's all gone wrong, hasn't it? [*To Steve.*] He had such high hopes for this reunion with you. I wasn't exaggerating when I said he talks to his aloes. That's all he's got left for company. You see, the others have been avoiding us as if we had the plague. At first I thought it was because of me . . . I haven't been too well lately . . . but we know the real reason now, not that it helps very much.

They all suspect Peter of being a police informer. Did you know that? Yes. They all think he is the one who told them you were going to be at that party. [*Gladys goes into the house with another load from the table. The two men stare at each other. Glays returns.*] What about you, Steven?

PIET. No, Gladys! Enough's been said.

GLADYS [*ignoring Piet*]. I think he does as well, Peter. Or at least has doubts. That's why Mavis didn't come, isn't it? Have I embarrassed you, Steven? There's no need to be. We're all old friends, and anyway, it's better to have these things out in the open. I'm sure you've been thinking about it. Watching him all night and trying to decide.

PIET. Please, Gladys!

GLADYS [*violently*]. No. No! Haven't you had enough lies! Who are they meant to protect this time? Him? Your beautiful friendship? Can't you see it's rotten with doubt? Don't leave us in suspense, Steven. What have you decided? Take a good look at him. Nothing? Still just doubts? Then let me settle them for you. [*She pauses, then turns and stares at Piet.*] It happens to be the truth. Yes. He is an informer. Peter is the one who went to the police and told them you were going to break your Banning Order and be at the party.

PIET [*staring at her in disbelief*]. No . . .

GLADYS.  Yes! I'll swear to it on your Bible if you want me to!

PIET.  Gladys . . .

GLADYS.  Don't touch me!

STEVE.  Hell! Wine has gone to my head. This is quite a party. Ja, you guessed right, Gladys. That's why Mavis isn't here. There's nothing wrong with the children. It's just that she's got *no* doubts. She is certain it was you, Piet. I had a hell of an argument with her before coming here. She said it was a trap. I told her and the kids to go to hell . . . nearly tore up the boat tickets. That's why I was late . . . plus the fact that I had a few drinks on the way. I needed Dutch courage to face you. [*He pauses.*] Piet?

PIET.  Nothing to say.

STEVE [*disbelief shows on his face*]. Nothing . . . ? You're joking, Piet.

PIET.  I got nothing to say, Steve.

[*A few seconds of silence and then Steve starts laughing.*]

STEVE.  Jesus, that's funny! I'm sorry, Piet, but I mean it. That's very, very funny. I think those were my exact words when they started questioning me after the party. They made a few jokes in the car, but I kept quiet . . . you see, hiding there in Betty's wardrobe while they searched the place . . . squashed in the dark there among her clothes . . . with her perfume and me shit-scared . . . it came up, man. Hard! I was trying to hit the damned thing down when they found me. And they saw it. In the car one of them said: 'If you don't teach it to behave, Daniels, we'll take it away from you.' I was scared, Piet. I knew where I was going. Anyway, up there on the fifth floor the questions really started. And Steve Daniels replied: 'I've got nothing to say.' [*He laughs again.*] You want to know how they made me change my mind? There's a room up there on the fifth floor . . . they call it the waiting room. All it's got is a chair by an open window. Every time I said that . . . 'Nothing to say!' . . . and I kept it up for a long time, Piet! . . . they put me in there and left me alone. Every half hour or so a couple of them would stick

their heads in, look at me . . . and laugh. I got no bruises to show
you. That's all they ever did to me. Just laugh. But they kept it
up. One night back in my cell, after another day of that, I knew
that if they put me in there once more . . . I'd jump. And I
wasn't thinking of escape from five floors up. Ja! They had
laughed at my manhood and every reason I had for diving out
of that window. When they came to fetch me the next morning
I was crying like a baby. And they comforted me like I was one.
When they started their questions again, I wiped my eyes and
answered . . . for the first time. I told them everything. Every
bloody thing I knew. And if they'd wanted it, I would have told
them things I didn't know. But wait . . . the really *big* laugh is still
coming. When I had finished and signed my statement, they
patted me on the back and said: 'Well done, Daniels! But now
tell us something we don't know.' And they weren't fooling.
They knew everything. Somebody had been talking to them for
a long time, and about a hell of a lot more than Steve Daniels
sneaking out to have a good time. So for Christ's sake, Piet,
anything you like . . . a lie if it's necessary . . . but don't tell me
you got nothing to say!

PIET. A lie?

STEVE. All right! I'll admit it. I've got doubts. So I'm asking you
straight: Is Gladys telling the truth?

PIET. Why me, Steve?

GLADYS. Careful, Steven! He looks like one of them, doesn't he?
The same gross certainty in himself! He certainly sounds like
them. He speaks English with a dreadful accent. What else,
Steven? He's poor enough to do it for money.

STEVE. All right Gladys! [*He grabs his jacket, hesitates for a second, then
goes over to confront Piet directly.*] Relax, Piet. I've solved our problem. I'm going to hope it was you. I mean it. I'm going to try
hard, because, hell, man! . . . will that make it easier going next
week . . . if I can throw away our friendship like all that junk on
my lounge floor.

[*He turns to go.*]

GLADYS [*to Piet*]. You're not going to defend yourself and deny it?

PIET. No.

GLADYS. My God, are you that safe? Can nothing threaten you? I'm so jealous, Peter. Aren't you, Steven?

STEVE. Gladys?

GLADYS. Wouldn't you like to be as safe as he is? Because we aren't, you know.

STEVE. Please, Gladys! What's going on? Are you playing games?

GLADYS. You wouldn't be doubting him if you were. I doubt everything now. But not him. When you come to think of it, it's almost stupid. He's lost a farm, his friends . . . you! . . . the great purpose in his life, and he's going to lose a lot more before it's all over, but his faith in himself refuses to be shaken. Of course he didn't do it! What's happened to you, Steven? He isn't an informer. It must have been one of your other trusted comrades. Go back to Mavis and start all over again, because it wasn't him.

STEVE [angrily]. Then why did you . . . ?

GLADYS [violently]. That's my business. Yes, mine! My reason for telling you an ugly lie, which you were ready to believe! . . . is *my* business. I accept, Steven, that I am just a white face on the outskirts of your terrible life, but I'm in the middle of mine and yours is just a brown face on the outskirts of that. Do you understand what I'm saying? I've got my own story. I don't need yours. I've discovered hell for myself. It might be hard for you to accept, Steven, but you are not the only one who has been hurt. Politics and black skins don't make the only victims in this country.

STEVE. Gladys . . .

PIET. Leave her alone, Steve.

GLADYS [turning on him with equal violence]. I don't need you! I don't need you to protect me anymore! You never did, anyway. When they took away my diaries you did nothing. When the others took away my false teeth and held me down and blew my mind to pieces, you weren't even there! I called for you, Peter, but you weren't there.

PIET [*restraining Gladys physically*]. I think you'd better go, Steve!

GLADYS. No, he can't! [*She stops struggling and speaks pleadingly.*] Please ... please ... I promised to tell him about England. I was taught to keep my promises. [*Piet releases her. She steadies herself and speaks calmly.*] It's very green. There are mountains in the distance, but you can't see them too clearly because of a soft, soft mist and the rays of the setting sun. There's a lovely little cottage with a thatch roof, and flowers in the garden, and winding past it an old country road with tall trees along the side. An old shepherd and his dog are herding a little flock of sheep along it and watching them, at the garden gate, is a little girl ... It's called 'Sunset in Somerset' and it hangs on a wall in a room where you sit and wait for your turn. I always tried to forget what was coming by looking at it and imagining that I was the little girl and that I lived in that cottage. But it didn't really help because the door to the room where they do it goes on opening and closing, opening and closing and you get nearer and nearer ... I had a friend. Marlene. She'd been there for a long time already. We used to sit together. She saw I was frightened. 'Do you know any swear words?' she asked me. 'It will make you feel better. Go on, swear, man. As hard as you can.'

She taught me. Oh shit! Oh fucking, almighty, bloody, Jesus Christ ...! But even that didn't help, because when your turn does come and they call your name and you sit down on the floor and say 'No,' they pick you up and carry you inside ... and do it. They've burned my brain as brown as yours, Steven. [*Her little present for Mavis is in front of her on the table. She examines it vacantly for a few seconds, and then remembers. She gets up and goes over to Steve. She speaks quietly and calmly.*] A little something for Mavis. Tell her I wish her bon voyage. Good-bye, Steve.

[*She goes into the house. The two men avoid each other's eyes.*]

STEVE [*putting on his coat*]. What happened?

PIET. Those raids, after your arrest. They took away personal diaries she had been keeping. Then she started to get funny ... imagining things. Wouldn't go out because people were spying on her. She thought I was one of the Special Branch.

STEVE. Those bastards!

PIET. That's why I couldn't get to your trial. The doctors told me not to leave her alone. Anyway, it got worse, and they took her away to Fort England Clinic.*

STEVE [*he makes a half-hearted move to leave*]. I don't want to leave this country, Piet. I was born here. It's my home. But they won't give me a chance to live. And they'll do the same to my children. You were prepared to let me go believing that you . . .

PIET. Hell, Steve, you know why. If you could have believed it, there was no point in denying it.

STEVE. Ja. So that's it, then. No quotation for old time's sake?

PIET. No. I'd rather remember this as another occasion when I didn't know what to say.

[*Steve puts on his hat and goes. Piet goes into the house and joins Gladys in the bedroom. She is sitting at her dressing table with her diary.*]

GLADYS. Has he gone?

PIET. Yes.

GLADYS. Did he say anything more?

PIET. No. Just good-bye. There wasn't anything left to say.

GLADYS. I wrecked everything, didn't I?

PIET. Between Steve and me? No.

GLADYS. I tried.

PIET. There was nothing left to wreck.

GLADYS [*holding her diary*]. I should have wrapped this up as well and given it to him as his farewell present. It would have been appropriate. He's got to start his life again. I know what that means. In some ways that's the worst . . . starting again . . . waking up with nothing left, not even your name, and having to start again. You see, I wasn't able to use it. It's empty. Blank. [*Turning the pages.*] All of them . . . blank . . . blank. It wasn't for want of trying, Peter. I sat down every night, opened it . . . but then nothing. The ink used to clot and dry on the nib while I sat looking at the blank page. I've got no secrets left, except for one which I don't want. I've tried to find others in my life, but all I've got is this one, and I'm frightened of it.

There's a little ritual at the end of every meal in Fort England. You sit at your table and wait while the dirty cutlery is taken to the matron, so that she can count the knives. There are none missing tonight, but . . . You're a good man, Peter, and that has become a terrible provocation.* I want to destroy that goodness. Ironic, isn't it! That which I most hate and fear about this country is all I seem to have learned. [*She looks at her diary.*] I'll keep this and try next time. I've got to go back, Peter.

PIET. Are you sure?

GLADYS. Yes. Aren't you?

[*She opens a drawer and starts to take out bottles of pills and toilet articles.*]

PIET. If you take some pills now, do you think we'll be all right until the morning?

GLADYS. Yes. Will you stay awake?

PIET. Yes.

GLADYS. And pack a suitcase for me?

PIET. Yes.

GLADYS. I'll go quietly this time.

PIET. Do you want to go to bed now? [*She nods.*] Just call me if you want anything.

[*He leaves the bedroom. Gladys sits at her dressing table quietly sorting out bottles of pills and a few personal possessions, which she will take with her. Piet, in the backyard, sits with the unidentified aloe.*]

CURTAIN

S·C·R·A·T·C·H = this work is still evolving and we encourage audience feedback

## HIDDEN PLOT THEATRE COMPANY

# **THE STONING**

### BY GHAZI RABIHAVI

Translated by Lucy Williamson
Directed by Bijan Sheibani

*On a cold night in winter, a war is raging. A woman and a young man shelter from bombs falling on the city. But as they talk, they create something far more destructive...*

A sensuous, delicate and uncompromising piece of theatre that
cuts deep into the heart of sexual politics.

Ghazi Rabihavi is an award-winning children's writer, and author of a number of adult plays and novels, but due to censorship laws in Iran, few were ever published or performed. Rabihavi was arrested and imprisoned in 1983 after his first published work for adults was serialised (without permission), and subsequent works were effectively barred by the censor. He worked with the company in rehearsal for this production.

"a very strong and powerful piece of work, beautifully constructed"
*Harold Pinter on Rabihavi's text*

## **This is the first British scratch performance and will include live Iranian music.**

Bijan Sheibani is the runner-up in the James Menzies-Kitchin Memorial Trust Award for
Young Directors 2002.

### 21-25 August
### Tues - Sat 8.30pm, Sunday 6.30pm
### Tickets £6.75 (full price) £4.50 (concessions)

**BOX OFFICE 020 7223 2223    boxoffice@bac.org.uk**

**BAC, Lavender Hill, London SW11 5TN    www.bac.org.uk**

**Production commissioned by BAC**

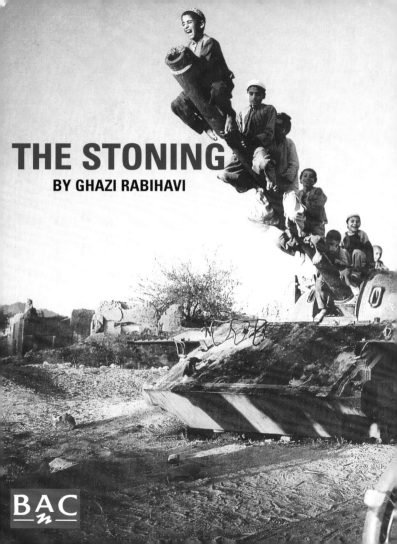

# THE STONING

## BY GHAZI RABIHAVI

# NOTES

*People Are Living There*

3   *Braamfontein*: inner-city area of Johannesburg where the Fugards lived in a seedy rooming-house on Hospital Hill in 1958. The sounds of cars driving past on Saturday nights, taking whites to the cinemas to 'have a good time', is alluded to later (p. 25); as is the sound of ambulances 'screaming past' (Act Two, p. 72).

10   *Native*: according to the Population Registration Act of 1950, one of the first major pieces of apartheid legislation, South Africans were classified as white, Coloured, or Native. 'Coloured' and 'Native' were also subdivided according to ethnic groups. 'Native' later became 'Bantu' and, later still, 'black' – the word used of themselves by the majority of those on the receiving end of apartheid, unless they preferred the cultural-linguistic identities of Zulu, Xhosa, etc. The word 'African', as in 'African National Congress', was officially taboo.

11   *Toweel*: Vic Toweel (1929– ) one of the best bantamweights in history, and the first South African to become a world boxing champion when he defeated Manuel Ortiz at Wembley Stadium, Johannesburg, on 31 May 1950. A quiet man who retired from the ring in the mid-1950s, and emigrated to Australia in 1987.

18   *Booysens*: Sissy comes from one of the poorer white suburbs, south of the city.

21   *Mario Lanza*: or Alfred Arnold Coccozza (1921–59), American tenor and actor, best known for his title role in film of *The Great Caruso* (1951) and for the voice singing the music to *The Student Prince* (1954).

29   *Southend Cemetery*: in Port Elizabeth, where the Fugard family lived. Milly therefore comes originally from the same part of the country, the Eastern Cape, and might be played with an appropriate accent, as she was by Yvonne Bryceland.

64   *To bed, to sleep, perchance no dreams*: see *Hamlet*, III. i. 64–5: 'To die, to sleep—To sleep, perchance to dream: ay, there's the rub.' A play on the most familiar of the quotations uttered in this scene: from the Victorian hymn 'All creatures great and small' to Tennyson's 'Charge of the Light Brigade' (Milly gets the number wrong: it was six hundred not four hundred who rode into the Valley of Death), and Psalm 23:1, 4: 'The Lord is my shepherd . . . Yea, though I walk through the valley of the shadow of death . . .' See also note to *A Lesson from Aloes*.

NOTES

## Statements after an Arrest under the Immorality Act

78 *Bontrug house*: i.e. a typical single-roomed 'location' house, built by the local authority for people designated 'Coloured'.

79 *Graaff Reinet*: founded 1786, named after governor Van der Graaff and his wife Reinet; the oldest town in the Eastern Cape, formerly an important trading centre on the frontier. It lies in a green and fertile spot in the arid semi-desert Karroo region, not far from the small towns of Cradock (see note to p. 83) and Middelburg; and the village of Nieu Bethesda (see *Dimetos* notes).

80 *Australopithecus ... Raymond Dart. 1930*: in 1924 the Australian-born Witwatersrand University Professor of Anatomy Raymond Dart (1893–1988) found the complete fossilized skull of one of humanity's extinct ancestors near the railway siding of Taung ('lion' in Sotho), in the northern Cape, on the fringe of the Kalahari Desert: he named it *Australopithecus Africanus* 'in commemoration first, of the extreme southern and unexpected horizon of its discovery, and secondly of the continent in which so many new and important discoveries have been made, thus vindicating the Darwinian claim that Africa would prove to be the cradle of mankind' (*Nature*, 7 Feb. 1925, p. 199). It was thought to be at least half a million years old; more recent examples of the ape-like species may be more than four million years old. Their precise relation to humans remains a question.

*Bishop Ussher*: James Ussher (1581–1656), Irish (Armagh) prelate and scholar whose system of chronology enabled him to calculate that God had created man, along with his universe, in seven days during the year 4004 BC, a date long accepted, even when geological studies of the late eighteenth and early nineteenth centuries made it evident that the past had to be measured in hundreds of thousands, if not millions of years.

*'no vestige of a beginning ... Charles Lyell ... Principles of Geology, 1830*: an example of the Man's (and Fugard's) shaky grasp of his sources here. It was the founder of modern geology, Scotsman James Hutton (1726–97), who concluded his epoch-making *The Theory of the Earth* (1795) thus: 'The result, therefore, of this physical inquiry [into the age of the earth] is, that we find no vestige of a beginning—no prospect of an end.' Charles Lyell (1797–1875) was another important Scottish geologist, whose *Principles of Geology* (1830–3) maintained that the causes of geological change in the remote past were those still operating at the time, discarding earlier assumption of catastrophic change, and thereby rendering the traditional Christian view based on the Old Testament even less credible. Microscopic, slow, but ceaseless change over unimaginable periods of time accomplished the effects revealed by geology.

81 *Julian Huxley's Principles of Evolution*: if the Man had asked for this, he

should have received a reply in the negative. There is no such book. Julian Huxley (1887–1975), grandson of T. H. Huxley (1825–95), Darwin's great defender, was best known for *Evolution: The Modern Synthesis* (1942). Perhaps a mistaken reference to Lyell's *Principles of Geology* (see above), or a conflation of that title and Huxley's *Evolution*.

83  *Cradock*: former frontier town in the Eastern Cape Karroo, best known today for its connections with the author Olive Schreiner (1855–1920), whose *The Story of an African Farm* (1883) was set in the surrounding district, and also contains speculations about the immense age of the earth and evolutionary theory, prompted by the stark, elementary landscape.

84  *'Give us this day . . . forgive those who . . .'*: from the Lord's Prayer. The first version of the play began with an extract from Genesis. Thus, biblical and scientific texts interweave in this play. The Man was based on a church missionary, although in Fugard's play he is a teacher. Either way, he would know his Bible well.

85  *correspondence course*: black or 'Coloured' characters learn in this way (e.g. Willie, in Fugard's *No-Good Friday*) because, at the time, the distance-teaching University of South Africa was generally the only avenue to higher education from which they were not excluded by apartheid legislation. Only gradually, during the 1980s and 1990s, did all the country's universities become 'open'.

91  *Immorality Act*: the Immorality Amendment Act, number 23 of 1957, forbade 'unlawful carnal intercourse' or 'any immoral or indecent act' between a white person and an African, Indian or Coloured person (as defined by the country's race laws). According to Section 16, an offender was liable to imprisonment for up to seven years' hard labour. Between 1950 and the end of 1980, more than 11,500 people were convicted, and more than twice that number charged. Mixed marriages were also prohibited by law. Many of those charged or convicted subsequently committed suicide or left the country. Offenders came from all classes of society. Special Force Order 025A/69 detailed the use of binoculars, tape recorders, cameras, and two-way radios to trap offenders; it also spelled out how bed-sheets should be felt for warmth and examined for stains. The Mixed Marriage and Immorality laws were finally abolished in June 1985. See Roger Omond, *The Apartheid Handbook: A Guide to South Africa's Everyday Racial Policies* (Harmondsworth: Penguin Books, 1985), 26–31.

*Noupoort*: railway junction between De Aar and Middelburg in the Eastern Cape Karroo district.

99  *Ugly feet . . . quite nice*: the details depend upon the physical realities of the performer, and how she reacts to and describes herself, working her way

up from her feet. The words of this speech were provided by Yvonne Bryceland, scrutinizing herself in the role as instructed by Fugard during rehearsal preparation.

*You say . . . rejected you?*: the indented words in this speech represent the performer speaking in the voice of the police interrogator. In some productions, a male voice off stage.

## Dimetos

109 *William Blake*: from Blake's visionary letter in verse to his friend and patron Thomas Butts (1802), which includes the lines:

> Now I a fourfold vision see,
> And a fourfold vision is given to me;
> 'Tis fourfold in my supreme delight
> And threefold in soft Beulah's night
> And twofold Always. May God us keep
> From Single vision & Newton's sleep.

110 *In a remote Province*: Nien Bethesda, for the revised (1976) version.

*Beside the Ocean*: Gaukamma Beach, a remote spot on the Eastern Cape seaboard, for the revised (1976) version.

130 *Daedalus . . . Theseus . . . twine*: Daedalus was the legendary Athenian craftsman who constructed the labyrinth for King Minos while in exile in Crete. There is an obvious parallel with Dimetos's situation. Theseus was the Athenian hero who found his way out of the labyrinth after killing the Minotaur, using a ball of thread given him by Ariadne – thereby saving the seven youths and seven maidens demanded from Athens by Minos as a tribute. The parallel here is with Danilo.

133 *chain . . . Prometheus*: in Greek myth, a Titan or one of the primordial gods, who stole fire from Olympus to give to mankind, and was punished by being chained to a rock, where an eagle tore at his liver.

151 *your fate*: anticipating the image of Hecate, the triformed goddess of fate conjured up by Sophia in Scene 6.

158 *sweet-smelling herb native to these parts*: not difficult in the eastern Cape, well known for its wide variety of indigenous medicinal herbs.

161 *I found her . . . She keeps company with a donkey, an owl, a griffin, a bat and an old, million-year-old turtle. There is a terrible familiarity between herself and the entrance to hell, which is just behind her*: the image of William Blake's *Hecate*, a colour print from 1795, which Fugard sent Yvonne Bryceland to look at in the Tate Gallery, London, in preparation for this scene. Blake depicts Hecate, the triformed moon goddess with power over heaven, earth, and the underworld, in her three phases, crescent, full, and waning, and surrounds her with creatures mentioned in his epigraph from *Macbeth*, IV.

i. 12–19, the inspiration for his picture (in Shakespeare's play, Hecate is 'Queen of the Witches').

## The Guest

170 *Advocate Marais*: In South Africa, an advocate is a lawyer who pleads the cause of a client before the Supreme and Appeal Courts; commonly used as a title before a surname. After his early career as a journalist in Pretoria, Eugène Marais (1871–1936) went to London to study medicine, but switched to law; by the time of his admission to the bar, the Boer War had begun, and with it his opposition to British imperialism.

171 *papers on the baboon*: Marais had begun to study the chacma baboons of the Waterberg in the years immediately following the Boer War, the basis of his volume *My Friends the Baboons*, which later became the more extended work on *The Soul of the Ape* (published posthumously in 1969, with an introduction by Robert Ardrey, who described it as a 'tragic masterpiece'). The chacma are the largest primates in southern Africa; their biggest enemy is the leopard. Highly gregarious, they occur in troops of up to 100, with a strict order of dominance.

175 *'de amandelboom zal bloeijen . . . straat omgaan'*: (Dutch) 'the almond tree shall flourish, and the grasshopper shall be a burden, and desire shall fail: because man goeth to his long home, and the mourners go about the streets' (Ecclesiastes 12:5).

179 *Zegen Heer . . . Amen*: a Dutch Grace, literally, 'Blessed God, for what we eat, let us never forget You. Amen.'

180 *'That's how it all started'*: Morais's addiction began in 1892, ten years before the ill-fated expedition to bring munitions and medical supplies to his countrymen.

195 *'Thou hast . . . dreaming on both'*: from Shakespeare's *Measure for Measure*, III, i. 32–4.

196 *concentration camp*: towards the end of the Boer War, Lord Kitchener removed the civilian Afrikaner population to camps, where nearly 28,000, mostly children, died of disease; an event scorched into Afrikaner history, creating a long-standing sense of bitter grievance towards the Bntish. It has recently been acknowledged that black people also died in these camps.

197 *'n Windjie . . . glad vervoer!*: (Afrikaans: 'Die Spinerak-rokkie', 'The Cobweb-dress') a fairy made herself a dress out of cobwebs, but had no sooner put it on, when a breeze carried her away. There's a lesson in the story: if ever you have a dress made of anything as fine as cobwebs, make sure there isn't a breeze when you put it on (Fugard–Devenish note).

199 *' 'n salige niksdoen en droom'*: (Afrikaans) 'a blessed idleness and dream'.

200 *'n Vyand . . . Vet-rivier!*: (Afrikaans: 'Lotos-land') Naudé warns the nation that Lotosland is a terrible trap. Contentment will be their undoing. He urges the Trekkers to shake off their sloth and return to the ordinary world. Only he and Koos van der Merwe do so, and after years of hardship they lose their Lotosland obesity. The fate of the others is not known. One rumour has it that they all ended up so fat they melted, hence the placename 'Fat River' (Fugard–Devenish note). One of the popular A. G. Visser's most popular poems.

*Cogito ergo sum*: (Latin) the basis of Descartes's philosophy: 'I think, therefore I am.'

203 *'The wilderness was like Eden . . . found therein'*: a slight rephrasing of Isaiah 51:3.

205 *The Soul of the Ape*: referring to Marais's pioneering study of the chacma baboons, an incomplete manuscript rediscovered and published with an introduction by Robert Ardrey in 1969. It begins: 'Shortly after the War, I had the opportunity of living for three years in very close proximity to a troop of wild chacma baboons (*Papio Ursinus ursinus*).'

206 *Gustav Preller . . . Malan, Minister of the Interior*: i.e. Dr D. F. Malan (1874–1959), who became a minister in the Pact government of 1924; better known as leader of the National Party and Prime Minister (1948–54). Gustav Preller (1875–1943) was a journalist active in nationalist Afrikaner circles, and a close friend of Marais.

207 *She's the soul*: Marais's theory that the individual nest of termites is like the organism of an animal, with the queen the 'soul' or governing spirit, first appeared in a series of articles for a popular Afrikaans periodical called *Die Huisgenoot* in 1925–6, followed by excerpts in the Belgian and French press; about six years after which the Belgian Maurice Maeterlinck (1862–1949) published *The Life of the White Ant*, describing the organic unity of the termitary, comparing it with the human body—an idea which aroused great interest, and which was supposed to be his. *Die Siel van die Mier* (1937) was first published as *The Soul of the White Ant* in Britain in 1971, translated by Winifred de Kok.

208 *the Preacher . . . increaseth sorrow*: from Ecclesiastes (the Preacher) 1: 18.

210 *'Die Sanger van die Suikerbosrand'*: (Afrikaans) literally 'The Singer of the Sugarbushborder' (sugarbush = protea): Suikerbosrand is also a place name.

*There is one mystery . . . one song all of his own*: Marais's fascination with 'Bushman' ideas he came across issued in several poems. A famous San lament is called in translation 'The Broken String'.

213 *Blus uit, O Diep Rivier . . . verlaat*: (Afrikaans) the poet addresses himself to oblivion in the image of a deep and dark river (Fugard–Devenish note).

'. . . *de priester en de profeet . . . gerigt*': (Dutch) '. . . the priest and the prophet have erred through strong drink, they are swallowed up of wine, they are out of the way through strong drink; they err in vision, they stumble in judgement' (Isaiah 28: 7).

*Ek sien . . . snel*: (Afrikaans) I see from far the glint of steel and gold | I hear the soft rumble of waters deep and cold; | hear your voice as whispering in a dream, | Come quickly . . . ('Diep Rivier').

'*Want alle tafels . . . leeren?*': (Dutch) 'For all tables are full of vomit and filthiness, so that there is no place clean'; 'So that there is no place clean. Whom shall he teach knowledge?' (Isaiah 28: 8–9).

'. . . *en wien zou Hij . . . lippen*': (Dutch) 'and whom shall he make to understand doctrine? Them that are weaned from the milk?'; 'and drawn from the breasts. For precept must be upon precept; line upon line, line upon line; here a little, and there a little: For with stammering lips . . .' (Isaiah 28: 9–11).

*If I quench thee, thou flaming minister, I can thy former light restore*': see Shakespeare, *Othello*, v. ii. 8–9, moments before Othello murders Desdemona.

214   *Put out the light . . . thy light*: *Othello*, v. ii. 7.

215   *Sy sê: 'Ek vorder . . . sandwoestyn*': (Afrikaans) South Africa, a female voice, speaks about herself and her people. She has no compassion for them. She has thrown them down from mountain tops and smothered them in deserts. She gives nothing, but demands everything. Tears, the listing of the names of the dead, the widow's lament, the dumb gestures of children—these are all to no avail. She claims as her holy right the fruits of endless pain ('Die Lied van Suid-Afrika'/'The Song of South Africa') (Fugard–Devenish note).

## A Lesson from Aloes

219   *Elizabeth Magdalena Potgieter*: Fugard's mother, who died in 1980.

220   *Algoa Park*: lower-middle-class, predominantly Afrikaans suburb.

221   *aloes*: indigenous succulent plants with thick tapering leaves and bell-shaped or tubular flowers on thick stems, common in the Eastern Cape.

    *a small field book on the plants*: according to a MS note, G. W. Reynolds' *The Aloes of South Africa* (1950), 516 pages not counting General Smuts's foreward.

222   '*What's in a name . . . sweet*': *Romeo and Juliet*, II. ii. 43: as with the other numerous literary allusions in this play, Fugard allows his character to identify the source.

223   *season . . . of the maturing sun*: John Keats, 'To Autumn'.

228   *Ay, there's the rub*: *Hamlet*, II. i. 65: used elsewhere by Fugard, e.g. in *People*.

229 *Damp clods . . . rainless glare*: from 'The Snake', by one of South Africa's premier poets, Roy Campbell (1901–57), which celebrates the aloe's ability to survive the harshest conditions.

232 *Watchtower Society*: i.e. from Jehovah's Witnesses.

233 *The police raids . . . little shell*: this refers to the immediately post-Sharpeville (1960) atmosphere in the country: a government clampdown ensured most resistance was silenced or driven abroad.

234 *Thoreau*: i.e. Henry David Thoreau (1817-62), American essayist best known for *Walden, or A Walk in the Woods* (1854), an account of his experiment in self-sufficiency.

235 *Henry Wadsworth Longfellow*: American poet (1807–82), best known for 'The Wreck of the Hesperus', 'The Village Blacksmith', and *The Song of Hiawatha* (1855); also for 'The Slave's Dream', rendered in its entirety later in the play (pp. 249–50), as a link between Piet and Steve.

240 *Sweet is the scene . . . Blake*: Oliver Wendell Holmes (1809–94), American physician, poet and essayist, best-known for his 'table talks', but this is from 'An After-Dinner Poem'; Dick Swiveller's famous remark is from Dickens's *The Old Curiosity Shop* (1841); and Blake's is from 'On Friends and Foes'.

241 *bus boycott started*: see Introduction, p. xxix. This was a common form of protest in the late 1950s and early 1960s, anticipating much more widespread disruption in later years. Cadles is the 'ugly Coloured area with all the factories' adjoining Algoa Park in Port Elizabeth.

242 *It's as simple as that*: from Ernst Fischer's *The Necessity of Art: A Marxist Approach* (1963) according to Fugard's 1968 notes: see Introduction, p. xxviii.

245 *not in our ideals, but in ourselves*: misquoting from *Julius Caesar*, I. ii. 140–1.

256 *'Put out the light . . . put out thy light'*: referring to the same moment referred to in *The Guest*, from *Othello*, v. ii. 7–10.

259 *Separate Group Areas*: the Group Areas Act, a mainstay of apartheid, was introduced in 1950, repealed in 1990: under this act, and numerous amendments, urban areas were divided into zones where specified racial groups were obliged to live and work. Many of the removals were enforced by violent means. *Boesman and Lena* displays the results perhaps most graphically among Fugard's works.

263 *Humewood*: wealthy white suburb of Port Elizabeth.

269 *Fort England Clinic*: Fort England Hospital in Grahamstown, a 470-bed mental hospital, the largest in the Eastern Cape. Sheila Fugard was a patient before this play appeared.

270 *and that has become a terrible provocation*: words omitted from the first (Market) production, and some others.

# GLOSSARY

African and Afrikaans words or phrases printed in bold, other South African expressions in bold italic. I have found *The Dictionary of South African English on Historical Principles* (Oxford: Oxford University Press, 1996) particularly useful.

**Ag**: (pronounced like German 'Ach'): 'Oh'

**Bakoond**: brick or clay oven, built into the side of a wide kitchen hearth, or free-standing outside the house

***Banning order***: order restricting an individual's freedom of movement, association, and/or speech, by ministerial decree according to 'security' legislation; a concept introduced by the Suppression of Communism Act of 1950, and subsequent legislation designed to limit dissent

***Bioscope***: cinema

**Bliksem**: scoundrel; or merely an expression of disgust

**Boetie**: little brother, a familiar form of address to a boy or man

**Brak**: mongrel dog

**Brandsiekte**: mange

***Congress***: shortened form of name of a number of oppositional political organizations, particularly the African National Congress, but also the Congress of Democrats

***Cool-drink, cooldrink***: a soft drink, usually carbonated

**Dop**: colloquial, a 'tot' or drink of spirits

**Dronklap**: drunk (noun)

***Exit permit***: travel document granted to somebody whose passport had been withdrawn, permitting departure from South Africa, but not the right to return; common in the 1960s and 1970s as a means of ridding the country of those the government thought (often mistakenly) would cause less harm to it abroad than at home

**Ja**: yes

**Ja, baas**: yes, boss

**Karmenaadjie**: a present of cooked meat

**Kom**: come

**Kierie**: traditional weapon of indigenous peoples of South Africa; short, thick stick with a knobbed head; a walking-stick

**Laat lammetjie**: child born long after the others in a family; literally, little late lamb

***Location***: segregated area for blacks outside town or city (later replaced by 'township')

**Maar**: but

**Mampoer**: raw brandy originating in the Transvaal, distilled, often illicitly, from fruit such as peaches or marula-fruit

***Meester***: master, or specifically schoolmaster

***Miesies***: missus, mistress: term of

(respectful) address, usually to a white woman

**Mos**: colloquial: actually, really, truly

**Naar**: colloquial: unpleasant, disagreeable

**Oom**: uncle; used respectfully or affectionately for an older man

**Oupa**: grandfather; informally, any elderly man, especially if Afrikaans

**Pikkie**: small person, child (perhaps from **piccanin**, but not necessarily black)

**Poep**: derogatory slang, a stupid person, from **poephol**, Afrikaans for anus

*Polony*: from Bologna sausage, a large, smoked sausage of mixed meats

**Randjies**: small ridges

**Rinkhals**: large venemous spitting-cobra, common in the Cape

*Rondavel*: traditional circular African dwelling, usually with a conical thatched roof; also any small one-roomed building of the same design

**Rooinek**: literally red-neck; among Afrikaners, often derogatory for an Englishman, or English-speaking South African

**Spruit**: small stream, usually containing little water except after rain

*Stoep*: verandah or porch

*Tackies*: canvas shoes

**Tant**: abbreviated form of **Tante**, or aunt: used respectfully or affectionately of an older woman, as well as for a relation

**Voorkamer**: any front room of a house

**Waenhuis**: coach house

**Wragtie**: from **wragtig**, truly, really

| | |
|---|---|
| GEORGE ELIOT | **Adam Bede** |
| | **Daniel Deronda** |
| | **Middlemarch** |
| | **The Mill on the Floss** |
| | **Silas Marner** |
| ELIZABETH GASKELL | **Cranford** |
| | **The Life of Charlotte Brontë** |
| | **Mary Barton** |
| | **North and South** |
| | **Wives and Daughters** |
| THOMAS HARDY | **Far from the Madding Crowd** |
| | **Jude the Obscure** |
| | **The Mayor of Casterbridge** |
| | **A Pair of Blue Eyes** |
| | **The Return of the Native** |
| | **Tess of the d'Urbervilles** |
| | **The Woodlanders** |
| WALTER SCOTT | **Ivanhoe** |
| | **Rob Roy** |
| | **Waverley** |
| MARY SHELLEY | **Frankenstein** |
| | **The Last Man** |
| ROBERT LOUIS STEVENSON | **Kidnapped and Catriona** |
| | **The Strange Case of Dr Jekyll and Mr Hyde and Weir of Hermiston** |
| | **Treasure Island** |
| BRAM STOKER | **Dracula** |
| WILLIAM MAKEPEACE THACKERAY | **Barry Lyndon** |
| | **Vanity Fair** |
| OSCAR WILDE | **Complete Shorter Fiction** |
| | **The Picture of Dorian Gray** |

OXFORD

# MORE OXFORD PAPERBACKS

This book is just one of nearly 1000 Oxford Paperbacks currently in print. If you would like details of other Oxford Paperbacks, including titles in the World's Classics, Oxford Reference, Oxford Books, OPUS, Past Masters, Oxford Authors, and Oxford Shakespeare series, please write to:

**UK and Europe:** Oxford Paperbacks Publicity Manager, Arts and Reference Publicity Department, Oxford University Press, Walton Street, Oxford OX2 6DP.

Customers in UK and Europe will find Oxford Paperbacks available in all good bookshops. But in case of difficulty please send orders to the Cash-with-Order Department, Oxford University Press Distribution Services, Saxon Way West, Corby, Northants NN18 9ES. Tel: 01536 741519; Fax: 01536 746337. Please send a cheque for the total cost of the books, plus £1.75 postage and packing for orders under £20; £2.75 for orders over £20. Customers outside the UK should add 10% of the cost of the books for postage and packing.

**USA:** Oxford Paperbacks Marketing Manager, Oxford University Press, Inc., 200 Madison Avenue, New York, N.Y. 10016.

**Canada:** Trade Department, Oxford University Press, 70 Wynford Drive, Don Mills, Ontario M3C 1J9.

**Australia:** Trade Marketing Manager, Oxford University Press, G.P.O. Box 2784Y, Melbourne 3001, Victoria.

**South Africa:** Oxford University Press, P.O. Box 1141, Cape Town 8000.

Expand your collection of

# VERY SHORT INTRODUCTIONS

## Available now

1. Classics
2. Music
3. Buddhism
4. Literary Theory
5. Hinduism
6. Psychology
7. Islam
8. Politics
9. Theology
10. Archaeology
11. Judaism
12. Sociology
13. The Koran
14. The Bible
15. Social and
    Cultural Anthropology
16. History

## Available soon

Ancient Philosophy
Animal Rights
Art Theory
Bioethics
Chaos
Continental Philosophy
Economics
Emotion
Ethics
The European Union
The First World War
Free Will
Indian Philosophy
Intelligence
Logic
Mathematics
Opera
Philosophy of Religion

**A complete list of Oxford Paperbacks**, including Oxford
World's Classics, Oxford History of Art, Past Masters, and Oxford
Paperback Reference, is available in the UK from the Trade and
Reference Publicity Department, Oxford University Press, Great
Clarendon Street, Oxford OX2 6DP.

In the USA, complete lists are available from the Paperbacks
Marketing Manager, Oxford University Press, 198 Madison Avenue,
New York, NY 10016.

Oxford Paperbacks are available from all good bookshops. In
case of difficulty, customers in the UK can order direct from Oxford
University Press bookshop, Freepost, 116 High Street, Oxford OX1
4BR, enclosing full payment. Please add 10% of published price for
postage and packing.

# LITERARY THEORY
## A Very Short Introduction
Jonathan Culler

Literary Theory is a controversial subject. Said to
have transformed the study of culture and society in
the past two decades, it is accused of undermining
respect for tradition and truth, encouraging suspicion
about the political and psychological implications of cultural products instead of admiration for great literature.
In this Very Short Introduction, Jonathan Culler explains
'theory', not by describing warring 'schools' but by
sketching key 'moves' that theory has encouraged and
speaking directly about the implications of cultural theory
for thinking about literature, about the power of language,
and about human identity. This lucid introduction will be
useful for anyone who has wondered what all the fuss is
about or who wants to think about literature today.

> 'It is impossible to imagine a clearer treatment of the sub-
> ject, or one that is, within the given limits of length, more
> comprehensive. Culler has always been remarkable for
> his expository skills, and here he has found exactly the
> right method and tone for his purposes.'
> **Frank Kermode**

www.oup.co.uk/vsi/literarytheory

# HISTORY

## A Very Short Introduction

John H. Arnold

*History: A Very Short Introduction* is a stimulating essay about how we understand the past. The book explores various questions provoked by our understanding of history, and examines how these questions have been answered in the past. Using examples of how historians work, the book shares the sense of excitement at discovering not only the past, but also ourselves.

'A stimulating and provocative introduction to one of collective humanity's most important quests – understanding the past and its relation to the present. A vivid mix of telling examples and clear cut analysis.'

**David Lowenthal, University College London**

'This is an extremely engaging book, lively, enthusiastic and highly readable, which presents some of the fundamental problems of historical writing in a lucid and accessible manner. As an invitation to the study of history it should be difficult to resist.'

**Peter Burke, Emmanuel College, Cambridge**

www.oup.co.uk/vsi/history